Geoff Tibballs is the author of a number of bestselling humour titles, including *The Mammoth Book of Jokes*, *The Mammoth Book of Dirty Jokes*, *The Mammoth Book of Comic Quotes*, *The Mammoth Book of One-Liners*, *The Senior Survival Guide* and *The Bowler's Holding, The Batsman's Willey*. He lives in Nottingham, where he struggles to convince people – especially his family – that what he does for a living constitutes real work.

Recent Mammoth titles

THE MAMMOTH BOOK OF

NEW COMIC QUOTES

Over 3,500 modern
gems of wit and wisdom from
TV, films and stand-up

GEOFF TIBBALLS

ROBINSON

ROBINSON

First published in Great Britain in 2017 by Robinson

1 3 5 7 9 10 8 6 4 2

A CIP catalogue record for this book is available from the British Library

ISBN: 978-1-47213-945-0

Typeset in Whitman by Hewer Text UK Ltd, Edinburgh
Printed and bound in Great Britain by CPI Group (UK) Ltd, Croydon CR0 4YY

Papers used by Robinson are from well-managed
forests and other responsible sources

Robinson
An imprint of
Little, Brown Book Group
Carmelite House
50 Victoria Embankment
London EC4Y 0DZ

An Hachette UK Company
www.hachette.co.uk

www.littlebrown.co.uk

Contents

Accidents

Electricity can be dangerous. My nephew tried to stick a penny into a plug. Whoever said a penny doesn't go far didn't see him shoot across that floor. I told him he was grounded.

Tim Allen

Sorry I poured three pints of strong European lager over you – it was an accident.

Becky (Rachael Stirling), *Detectorists*

Why do people in the media always focus on the negative side of things, when so much of what happens at this leisure centre is a success story? Last year, six hundred people visited this centre and nearly five hundred returned home without any loss of life or serious injury.

Gordon Brittas (Chris Barrie), *The Brittas Empire*

There are no accidents. God's just trying to remain anonymous.

Brett Butler

Speed has never killed anyone. Suddenly becoming stationary, that's what gets you.

Jeremy Clarkson

Last night I reached for my liquid Viagra but accidentally drank from a bottle of Tipp-Ex instead. I woke up this morning with a huge correction.

Alan Davies

Through no fault of his own, my uncle crashed his car into a lemon tree. He is still bitter and twisted.

Stewart Francis

When I finished high school I wanted to take all my graduation money and buy myself a motorcycle. But my mom said, 'No'. See, she had a brother who died in a horrible motorcycle accident when he was eighteen. And I could just have his motorcycle.

Anthony Jeselnik

(of the crew of the *Titanic*): I would imagine that in a sinking situation, you'd hope to be getting time and a half.

Phill Jupitus, *QI*

BP has put more birds in oil than Colonel Sanders.

David Letterman

Arnold Rimmer (Chris Barrie): You've got a scar. When did you get that?
Dave Lister (Craig Charles): Those complimentary pens that the hospital were giving out – you know, 'Most accidents happen in the home, so be careful' ones. I accidentally stabbed myself in the head with one.
Arnold: Where were you?
Dave: I wasn't at home, so I didn't feel stupid or anything.

Red Dwarf

Apparently fifty thousand people died from driving last year and ten thousand died from drinking. Yet only five hundred died from drink-driving. Then again, only two people died from drink-driving and juggling. I think that's my safest way home then.

Lee Mack

(explaining why she can no longer dance): I had an unfortunate incident with an apple pie in a well-known fast food chain. I can't tell you the name for libel reasons, but he was old . . . and he had a farm.

Beryl Merit (Rosalind Knight), *Gimme Gimme Gimme*

Ukraine announced plans to open Chernobyl, their nuclear disaster site, to tourists. They say it's just like Disneyland, except the six-foot mouse is real.

Conan O'Brien

I bought the journal of the Titanic Society. It's about a hundred pages, lots of stuff about the captain and how it was put together, but not one reference in the entire book to the fact that it sank. I love it when people are positive. With the Titanic Society, their ship is always half *empty* of water.

Frank Skinner, *QI*

After her accident, my nan had a plastic hip put in. But I thought they should have replaced it with a Slinky, 'cause if she did fall down the stairs again . . .

Steve Williams

I just got out of hospital. I was in a speed-reading accident. I hit a bookmark and flew across the room.

Steven Wright

If there is anything that this horrible tragedy can teach us, it's that a male model's life is a precious, precious commodity. Just because we have chiselled abs and stunning features, it doesn't mean that we, too, can't not die in a freak gasoline fight accident.

Derek Zoolander (Ben Stiller), *Zoolander*

Actors and Acting

I used to get the girl and the part. These days I'm lucky to get the part.

Sir Michael Caine, 2001/2

Theatre actors look down on film actors, who look down on TV actors. Thank God for reality shows or we wouldn't have anybody to look down on.

George Clooney, 2008

One of the fringe benefits of my work is that I often get to see people close up I once thought were ten feet tall on movie screens – or ten inches tall on TV. Most of them turn out to be somewhere in between.

Billy Crystal, *Absolutely Mahvelous*

Danny Dyer hasn't always been in *EastEnders* even though he feels like part of the furniture, especially when he's trying to act.

Philomena Cunk (Diane Morgan), *Cunk on Christmas*

I did a little bit of research and between all the nominees here tonight, you've made fourteen hundred films. And you've gone to a total of six years of college.

Ellen DeGeneres, hosting the 2014 Academy Awards

Come on, if you don't win tonight it doesn't mean you're not a good person. It just means you're not a good actor.

Ellen DeGeneres

Whenever I see a respected actor in panto I always like to shout out, 'It's beneath you!'

Gary Delaney, Twitter

Acting is really about lying and, in my case, drinking coffee.

Johnny Depp

I always fasted on Yom Kippur. I still worked on the movie sets but I fasted. And let me tell you, it wasn't easy making love to Lana Turner on an empty stomach.

Kirk Douglas

Just looking at all the wonderful faces here reminds me of some of the great work that was done this year . . . by cosmetic surgeons.

Ricky Gervais, hosting the 2010 Golden Globes

It's going to be a night of partying and heavy drinking. Or as Charlie Sheen calls it, breakfast.

Ricky Gervais, hosting the 2011 Golden Globes

(introducing Robert Downey Jr): Many of you in this room probably know him best from such facilities as the Betty Ford Clinic and Los Angeles county jail . . .

Ricky Gervais, hosting the 2011 Golden Globes

My sister wanted to be an actress, but she never made it. She does live in a trailer. She got halfway. She's an actress; she just never gets called to the set.

Mitch Hedberg

I lost a Tony award to Broadway legend Audra McDonald when I was twelve, so I've been a bitter bitch since before my first period.

Anna Kendrick, *Scrappy Little Nobody*

(to Charles Dance): Your fans are known as Charlie's Angels. Is that because there are only three of them?

Sushil Kumar (Meera Syal), *The Kumars at No. 42*

People are falling all over themselves to send you free shoes and free cufflinks and colonic irrigations for two, but nobody ever offers you a free acceptance speech. There just seems to be a gap in the market. I would love to be able to pull out a speech by Dolce & Gabbana.

Hugh Laurie

I don't think you can be really posh and be an interesting actor. I'm a bit of posh rough.

Damian Lewis

That's what I love about you, Barbara, you're one of us. You're like a big film star, but you're still common as muck!

Mrs Merton (Caroline Aherne) to Barbara Windsor, *The Mrs Merton Show*

When your leading ladies look like your granddaughter, it's time to move on.

Sir Roger Moore

Movie acting suits me because I only need to be good for ninety seconds at a time.

Bill Murray

In this industry, there are only two ways up the ladder: rung by rung or claw your way to the top. It's sure been tough on my nails.

Jack Nicholson

When people warned me there would be long periods out of work if I became an actor, I couldn't keep a straight face because that was exactly what I had in mind.

Bill Nighy

Sean Connery has such a deep love of Scotland that he refuses to use anything other than a Scottish accent no matter what role he is taking.

Graham Norton

Katie Holmes is not a very good actress. Did you see her try and play John F. Kennedy's wife? She was so bad he shot *himself* in it.

Joan Rivers

Ellen Barkin, you've always been ahead of your time. You were voted hottest woman over fifty at age thirty-six.

Jeff Ross

Theatricals can be irritating, but will provide a better night out than mobile phone salespeople.

Arthur Smith

Hugh [Laurie] is one of those people who manages to be lugubriously sexy – like a well-hung eel.

Emma Thompson

Raquel Turner (Tessa Peake-Jones): The tour doesn't start for another three months.
Del Trotter (David Jason): Oh well, gives you plenty of time to meet more of them intelligent, sensitive actor people, doesn't it?
Raquel: Derek, will you get it into your thick skull: I'm not trying to meet intelligent and sensitive people, I'm happy with you!

Only Fools and Horses

I've lost a lot of roles because of my height. I'm six-foot-three in heels. Producers are short and I was never their sexual fantasy.

Sigourney Weaver

They say an actor is only as good as his parts; well, my parts have done me pretty well, darling!

Barbara Windsor

Advice

_____

Keep the fights clean and the sex dirty.

> Kevin Bacon, on the basis for a happy marriage

Advice for when a child under four is having a tantrum is, 'Throw some water on them'. I tried it and my kid screamed even more. His mum said I shouldn't have used the kettle.

> John Bishop

Never do today that which will become someone else's responsibility tomorrow.

> David Brent (Ricky Gervais), _The Office_

Don't assume. It makes an 'ass' out of 'u' and 'me'.

> David Brent (Ricky Gervais), _The Office_

My mum told me the best time to ask my dad for anything was during sex. Not the best advice I'd ever been given. I burst in through the bedroom door saying, 'Can I have a new bike?' He was very upset. His secretary was surprisingly nice about it. I got the bike.

> Jimmy Carr

Never come out to your father in a moving vehicle.

> Kate Clinton

Never make a decision when you need to pee.

> Leonard Cohen, _Beautiful Losers_

Never follow anyone else's path, unless you're in the woods and you're lost and you see a path. Then by all means follow that path.

> Ellen DeGeneres

The only advice I ever got from my dad is this: sex is like pizza, even when it's bad, you still gotta pay for it.

> Nick Di Paolo

The one thing you shouldn't do is tell a cab driver how to get somewhere.

> Jimmy Fallon

When you encounter seemingly good advice that contradicts other seemingly good advice, ignore them both.

Al Franken, *Oh, the Things I Know!*

Live each day as if it were the last day of your life because, so far, it is.

Richard Jeni

Write the name of someone you hate on your body every day in permanent marker, so no matter how you die they'll become a suspect.

Mark Leggett, Twitter

A bit of advice: never read a pop-up book about giraffes.

Sean Lock

In a sexual situation, never use cute language when you can be obscene and insulting. (I mean insulting to her dignity – 'Get over that bed. You know you want it,' rather than 'Ooh, I think you've got a spot coming.')

Victoria Coren Mitchell

Don't play dead with a vulture. That's exactly what they want.

Kevin Nealon

Don't put your trust in revolutions. They always come around again. That's why they're called revolutions.

Sir Terry Pratchett, *Night Watch*

My dad used to say: 'Keep your chin up, son.' He once broke his jaw walking into a lamp-post.

Adam Sandler

Wear only a towel around your waist and you can get into just about anywhere if you just repeat, 'So sorry, so sorry' and keep moving forward.

Ted Travelstead, Twitter

If you're behind someone at an ATM at night, let them know you're not a threat by gently kissing their neck.

Bridger Winegar, Twitter

Worried that your teeth will be stained after a heavy night drinking red wine? Drink a bottle of white wine before going to bed, to remove the stains.

Top Tips, *Viz*

Age and Ageing

Mary Albright (Jane Curtin): When men get grey hair, they look distinguished. When women get grey hair, they look old.
Dick Solomon (John Lithgow): When women get breasts, they look sexy. When men get breasts, they look old.
Mary: Good point!

3rd Rock from the Sun

Birthdays are nature's way of telling us to eat more cake.

Jo Brand

After a certain age you get the face you deserve.

Joan Collins

After fifty, you have to stop seeing your heart as a muscle and more as an unexploded bomb.

Hal Cruttenden

Women your age are more likely to be mauled at the zoo than get married.

Jack Donaghy (Alec Baldwin), *30 Rock*

Sex for the woman in her fifties is a bit like making your own pastry; you know you should, but you're not sure if you can be bothered.

Jenny Eclair

I'm stuck in that awkward in-between stage where my hair is just starting to fall out but I'm still maintaining my youthful acne.

Greg Fitzsimmons

I'm twenty-six and my girlfriend is thirty-six. Is ten years' age gap a big difference to have sex? Because her sixteen-year-old sister is hot!

Micky Flanagan

I don't need you to remind me of my age. I have a bladder to do that for me.

Stephen Fry

I thought when I was forty-one, I would be married with kids. Well, to be honest, I thought I would be married with weekend access.

Sean Hughes

Age to women is like Kryptonite to Superman.

Kathy Lette

The way to stay young is to have early nights, give up booze and lie your head off about how old you are.

Kathy Lette

Having sex with men in their thirties is generally much better, but you've got to rub their legs afterwards for cramp.

Sarah Millican

I'm at the age where I don't have to kiss arse or play nice!

Sharon Osbourne

Adulthood is probably when you stop taking drugs to trip out and start taking drugs to feel normal.

Kelly Oxford, Twitter

Joan Collins lies about her age so much, we should have her body carbon-dated.

Joan Rivers

Ed, have you noticed that the older you get, the younger your girlfriends get? Soon you'll be dating sperm.

Mitch Robbins (Billy Crystal), *City Slickers*

Forty is only young if you die at forty. Or if you're sleeping with Cher.

Chris Rock

I'm going to be fifty this year. Soon I'm going to meet somebody around my own age, and she's going to be smart and beautiful, and I'm going to date her daughter.

Bob Saget

I'm at the age now where the roles reverse with my parents. I go shopping with them and it's like trying to organise little ducklings. They're wandering all over.

Jerry Seinfeld

I keep reading that I'm over the hill sexually. I don't even remember having a sexual peak when I was nineteen; I just remember apologising a lot.

Jeff Stilson

I've started wearing cardigans and saying things like, 'Whoops-a-daisy' and, when I take a first sip of tea, 'Ooh, that hits the spot!'

Gary Strang (Martin Clunes), Men Behaving Badly

You know your girlfriend is too young when she'll do everything in bed but go upside-down, because it's too scary.

Daniel Tosh

God, you look old, Sue! If you weren't talking, I might try and bury you.

Jill Tyrell (Julia Davis), Nighty Night

My father was never proud of me. One day he asked me, 'How old are you?' I said, 'I'm five.' He said, 'When I was your age, I was six.'

Steven Wright

Air Travel

It can hardly be a coincidence that no language on Earth has ever produced the expression, 'As pretty as an airport.'

Douglas Adams, The Long Dark Tea-Time of the Soul

The only way to explain how some people dress for the airport is they think no one else will be there.

Andy Borowitz

Unsettling things to hear from the cockpit of a plane: 'This is your captain speaking, we're out at the moment, please leave a message after the tone.'

Rory Bremner, *Mock the Week*

This is just a hunch, but I bet airplanes think helicopters are assholes.

Dana Gould

On a flight to Belfast, I was upgraded to business class. I was a bit scared. I thought, 'Will I have to play golf?'

Jeremy Hardy

I wonder how long it will be until airlines aren't only charging for physical baggage, but for emotional baggage too. Not that it'd bother me. I'm fine. Just ask my dad. WHO'S NEVER THERE!

Tegan Higginbotham

I'm absolutely terrified of flying. I don't mean nervous. I don't mean jumpy. I mean sobbing as the plane taxis down the runway. I mean strangers offering to hold my hand. I mean people ten rows behind going: 'Is that the woman from *Have I Got News For You* shouting the Lord's Prayer at the drinks trolley?'

Victoria Coren Mitchell

Experience has taught me that you feel better on a flight if you avoid chicken fat in plastic sauce.

Sir Terry Pratchett

On the plane across the aisle from us was a baby boy who, though tiny in stature, had a crying scream so piercing, it was annoying people on other planes.

Paul Reiser

Chocolates, perfume, cigarettes, alcohol: the airport duty-free shop is like a *Loose Women* theme park.

Frank Skinner, *Room 101*

Much of my dislike for aviation stems from the associated language. I don't like to depart from somewhere labelled 'terminal' and I hate the idea of a 'non-stop' flight.

Sandi Toksvig, *The Chain of Curiosity*

Airports are one of the few places where you can be sat in a Wetherspoons on your own, on a Sunday, and not feel like life hasn't turned out right.

Jack Whitehall

If God had intended us to fly he would have made it easier to get to the airport.

Jonathan Winters

Alcohol

It's scotch whisky, Glenlivet, single malt. When you die, you'll go to heaven, say 'Hello' to God. And when God says 'Hello' to you, this is what you'll smell on his breath.

Artie (Rip Torn), *The Larry Sanders Show*

Eggnog, who thought that one up? 'I want to get a little drunk, but I also want some pancakes.'

Dave Attell

Lucille Bluth (Jessica Walter): Get me a vodka rocks.
Michael Bluth (Jason Bateman): Mom, it's breakfast.
Lucille: And a piece of toast.

Arrested Development

Beer with no alcohol – what a waste. That's like a nun with a D-cup.

Brett Butler

I think the warning labels on alcohol beverages are too bland. They should be more vivid. Here is one I would suggest: 'Alcohol will turn you into the same asshole your father was.'

George Carlin, *When Will Jesus Bring the Pork Chops?*

I've had my run-ins with booze; it's well-documented. So what I can say from experience is that it takes a lot of guts and perseverance and courage to stop drinking. Which is why I haven't.

Jack Dee

For the past seventeen years, I have been experimenting with lager. I am a lager user and one drug leads to another. If you do lager, as night follows day, you'll end up doing Kentucky Fried Chicken.

Ben Elton

The closest thing I have to a nutritionist is the Carlsberg beer company.

Colin Farrell

When you don't drink, people always need to know why. They're like: 'You don't drink? Why?' This never happens with anything else. 'You don't use mayonnaise? Why? Are you addicted to mayonnaise? Is it OK if I use mayonnaise?'

Jim Gaffigan

Why do you need a driver's licence to buy liquor when you're not supposed to drink and drive?

Gallagher

I like a drink as much as the next man. Unless the next man is Mel Gibson.

Ricky Gervais

(after a customer uses the word 'alcoholic'): Old man, you know we don't use the 'A' word in here. We refer to them as the 'Liquid crusaders fighting the holy war against the teetotal Taliban'.

Guv (Al Murray), *Time Gentlemen Please*

I went out with a guy who once told me I didn't need to drink to make myself more fun to be around. I told him, 'I'm drinking so that you're more fun to be around.'

Chelsea Handler

Alcohol is like pouring smiles on your brain.

Chris Hardwick

(to his nephew Jake): Alcohol is for people who can afford to lose some brain cells.

Charlie Harper (Charlie Sheen), *Two and a Half Men*

There are these machines now that tell you when to stop drinking. They're called cashpoint machines.

Harry Hill

I did have a drinking problem. Southern Comfort tasted quite nice; ordinary Comfort tasted like fabric softener.

Milton Jones

Ever have trouble opening a bottle of champagne? My advice: hit it with a ship. I've seen people do that. It works.

Russell Kane

In Alaska, it's illegal to give an alcoholic beverage to a moose. How lonely are the guys in Alaska? If you're with a moose, wouldn't you want to be the drunk one?

Jay Leno

Sam Malone (Ted Danson): How's a beer sound, Norm?
Norm Peterson (George Wendt): I don't know. I usually finish them before they get a word in.

Cheers

There are better things in life than alcohol, but it makes up for not having them.

Sir Terry Pratchett

A weekend without drinking is no big deal. I did it that time I was in an alcohol-induced coma.

Homer Simpson (Dan Castellaneta), *The Simpsons*

Darling, if you want to talk bollocks and discover the meaning of life, you're better off downing a bottle of whisky. At least that way, you're unconscious by the time you start to take yourself seriously.

Patsy Stone (Joanna Lumley), *Absolutely Fabulous*

That's like saying Prada are just shoes, or vodka is just a morning beverage.

> Karen Walker (Megan Mullally), *Will & Grace*

Somebody's gotta be the designated drinker.

> Karen Walker (Megan Mullally), *Will & Grace*

Ben Doucette (Gregory Hines): Let's talk wine. Karen, have you any preferences?
Karen Walker: Honey, I'd suck the alcohol out of a deodorant stick, so you're asking the wrong gal, OK?

> *Will & Grace*

The easiest way to tell the difference between a chardonnay and a sauvignon blanc is to read the bottle.

> Bradley Walsh

My friends drink real ale, so I know how much better they are than me.

> Josh Widdicombe

Allergies

I can give you the cause of anaphylactic shock in a nutshell.

> Gary Delaney

We just found out my little brother has a peanut allergy, which is very serious I know. But still I feel like my parents are totally overreacting. They caught me eating a tiny bag of airline peanuts and they kicked me out of his funeral.

> Anthony Jeselnik

When the boys at school found out I had a potentially fatal peanut allergy, they used to hold me up against a wall and play Russian roulette with a bag of Revels.

> Milton Jones

My dad's allergic to cotton. He has pills he can take but he can't get them out of the bottle.

Brian Kiley

There is always someone worse off than yourself. At least you are not a monkey with an allergy to nuts.

Miles Kington

Margaret Tate (Sandra Bullock): What am I allergic to?
Andrew Paxton (Ryan Reynolds): Pine nuts and the full spectrum of human emotion.

The Proposal

We got so much food in America we're allergic to food. Allergic to food! Hungry people ain't allergic to shit. You think anyone in Rwanda's got a lactose intolerance?

Chris Rock

I'm allergic to rocks hitting me in the face.

Mike Rowe

Ambition

Keep the dream alive: hit the snooze button.

Anon

I used to want to be a movie star so I wouldn't have to live in trailers anymore. And now that I make movies, I spend a lot of my life living in trailers.

Roseanne Barr

If you find yourself born in Barnsley and then set your sights on being Virginia Woolf, it is not going to be roses all the way.

Alan Bennett

As a child I wanted to be abducted by aliens.

Russell Brand

I like when a woman has ambition. It's like seeing a dog wearing clothes.

Jack Donaghy (Alec Baldwin), *30 Rock*

I'm sick of following my dreams: I'm just going to ask them where they are going and hook up with them later.

Mitch Hedberg

I want to succeed in America where, unlike Britain, they do not regard ambition as being the same as eating babies.

Eddie Izzard

Resolution 1: will obviously lose twenty pounds. 2: always put last night's panties in the laundry basket. Equally important: will find nice sensible boyfriend and stop forming romantic attachments to any of the following: alcoholics, workaholics, sexaholics, commitment phobics, peeping toms, megalomaniacs, emotional fuckwits or perverts.

Bridget Jones (Renée Zellweger), *Bridget Jones's Diary*

Make a sex tape, upload it, get on a reality show, release a perfume, retire – that's the new American dream.

Natasha Leggero

It's easier to put on slippers than to carpet the whole world.

Stuart Smalley (Al Franken), *Stuart Saves His Family*

I always wanted to open a delicatessen in Jerusalem and call it Cheeses of Nazareth.

Sandi Toksvig

America

I am tired of hearing discrimination against Americans. Everybody hates Americans until they need to watch a good film, listen to some decent hip hop or go to war. What do you get when you add sunshine and personal space to a Brit? An American. Add health care and education and you get a Canadian.

Dana Alexander

When you move to New York, you realise it's not a melting pot at all. It's actually a bunch of pots that want to live next to their own kinds of pots and not talk to other pots.

Nate Bargatze

During the warm season (8 and 9 August), Maine is a true 'vacation paradise', offering visitors a chance to jump into crystal-clear mountain lakes and see if they can get back out again before their bodily tissue is frozen as solid as a supermarket turkey.

Dave Barry, *Dave Barry's Only Travel Guide You'll Ever Need*

In New York, tip the taxicab driver forty dollars if he does *not* mention his haemorrhoids.

Dave Barry

Just get on any major highway and eventually it will dead-end in a Disney parking area large enough to have its own climate, populated by large nomadic families who have been trying to find their cars since the Carter administration.

Dave Barry

Some people say America is not ready for a black president. But I know America to be a forward-thinking country, because otherwise would you have let that retarded cowboy fella be president for eight years? We were very impressed. We thought it was nice of you to let him have a go because in England, he wouldn't be trusted with a pair of scissors.

Russell Brand, hosting the 2008 MTV Video Music Awards

Stand on two phone books almost anywhere in Iowa and you get a view.

Bill Bryson, *The Lost Continent: Travels in Small-Town America*

There. Right there, Peg, is the problem with America. We've lost our spirit of self-reliance. Something's broken, call someone. Something's leaking, call someone. One of the kids suffers a ruptured appendix, call someone. Whatever happened to rugged American manhood?

Al Bundy (Ed O'Neill), *Married . . . With Children*

My problem with the Grand Canyon is Americans are too proud of it for my liking. The Grand Canyon was like that when they found it. And it's not like it was hard to find.

Ed Byrne

Selina Meyer (Julia Louis-Dreyfus): Can I really blame another country for something they didn't do?
Ben Cafferty (Kevin Dunn): It's been the cornerstone of American foreign policy since the Spanish-American War.

Veep

When you're born, you get a ticket to the freak show. When you're born in America, you get a front row seat.

George Carlin

(on the invention of Segways): They're made in America, of course, so fat Yanks can go to the fridge without expending any energy.

Jeremy Clarkson

Most Americans barely have the brains to walk on their back legs.

Jeremy Clarkson

Americans are good at herding bison. The end.

Jeremy Clarkson

New York, the city that never sleeps . . . with the same person two nights running. My favourite place in America, where *Sex and the City* isn't just a programme, it's a promise.

Daniel Cleaver (Hugh Grant), *Bridget Jones: The Edge of Reason*

New Yorkers weren't rude so much as tense. If I went into a tobacconist and started with my public school patter, 'I'm so sorry to bother you, but I'd rather like to buy some cigarettes, so if you'd be so good as to allow me to intrude upon your time . . .' they'd shout 'Whaddyawant?' as though you'd insulted them. But if you strode into the store, fixed them with a look of pure hatred and hissed the word 'Larks!', they'd smile and chat and tell you why they'd just left their wife.

John Cleese, *So Anyway . . .*

There's nothing more American tourists like than stuff they can get at home.

Stephen Colbert

I often confuse Americans and Canadians. By using long words.

Gary Delaney

Iowa is the only state in the country where you can stand on your front porch and actually watch your dog run away for three days.

Greg Fitzsimmons

It only takes a room of Americans for the English and Australians to realise how much we have in common.

Stephen Fry

In Montana, a policeman will pull you over because he is lonely.

Rich Hall

Living in New York is like being at some terrible late-night party. You're tired, you have had a headache since you arrived, but you can't leave, because you'd miss the party.

Simon Hoggart, *America: A User's Guide*

I dearly love the state of Texas, but I consider that a harmless perversion on my part and discuss it only with consenting adults.

Molly Ivins

The thing about making a documentary in Las Vegas is there isn't much to film apart from other people making documentaries about Las Vegas.

Clive James

In New York, the principal leisure activity is internal bleeding.

Richard Jeni

The United States has a kick-ass military and really good bullshit marketing people. If this country was a person, it would be a used car salesman with a flame-thrower.

Richard Jeni

When I was in America, I really got into the culture. I went into a shop and the guy said, 'Have a nice day' and I didn't, so I sued him.

Milton Jones

Las Vegas is like Blackpool, but on speed.

Peter Kay

The crime problem in New York is getting really serious. The other day the Statue of Liberty had both hands up.

Jay Leno

America is the only country where a significant proportion of the population believes that professional wrestling is real but the moon landing was faked.

David Letterman

Labor Day is a great American holiday that people celebrate by going out and buying products made in China.

David Letterman

New York is great. If you're here and want a one-of-a-kind souvenir, be sure to take home the police sketch of your assailant.

David Letterman

Don't you miss the days when America was just *morally* bankrupt?

Bill Maher, 2010

I live in Los Angeles. I know you're not supposed to be able to taste air . . .

Marc Maron

The American legal system sucks worse than a Celine Dion cover version of 'Whole Lotta Love'.

Dennis Miller

I moved to LA, so I joined a gym, because it was either that or a gang.

Sue Murphy

Have you ever watched footage of the destruction caused by hurricanes in America? When a big wind sweeps across America, there isn't a building left standing. And you can't help thinking the southern states of America must have been built by the first two little piggies.

Dara O'Briain

You can't smoke in a restaurant in Los Angeles, which is mildly ironic when you consider the fact that you can't breathe outside a restaurant in Los Angeles.

Greg Proops

People in LA are deathly afraid of gluten. I swear to God, you could rob a liquor store in this city with a bagel.

Ryan Reynolds

This is America! Anyone can eat what they want as long as it's too much.

Homer Simpson (Dan Castellaneta), *The Simpsons*

If America leads a blessed life, then why did God put all of our oil under people who hate us?

Jon Stewart

The difference between the North and the South: in the North, there's a cutoff age for sleeping with your parents.

Judy Tenuta, *The Power of Judyism*

Nebraska is proof that hell is full and the dead are walking the Earth.

Lizz Winstead

People in London think of London as the centre of the world, whereas New Yorkers think the world ends three miles outside of Manhattan.

Toby Young

Anger

When Mom got mad, she'd threaten me, 'Wait till your father gets home.'
I'd say, 'Mom, it's been eight years . . .'

Brett Butler

To have a grievance is to have a purpose in life.

Alan Coren

I'm the police dog of finding stuff to complain about.

Anna Kendrick, Twitter

What I hear when I'm being yelled at is people caring loudly at me.

Leslie Knope (Amy Poehler), *Parks and Recreation*

I told myself that it took forty-two facial muscles to frown and only four to
stretch out my arm and bitch-slap the witch.

Kathy Lette, *To Love, Honour and Betray*

Whining is anger through a small opening.

Stuart Smalley (Al Franken)

You're in a tizzy. Your nostrils are that flared, you could park a bus up 'em.

Rita Sullivan (Barbara Knox), *Coronation Street*

Well, remember what you said because in a day or two I'll have a witty
and blistering retort! You'll be devastated *then*.

Bill Watterson, *Calvin and Hobbes*

Animals

Why do people want to swim with dolphins? The equivalent would be an
Indonesian fellow coming over here, going up to a farmer and saying:
'Can I get in with the cows? I just fancy scuffling about with them.'

Bill Bailey

So many pigs seem to die while eating an apple.

John Brennan, Twitter

Stephen Fry: How do otters kill crocodiles?
Rob Brydon: Softly with their songs.

QI

In pursuit of scientific answers, animals have been tortured for the past hundred years. They're still not talking. I'm starting to think they don't know anything.

Jimmy Carr

I don't often agree with the RSPCA as I believe it's an animal's duty to be on my plate at suppertime.

Jeremy Clarkson

Is the underneath of an elephant its chest or its torso? It's a huge grey area.

Tony Cowards, Twitter

Animals look at people the way people look at people who might mug them.

Dov Davidoff

So it turns out that if you bang two halves of a horse together, it doesn't make the sound of a coconut.

Ken Dodd

A polar bear is one of the few animals that will stalk a human. If you go to where polar bears live, it might stalk you and when you're on the plane going home, it might be behind you reading.

Craig Ferguson

Kids: if a bear is wearing a ranger hat, it's because he ate the ranger!

Craig Ferguson, on cute US advertising mascot Smokey Bear, created to educate the public about the danger of forest fires

Animals: fun to pet, better to chew.

Jim Gaffigan

My favourite animal is the manatee, the sea cow. Have you ever seen that animal? The manatee is endangered, and I think it's because it's out of shape. It looks like a retired football player.

Jim Gaffigan

The giant panda: what a beautiful, beautiful creature. A word of warning, though, its fur is not machine-washable.

Brüno Gehard (Sacha Baron Cohen)

What's the difference between a hippo and a Zippo? One is really heavy, the other is a little lighter.

Masai Graham

Chris Griffin (Seth Green): Dad, what's the blowhole for?
Peter Griffin (Seth MacFarlane): I'll tell you what it's *not* for, son. And when I do, you'll understand why I can never go back to Sea World.

Family Guy

Animals are happier than humans because they're like furry little existentialists, all living in the moment. Their collective motto: live fast, die young and leave a good-looking pelt.

Richard Jeni

Jerry (Jerry Seinfeld): They're cloning sheep now.
Cosmo Kramer (Michael Richards): No, they're not cloning sheep. It's the same sheep! I saw Harry Blackstone do that trick with two goats and a handkerchief on the old Dean Martin show!

Seinfeld

I had to take the RSPCA advice quite seriously because they said you should check under your bonfire [on Guy Fawkes night] for sleeping hedgehogs. I couldn't find any, but luckily I had some in the freezer.

Sean Lock

How fast does a zebra have to run before it looks grey?

Demetri Martin

I used to go out with a giraffe. I used to take it to the pictures. You'd always get some bloke complaining that he couldn't see the screen. 'It's a giraffe, mate. What do you expect?' 'Well, he can take his hat off for a start.'

Paul Merton, *Have I Got News for You*

What do you think you should do if you're attacked by a bear? Play dead? No, that's a lie promoted by bears.

Eugene Mirman

Guide dogs for the blind. It's cruel really, isn't it? Getting a dog to lead a man around all day. Not fair on either of them.

Alan Partridge (Steve Coogan), *I'm Alan Partridge*

If only someone would do for cows what Bambi did for deer. Cows have been in films, but they haven't starred. I'm still willing to eat a species that is only a supporting player.

Paula Poundstone

Animals have two vital functions in today's society: to be delicious and to fit well.

Greg Proops

I got involved with an animal charity recently and adopted a whale and a monkey, which is all very well, but sooner or later I'm gonna have to be the one who has to explain to them why they don't look like each other.

Mark Restuccia

I'm opposed to product testing on animals, especially in cosmetics research. What can we possibly learn from it? So what if a dog looks good in lipstick?

Jeff Stilson

It hit me how resentful it must make rats, knowing that they're just a bushy tail away from being hand-fed in the park.

Jeff Stilson

My grandfather once killed a bear. It was looking the other way, so he pushed it off a cliff.

Mark Watson

Animosity

Malcolm Tucker (Peter Capaldi): Don't take it personally.
Hugh Abbot (Chris Langham): You're telling me she doesn't like me as a person. How else am I supposed to take it?

The Thick of It

The great thing about forgetting people you hate is that when you remember them it's like hating them for the very first time.

Nina Bargiel, Twitter

Know someone you hate? Give their kid a kazoo.

Dana Gould

The only thing that will be remembered about my enemies after they're dead are the nasty things I've said about them.

Camille Paglia

There's only two things I hate in this world. People who are intolerant of other people's cultures and the Dutch.

Nigel Powers (Michael Caine), *Austin Powers in Goldmember*

I don't despise, because no one should live rent-free inside your head.

Anne Robinson

I don't hate you . . . I just don't like that you exist.

Gena Showalter, *Seduce the Darkness*

Apology

It's like I used to tell my wife: I do not apologise unless I think I'm wrong. And if you don't like it, you can leave. And I say the same thing to my current wife and I'll say it to my next one, too.

Stanley Hudson (Leslie David Baker), *The Office* (US)

George Costanza (Jason Alexander): You've got to apologise.

Jerry (Jerry Seinfeld): Why?

George: Because it's the mature and adult thing to do.

Jerry: How does that affect me?

Seinfeld

An apology is the superglue of life. It can repair just about anything.

Lynn Johnston

Saying 'I'm sorry' is the same as saying 'I apologise' . . , except at a funeral.

Demetri Martin

You know you're a true married couple when you have to apologise for what you did in her dream.

Ray Romano

The only other person I've apologised to is my mother, and that was court-ordered.

Karen Walker (Megan Mullally), *Will & Grace*

Appearance

Can you watch Andrew Lloyd Webber? He looks like he's had his face carved off by a diseased butcher, put in a piñata, beaten with hockey sticks for six hours and then the resulting slop piped back onto his head like the icing on the ugliest cake the world has ever seen.

Frankie Boyle

I would define my looks as a Victorian child-catcher.

Russell Brand

Beauty is in the eye of the beholder, which is a pity because this week the National Association of Beholders wrote to tell me that I've got a face like a rucksack full of dented bells.

Charlie Brooker

I just look like someone with a long face. Not just A. P. McCoy himself, but some of the horses he rides.

Rob Brydon

I always look skint. When I buy a *Big Issue*, people take it out of my hand and give me a pound.

Billy Connolly

Elliot Reid (Sarah Chalke): Oh, Dr Cox. Does this lipstick make me look like a clown?
Dr Perry Cox (John C. McGinley): No, it makes you look like a prostitute who caters exclusively to clowns.

Scrubs

I'd like to tell my wife I look like Brad Pitt, but unfortunately she can see.

Larry David (himself), *Curb Your Enthusiasm*

I am best viewed from a distance . . . and at night.

Jenny Eclair

I look like a troll wearing a woman's wig backwards.

Noel Fielding

Looking in the mirror, staring back at me isn't so much a face as the expression of a predicament.

Colin Firth

A woman with the kind of face that once seen is rarely remembered. Never was there a creature more appropriately placed to be the poster girl for euthanasia.

Dawn French, *A Tiny Bit Marvellous*

[comedian] Greg Davies looks like the bloated corpse of Rik Mayall.

Rhod Gilbert, *Never Mind the Buzzcocks*

I don't look like Halle Berry. But chances are she's going to end up looking like me.

Whoopi Goldberg

You always think people at the BBC are going to be glamorous and then you remember Nicholas Witchell works there.

> Rev. Geraldine Granger (Dawn French), *The Vicar of Dibley*

Saw a guy with three lip-ring piercings on the subway today. Took everything in my power not to attach a shower curtain.

> Sam Grittner, Twitter

I have a good side and a bad side. On my good side, I have a jaw and a chin, it's OK, but on my bad side, oh, dear, the neck goes away, my nose becomes this malformed thing and half a cheek sticks out. I go from Richard Gere to Richard Nixon.

> Tom Hanks

Skirt no bigger than a belt, too much eyeliner, and roots as dark as her soul.

> Blanche Hunt (Maggie Jones) on Liz McDonald
> (Beverley Callard), *Coronation Street*

His pear-shaped head, I could now see, was situated on top of a pear-shaped body, which his black gown caused to resemble a piece of fruit going to a funeral.

> Clive James, *May Week Was In June*

Say what you will about Charles Manson, but he's one of the only people with the decency to look like a dangerous maniac the first time you meet him.

> Richard Jeni

Michael Jackson is what happens when you keep fixing it until it's broke.

> Richard Jeni

He had a new girl and I told him she looked like Marilyn Monroe. He smiled because he thought I meant she was beautiful, and I smiled because I meant she looked like a corpse.

> Jarod Kintz, *The* Titanic *would never have
> sunk if it were made out of a sink*

Looking at my face is like reading in the car. It's all right for ten minutes, then you start to feel sick.

Andrew Lawrence

I've got enough crow's feet to start a bird sanctuary.

Kathy Lette

I don't like to watch myself on screen because, in my mind, there is a touch of George Clooney about me but, when I see it, there is more than a little Donkey from *Shrek* about me.

Stephen Mangan

I hate seeing people that look like me. Especially if God's living by the motto: 'If at first you don't succeed . . .'

Demetri Martin

Whenever I see a man with a beard, moustache and glasses, I think: There's a man who has taken every precaution to avoid people doodling on photographs of him.

Carey Marx

I don't worry about losing my looks. It's finding them on someone else that worries me.

Simon Munnery

With my sunglasses on, I'm Jack Nicholson. Without them, I'm fat and seventy.

Jack Nicholson

I speed up past mirrors.

Bill Nighy

When I was about thirteen, I realised girls weren't going to kiss me because I was a gigantic, weird-looking creature from the depths. I was like six foot, aged eleven.

Chris O'Dowd

I'm really white. I'm English white, that's basically turbo-white. My skin is borderline translucent. If I'm standing and the sun is behind me, I'm a functioning x-ray.

John Oliver

My face was designed as a leisure accessory.

Alan Partridge (Steve Coogan), *Knowing Me,*
Knowing You with Alan Partridge

I've spent my whole life being told I have a face like a horse.

Jeremy Paxman

When I was growing up, I knew I was different. The other girls were blonde and delicate, and I was a swarthy six-year-old with sideburns.

Toula Portokalos (Nia Vardalos), *My Big Fat Greek Wedding*

[at a comedy show in a prison] You look like what happens when the morning-after pill kind of works.

Jeff Ross

I usually feel pretty good about myself. I know what I look like. You'd bang me, but you wouldn't blog about it . . . It's fine.

Amy Schumer

I see my large nose, like half an avocado. I broke it falling downstairs when I was six and it now resembles a large blob of Play-Doh.

Arthur Smith

Michael Portillo seems to have his lips on inside out.

Linda Smith

Carla Tortelli (Rhea Perlman): Lilith, you look like a million bucks.
Dr Lilith Sternin-Crane (Bebe Neuwirth): Thank you, Carla.
Carla: You didn't let me finish. What I was going to say was you look like a million bucks just stampeded across your face.

Cheers

When I look in the mirror I don't see a rock star anymore. I see a little balding old guy who looks like someone's uncle.

Pete Townshend

I've got little ankles and a bit of a belly, so it makes me look rather like an egg on legs.

Johnny Vegas

I forget as many faces as I do names these days. I think I may have forgotten my own, because the face that looks out at me from the bathroom mirror doesn't look like the me I remember.

Sir Terry Wogan

Argument

Your argument is buttocks: it stinks, it has a large crack up the middle and frankly it's beneath you.

Marcus Brigstocke, *The Now Show*

Wil Wheaton (himself): Sheldon, do you really think we're going to fight?
Sheldon Cooper (Jim Parsons): My fists are not up here because I'm milking a giant, invisible cow.

The Big Bang Theory

. . . and I stormed out and slammed the door! Of course, it was that fourteenth-century Bavarian cathedral door, so I had to get two of the servants to help me, but what it lacked in spontaneity it made up for in resonance.

Niles Crane (David Hyde Pierce), *Frasier*

She gave me a bunch of crap about me not listening to her or something. I don't know, I wasn't really paying attention.

Harry Dunne (Jeff Daniels), *Dumb and Dumber*

I think I had an argument with a hypnotist this morning. It makes perfect sense as I have no memory of it.

Dana Gould

You'd better watch who you're calling a child, Lois. Because if I'm a child, you know what that makes you? A paedophile. And I'll be damned if I'm gonna be lectured by a pervert!

Peter Griffin (Seth MacFarlane), *Family Guy*

Richard, I'm warning you. If you don't shut up and let me watch *Miss World*, I'm going to stuff your head up your bum! And you'll spend the rest of your life wandering around on all fours looking for the light switch.

Eddie Hitler (Adrian Edmondson), *Bottom*

My parents only had one argument in forty-five years. It lasted forty-three years.

Cathy Ladman

Lucy (Sally Bretton): So what if I forgot our poxy anniversary?
Lee (Lee Mack): I think this year is copper; fourteenth is poxy.

Not Going Out

I was stuck in traffic and I looked in the mirror and in the car behind me there was a couple having a horrible argument, and right below their image it said, 'Objects in mirror are closer than they appear'. I just thought, Man, I hope so because she was pretty mad.

Demetri Martin

Unlike your thighs, your argument doesn't retain water.

Jack McFarland (Sean Hayes) to Karen Walker
(Megan Mullally), *Will & Grace*

I'm not a fighter, I'm a bleeder.

Dylan Moran

He who disagrees with me in private, call him a fool. He who disagrees with me in public, call him an ambulance.

Simon Munnery

Homer Simpson (Dan Castellaneta): Can you yell at me now and get it over with?
Marge Simpson (Julie Kavner): No, I'm going to parcel my anger out over the next few days and weeks, jabbing at you just when you seem the most content.

The Simpsons

When my wife and I argue, we're like a band in concert: we start with some new stuff and then we roll out our greatest hits.

Frank Skinner

When you see a married couple walking down the street, the one that's a few steps ahead is the one that's mad.

Daniel Tosh

Art

Subsidy is for art, for culture. It is not to be given to what the people *want*. It is for what the people *don't* want but ought to have!

Sir Humphrey Appleby (Nigel Hawthorne), *Yes, Minister*

The windmill was invented for the sole purpose of filling up the blank bits in the back of sixteenth-century Flemish paintings.

Alan Coren

A picture is worth a thousand words, but conversations with them generally end in disappointment.

Dov Davidoff

Why do they call that funny little statue a bust when it stops right before the part of the body that it's named after?

Gallagher

What's the difference between art and pornography? A government grant.

Peter Griffin (Seth MacFarlane), *Family Guy*

Good art is in the wallet of the beholder.

Kathy Lette

The thing about glitter is if you get it on you, be prepared to have it on you forever. Glitter is the herpes of craft supplies.

Demetri Martin

To me, the *Mona Lisa* looks like she's chewing a toffee.

Justin Moorhouse

In the gents a couple of weeks ago I did see someone had drawn a lady's part. Quite detailed. The guy obviously had talent.

Alan Partridge (Steve Coogan), *I'm Alan Partridge*

Originality is for people with short memories.

Grayson Perry

(of Anthony Williams' portrait of Queen Elizabeth II for her seventieth birthday): She deserves better than to be perpetuated as an old age pensioner about to lose her bungalow.

Brian Sewell

Hey, what's the worst that can happen if you piss off a German painter? Sandi Toksvig, on Queen Elizabeth's lukewarm response to the gift of a royal portrait by German artist Nicole Leidenfrost in 2015

Astrology

Astrology really annoys me. When people say to me, 'What sign are you?', I usually say, 'No overtaking, humpback bridge.'

Alexei Sayle

The margin of error in astrology is plus or minus one hundred per cent.

Calvin Trillin

Atheism

Isn't an agnostic just an atheist without balls?

Stephen Colbert

Atheism is a religion like abstinence is a sex position.

Bill Maher

I do remember once going out with a lady who was raised atheist and was an utter chore to walk around an art gallery with. She'd go, 'Who's the guy on the sticks? Is he the same guy who was in the shed earlier on?'

Dara O'Briain, QI

The annoying thing about being an atheist is that you'll never have the satisfaction of saying to believers: 'I told you so.'

Mark Steel

Australia

Every country is like a particular type of person. America is like a belligerent, adolescent boy, Canada is like an intelligent, thirty-five-year-old woman, Australia is like Jack Nicholson.

Douglas Adams

I decided to come up with a new slogan for Canberra. First I wrote: 'Canberra – there's nothing to it!' and then 'Canberra – why wait for death?'

Bill Bryson, *Down Under: Travels in a Sunburned Country*

Stone, paper, scissors: to most of us it's a game, but to Australians it's a wedding list.

Angus Deayton

The land that foreplay forgot.

Germaine Greer

I've got a sister in Australia, so when I phone her up there is a slight delay on the line after I've spoken, because she's a bit thick.

Harry Hill

Bret (Bret McKenzie): I would never go out with an Australian!
Jemaine (Jemaine Clement): But if you were to, I would be fine with it.
Bret: When I first met you, you tried to have me deported from New Zealand because you thought I was an Australian.
Jemaine: That was a misunderstanding; you were wearing a vest top.

Flight of the Conchords

The use of the word 'just' by an Australian means that whatever it is you have to do, it will not be easy, as in, 'Just pull that sword out of the stone,' or 'Just split that atom.'

Michael Palin, *Full Circle with Michael Palin*

One thing I'm very concerned about Australia is that we lack the ability to name cyclones properly. We're really bad at it. I mean, no one is scared of Cyclone Pam!

Andy Saunders

Automobiles

Cars will soon have the internet on the dashboard. I worry that this will distract me from my texting.

Andy Borowitz

My favourite road sign is 'Falling rocks'. What exactly am I supposed to do with that information? They may as well have a sign saying, 'Random accidents ahead. Life's a lottery. Be lucky.'

Jimmy Carr

You think it's possible for them to design an electric car that doesn't look like a gay spaceship?

Jeff Cesario

Racing cars which have been converted for road use never really work. It's like making a hardcore adult film, and then editing it so that it can be shown in British hotels. You'd just end up with a sort of half-hour close-up of some bloke's sweaty face.

Jeremy Clarkson, *Top Gear*

(of the Porsche Cayenne): I've seen gangrenous wounds better looking than this.

Jeremy Clarkson, *Top Gear*

(of a family car): Much more of a hoot to drive than you might imagine. Think of it, if you like, as a librarian with a G-string under the tweed. I do, and it helps.

Jeremy Clarkson

The Suzuki Wagon R should be avoided like unprotected sex with an Ethiopian transvestite.

Jeremy Clarkson

I'm sorry, but having an Aston Martin DB9 on the drive and not driving it is a bit like having Keira Knightley in your bed and sleeping on the couch.

Jeremy Clarkson, *Top Gear*

I wish they'd stop improving car washes. They just keep adding to the choice on that menu: the super valet, super foam valet, super wax valet. When all you want is a button that says: 'Get this shit off my bonnet.'

Jack Dee

Ever drive by one of those things on the highway that tells you how fast you're going? I don't even pay attention to them anymore because I found a similar gadget in my dashboard.

Gary Gulman

You could stick a BMW badge on a dead cat and people would still buy it.

Richard Hammond, *Top Gear*

Unless I have been sorely misinformed, supermodels are powerless to resist a man with illuminated door sills.

Richard Hammond

I know a lot about cars. I can look at any car's headlights and tell you exactly which way it's travelling.

Mitch Hedberg

Surely every car is a people carrier?

Adam Hess

There's an undeniable pleasure in stepping into an open-top sports car driven by a beautiful woman. It feels like you're climbing into a metaphor.

Hugh Laurie, *The Gun Seller*

If you asked my father about cars, he could have told you everything from the engine capacity to the diameter of the wheel arch on every vehicle he ever owned. I think my first car – or was it the second? – might have been blue.

Victoria Coren Mitchell

It is better to travel than to arrive, said someone who'd never gone very far in an Austin Maestro.

Tim Moore, *You Are Awful (But I Like You): Travels Through Unloved Britain*

I put so much petrol in my car the other day, I couldn't get in.

Vic Reeves

You know what I never get with the limo? The tinted windows. Is that so people don't see you? Yeah, what better way not to have people notice you than taking a thirty-foot Cadillac with a TV antenna and a uniformed driver? You see a limo go by, you know it's either some rich jerk or fifty prom kids with one dollar seventy-five each.

Jerry Seinfeld

Gabrielle Solis (Eva Longoria): We had sex in his limo yesterday.
Edie Britt (Nicollette Sheridan): Ooh, I love limo sex. Town car or stretch?
Gabrielle: Well, stretch, of course. I'm not a complete slut.

Desperate Housewives

Every weekend, I would get the drunk-driving lecture. Of course, Dad drank and drove all the time. I guess it wasn't a lecture; it was helpful tips from the master.

Christopher Titus

Here, Boycie. You know this car's a GTI. If you rearrange the letters, then you got yourself a personalised number plate!

Del Trotter (David Jason), *Only Fools and Horses*

I welcome this new road and every blast of carbon monoxide it brings. If God had meant us to walk everywhere, he wouldn't have given us Little Chefs.

Rev. Bernice Woodall (Reece Shearsmith), *The League of Gentlemen*

I bought this thing for my car. You put it on your car, it sends out this little noise, so when you drive through the woods, deer won't run in front of your car. I installed it backwards by accident. Driving down the street with a herd of deer chasing me. Those were the days.

Steven Wright

Babies

Babies are equipped at birth with a number of instinctive reflexes and behaviour patterns that cause them to spend their first several years trying to kill themselves. If your home contains a sharp, toxic object, your baby will locate it; if your home contains no such object, your baby will try to obtain one via mail order.

Dave Barry

Ross Geller (David Schwimmer): I think it'll be a boy.
Phoebe Buffay (Lisa Kudrow): I think it'll be a girl.
Ross: Phoebe, you thought Ben would be a girl.
Phoebe: Have you seen him throw a ball?

Friends

It amazes me that a baby can be born unable to see, hear, speak, walk, or even solve the *Sun*'s coffee-time crossword, but is capable of generating a sound so loud it can dislodge masonry at forty paces.

Jeremy Clarkson

Crystal Anderson Conner (Natalie West): Why won't he sleep? I've tried everything, even the washing machine!
Darlene Conner (Sara Gilbert): You put him in the washing machine?!
Crystal: No, Darlene. You put him in his little baby seat *on* the washer and the vibrations are supposed to soothe him to sleep.
Roseanne Conner (Roseanne Barr): Yeah, you know, when you were a baby, we couldn't afford a washing machine, so I had to take you down to the river and beat you against a rock.

Roseanne

I don't want to get the same looks I give people when they get on a plane holding a baby: 'That's a cute baby, just keep walking, keep walking, keep going, keep going . . .'

Ellen DeGeneres

I hate when new parents ask who the baby looks like. It was born fifteen minutes ago: it looks like a potato.

Will Ferrell

A Harvard Medical School study has determined that rectal thermometers are still the best way to tell a baby's temperature. Plus, it really teaches the baby who's boss.

Tina Fey

Changing a diaper is a lot like getting a present from your grandmother – you're not sure what you've got but you're pretty sure you're not going to like it.

Jeff Foxworthy

Did you know babies are nauseated by the smell of a clean shirt?

Jeff Foxworthy

Son, when you have them, little babies, you love them. Even if they're real mingers. I mean, when Ian was born he looked like David Gest.

Frank Gallagher (David Threlfall), *Shameless*

Rachel and Ross are so irresponsible. Their baby is the product of a bottle of merlot and a five-year-old condom.

Monica Geller (Courteney Cox), *Friends*

If this baby's half as bad as our least bad one, we're still ruined.

Hal (Bryan Cranston), *Malcolm in the Middle*

People show you their babies on their phone now, and it's like a cashew with some hair coming out of it. The thing to say is, 'Nice phone.'

Rich Hall, *QI*

A tip to all new mothers: don't put your baby in bed with you because you might fall asleep, roll on it and put your back out.

Harry Hill

He has one ball and I have a lazy ovary! In what twisted world does that create a baby? It's like the Special Olympics of conception.

Miranda Hobbes (Cynthia Nixon), *Sex and the City*

Pamela Jones (Gemma Jones): Oh, no, Bridget. Who's the father? Is it Mark's?
Bridget Jones (Renée Zellweger): There's at least a fifty per cent chance.
Pamela: A fifty per cent chance? Did you have a three-way?

Bridget Jones's Baby

People who care about celebrity babies are creepy. 'What will her baby look like?' A baby. You've seen a baby, right? It'll look like that.

Anna Kendrick, Twitter

A balanced meal is whatever stays on the spoon en route to a baby's mouth.

Kathy Lette

As a breastfeeding mother, you are basically just meals on heels.

Kathy Lette

I find breastfeeding in public offensive. What particularly annoys me is when they turn away so you can't see.

Sean Lock

Me and my girlfriend had a lot of rows about the whole baby thing. I've wanted to have a baby for about five years. But she wants to keep it forever.

Lee Mack

You learn about humans when you have a baby. Like girls. Girls are so much more advanced than boys. I seriously think that girls are born in conversation. They come out of the womb talking: 'Are you my mother? Lovely to put a name to a face.'

Michael McIntyre

Social worker: Vicky, where is the baby?

Vicky Pollard (Matt Lucas): Swapped it for a Westlife CD.

Social worker: How could you do such a thing?

Vicky: I know, they're rubbish.

Little Britain

Babies awaken slightly disoriented, with a look that's half angel and half lost tourist.

Paul Reiser

All babies look like Renée Zellweger pushed against a glass window.

Joan Rivers

The baby advice says: 'It's safest to let them sleep alone, especially if you drink, use drugs or are overweight.' Yeah, I thought that was weird, too. But if you think about it, if you're drunk, stoned or really fat, in the middle of the night, that baby might look delicious. I've eaten weirder things.

Amy Schumer

My friend has a sixteen-month-old. The baby's crawling around and has an accident in his diaper. And the mother comes over and says, 'Isn't that adorable? Brandon made a gift for Daddy.' I'm thinking this guy must be real easy to shop for on Father's Day.

Garry Shandling

Babies aren't dishwasher-safe.

Daniel Tosh

Bankers and Banking

Following their financial meltdown, bankers in Iceland are being thrown in jail. The prosecution is using a little-known thing called 'justice'.

Jay Leno

If you have a gun, you can rob a bank, but if you have a bank, you can rob everyone.

Bill Maher

'Here you can shoot the bad guys,' a mercenary says in Baghdad. 'In America, we give them corporate bonuses.'

Michael Robotham, *The Wreckage*

Banks aren't neutral observers, they're . . . the people who caused this mess. It's like someone who's wet themselves in a public building insisting they choose which mop the librarian fetches to clear up the puddle.

Mark Steel

Baseball

If a tie is like kissing your sister, losing is like kissing your grandmother with her teeth out.

George Brett

Baseball fans love numbers. They love to swirl them around their mouths like Bordeaux wine.

Pat Conroy

The last time the Chicago Cubs won the World Series, people weren't able to clap because we still had flippers. What we now call humans were still evolving from the sea.

Jimmy Kimmel, after the Cubs' 2016 triumph, their first in 108 years

Major League baseball has asked its players to stop tossing baseballs into the stands during games, because they say fans fight over them and they get hurt. In fact, the Florida Marlins said that's why they never hit any home runs. It's a safety issue.

Jay Leno

My best advice to any player? Don't park in the spaces marked 'Reserved for umpires'.

Ex-umpire John McSherry

Basketball

We don't need referees in basketball, but it gives the white guys something to do.

Charles Barkley

I pray if I ever find out I have only about three minutes to live it's during a basketball game, because then I'll have, what, ten, twelve years to live?

Elayne Boosler

I'm six-foot-eleven. My birthday covers three days.

Darryl Dawkins

The first time I saw Dick Vitale, his hair was blowing in the breeze. And he was too proud to chase it.

Cliff Ellis

Basketball is a turn based strategy game in which teams attempt to damage a hoop with long distance projectile attacks or devastating melee.

Bevis Simpson, Twitter

Basketball is the second-most exciting indoor sport and the other one shouldn't have spectators.

Dick Vertlieb

We were so bad last year, the cheerleaders stayed home and phoned in their cheers.

Pat Williams

Manute Bol is so skinny, his pyjamas have only one pinstripe.

Pat Williams

When the list of great coaches is finally read out, I believe Frank Layden will be there . . . listening.

Pat Williams

Beauty

Beauty is fleeting, but a rent-controlled apartment overlooking the park is forever.

Carrie Bradshaw (Sarah Jessica Parker), *Sex and the City*

The first time I set eyes on Mary Swanson, I just got that old-fashioned, romantic feeling where I'd do anything to bone her.

Lloyd Christmas (Jim Carrey), *Dumb and Dumber*

The problem with beauty is that it's like being born rich and getting poorer.

Joan Collins

Manicures are basically just holding hands with a stranger for forty-five minutes whilst listening to Enya.

Miranda Hart, *Is It Just Me?*

Good looks are a curse, Deirdre. You and Kenneth should count your-selves lucky.

Blanche Hunt (Maggie Jones), *Coronation Street*

A woman's handbag is full of things which will make her look beautiful, plus a canister of mace to deal with men driven mad by her beauty.

Miles Kington

Make-up is such a weird concept. I'll wake up in the morning and look in the mirror: 'Gee, I really don't look so good. Maybe if my eyelids were blue, I'd be more attractive.'

Cathy Ladman

Max Reede (Justin Cooper): My teacher tells me beauty is on the inside.
Fletcher Reede (Jim Carrey): That's just something ugly people say.

Liar Liar

In a thousand years, archaeologists will dig up tanning beds and think we fried people as punishment.

Olivia Wilde

It's a problem being beautiful. It's only the handsome men that ask us out, because they're the only ones who think they have a chance. And handsome men are dolts. Life is unfair to us. At some point we have to face the certain reality: despite all the good the world seems to offer, true happiness can only be found in one thing – shopping.

Ling Woo (Lucy Liu), Ally McBeal

My girlfriend does her nails with white-out. When she's asleep, I go over there and write misspelled words on them.

Steven Wright

Birds

The internet says pigeons can fly at sixty-five miles per hour. They can, just not necessarily in a straight line. This is a myth created by crows.

Tim FitzHigham

I find that ducks' opinion of me is greatly influenced by whether or not I have bread.

Mitch Hedberg

I wonder what kind of bird Humpty Dumpty would have hatched out to, had he lived.

Harry Hill

Flamingos divorce each other every year. They are nature's version of Cheryl Cole, but with thicker legs.

Tom Hollander, Have I Got News for You

An Australian relief effort is knitting sweaters to protect the fur of penguins who are being affected by an oil spill. The sweaters are being refused by many penguins who would rather die than dress casual.

Conan O'Brien

You can't lose a homing pigeon. If your homing pigeon doesn't come back, then what you've lost is a pigeon.

Sara Pascoe

Good thing you put a swing in your bird's cage. He's probably on that thing like, 'Man this is way better than flying.'

@sad_tree, Twitter

Turkeys are peacocks that have really let themselves go.

Kristen Schaal

Birth

I used to think there was some sort of mix-up at the hospital when Frasier was born. Of course, when Niles came along, it shot that theory to hell.

Martin Crane (John Mahoney), Frasier

For a father a home birth is preferable. That way you're not missing anything on television.

Jeremy Hardy

The pain from a kick in the bollocks is worse than the pain from child-birth. How do I know? Because a few years down the line a woman will say to her partner, 'Do you want to try for another baby?' But I have never heard a man say, 'I'd like another kick in the bollocks.'

Jason Manford

I have tremendous respect for women after watching my wife give birth three times. I could never, ever raise a child to whom I gave birth. You know, because a newborn is about the size of a basketball, and if I had to expel a basketball from my body via a very restricted passageway, I would never want to see that basketball again. Not even on weekends.

Jeff Stilson

It's expected of men now: we've got to be there when the kids are born. I'm still not sure what our role is in the delivery room. As far as I can tell, it's like waiting for your luggage at baggage claim. You just stand there and peer into that void, 'God, I hope that one's mine.'

Jeff Stilson

I mean, look at the fuss women make about childbirth. Now, I'm not saying it doesn't smart a bit but, if blokes did it, I reckon you'd be looking at, what, give birth, have a couple of paracetamol, maybe a bit of a nap and then back to work within the hour.

Gary Strang (Martin Clunes), *Men Behaving Badly*

I told my wife I didn't want to be there at the birth. I don't see why my evening should be ruined too.

Dennis Wolfberg

Body

If your body is ninety per cent water, why have you got to drink water all the time? Why can't you just have some crisps?

Russell Brand

If you've got an ass like the North Star, men are gonna want to follow it.

Ron Burgundy (Will Ferrell), *Anchorman 2: The Legend Continues*

Dina Byrnes (Blythe Danner): I had no idea you could milk a cat.
Greg Focker (Ben Stiller): Oh, you can milk just about anything with nipples.
Jack Byrnes (Robert De Niro): I have nipples, Greg. Could you milk me?

Meet the Parents

I finally have the body I want. It's easy, actually. You just have to want a really shitty body.

Louis C.K.

I went to a masseur for physiotherapy. He said, 'Ooh, you're full of knots.' I said, 'Let me take my duffel coat off first.'

Alan Carr

I don't understand the whole concept of a massage. You get a woman to rub all over every single part of your body except the one part you really want rubbed.

Rodney Carrington

I've got the classic Italian male body; I got the ass of a two-hundred-and-seventy-pound man and the chest of a small Romanian gymnast.

Jeff Cesario

I like a woman with an arse you can park a bike in and balance a pint of beer on.

Mark Darcy (Colin Firth), Bridget Jones's Diary

I wonder what will happen if I put hand cream on my feet. Will they get confused and start clapping?

Ellen DeGeneres, Seriously . . . I'm Kidding

Without fake tan, I have the skin tones of a dead jellyfish.

Jenny Eclair

This double chin was grafted on to me in Brazil. It belonged to Elizabeth Taylor. It was her left love-handle.

Dame Edna Everage (Barry Humphries)

Nina Van Horn (Wendie Malick): I like to think of my body as a temple.
Dennis Finch (David Spade): Which explains why there's a line to get in on Friday nights.

Just Shoot Me!

The left side of the brain is responsible for speech, but then it would say that.

Harry Hill

All I can say is, if they show my butt in a movie, it better be a wide shot.

Jennifer Lopez

You're more than just a pair of bosoms, aren't you? Because you won Rear of the Year last year, didn't you?

Mrs Merton (Caroline Aherne) to Melinda
Messenger, The Mrs Merton Show

Couple of weeks I'll be bendy like Madonna, darling. Then I'll be able to kiss my own arse from both directions.

Edina Monsoon (Jennifer Saunders), Absolutely Fabulous

I just kind of hate him at the moment. I gave up my career for him, and my body. I have to wear a padded bra now just so my giant nipples don't poke through even when I'm wearing a leather jacket.

New mother Sharon Morris (Sharon Horgan), *Catastrophe*

I have a wandering eye and a lazy eye, so they cancel each other out.

Kevin Nealon

(on his appendix): Why would God put it in you when it does nothing but randomly kill you for no reason?

Dara O'Briain

Right, dry skin cream. I'm having an attack of the old flakes again. This morning my pillow looked like a flapjack.

Alan Partridge (Steve Coogan), *I'm Alan Partridge*

I wore a padded bra every single day and night from the age of fourteen until I was thirty-one. . . . I realised I was walking around with two lies on my chest: 'Wanna squeeze my tits? They're in the washing basket.'

Sara Pascoe, *Animal: The Autobiography of a Female Body*

Blanche Devereaux (Rue McClanahan): Who knows my body better than I do?
Sophia Petrillo (Estelle Getty): Any man in Miami not attached to a woman or a respirator.

The Golden Girls

My breasts are so low now, I can have a mammogram and a pedicure at the same time.

Joan Rivers

I used to be so flat, I wore angora sweaters just so the guys would have something to pet.

Joan Rivers

With age comes wisdom: you don't need big boobs to be feminine. Look at Liberace.

Joan Rivers

Barbara Royle (Sue Johnston): I haven't got bad boobs for a woman of my age.

Jim Royle (Ricky Tomlinson): Behave. They're like bloody spaniels' ears.

The Royle Family

Anna Scott (Julia Roberts): You know what they say about men with big feet.

Will Thacker (Hugh Grant): No, I don't actually. What's that?

Anna: Big feet . . . large shoes.

Notting Hill

I have never seen anyone sweat so much in my entire life. And I've been in a sauna with Pavarotti!

Malcolm Tucker (Peter Capaldi), *The Thick of It*

The only physical adornments which grow bigger with passing years are the nose and ears. The rest, regrettably, diminishes.

Sir Terry Wogan

I haven't got a waist. I've just got a sort of place, a bit like an unmarked level crossing.

Victoria Wood

Boredom

I don't know how long I could be a vet before I got bored and started shagging stuff.

Frankie Boyle

Boredom forces you to ring people you haven't seen for eighteen years and halfway through the conversation you remember why you left it so long. Boredom means you start to read not only mail order catalogues but also the advertising inserts that fall on the floor . . . Eventually boredom means you will take up golf.

Jeremy Clarkson, *The World According to Clarkson*

Boredom was my bedmate and it was hogging the sheets.

Andrew Davidson, *The Gargoyle*

Marie (Geraldine James): She's here to introduce us to the fascinating world of rugs . . . My apologies; I stand corrected, it's not just rugs, it is in fact all forms of carpeting.
Chris Harper (Helen Mirren): Oh, thank God. For a moment I thought it was going to be dull.

Calendar Girls

You can tell how boring a person is by the lack of fear in their eyes when someone is flipping through photos on their phone.

Bill Murray

God, I'm bored! Might as well be listening to Genesis.

Rick (Rik Mayall), *The Young Ones*

Do you know how bored I was today? I came this close to actually cleaning the house.

Gabrielle Solis (Eva Longoria), *Desperate Housewives*

Boxing

The noise that comes from the wretched throats of a boxing crowd indicates that brain damage is also in the head of the beholder.

Julie Burchill

When I was at school, I was perpetually punched in the head by other kids. So my dad sent me off to learn boxing . . . where I was perpetually punched in the head by other kids.

Lee Evans

There's more to boxing than hitting. There's not getting hit, for instance.

George Foreman

(on why he named all five of his sons George): In boxing, you have to prepare for memory loss. I wanted to make sure I didn't forget anybody's name.

George Foreman

The only way I'll ever fight again is if someone steals my last Rolo.

Lennox Lewis

It's hard to know what's gay in life. Boxing: that's two men fighting over a belt.

Demetri Martin

Jumbo Cummings: a name that sounds like an elephant ejaculating.

Rory McGrath

When it comes to ballyhoo, Muhammad Ali made Barnum & Bailey look like non-starters, and he had the incandescent quality of the real star which would have made him famous, even if his gift was knitting, not fighting.

Michael Parkinson

Britain

People are saying after Brexit that British people don't trust experts anymore. I don't think that's the problem. I think the problem is that British people have strong opinions based on . . . nothing at all.

Frankie Boyle

It is an interesting experience to become acquainted with a country through the eyes of the insane, and, if I may say so, a particularly useful grounding for life in Britain.

Bill Bryson, *Notes from a Small Island*

The UK officially voted to leave the European Union. It was such an important vote and it's good to know that people were making an informed decision. Check out the number two trending topic in the UK while people voted whether or not to leave the EU: 'What is the EU?'

Jimmy Fallon

Rain is the one thing the British do better than anybody else.

Marilyn French

(of the Isle of Man): The weather's foul, the food's medieval, it's covered in suicidal motorists and folk who believe in fairies . . . Everyone you actually see is Benny from *Crossroads* or Benny in drag.

A.A. Gill

Britain stopped evolving gastronomically around the year 1242.

John Oliver

British people would die for their right to drink themselves to death.

John Oliver

Talking to the British about sex is like talking to Americans about reading; nobody does it, so why talk about it?

Greg Proops

Apparently one in three Britons are conceived in an IKEA bed, which is mad because those places are really well lit.

Mark Smith

In Britain, a cup of tea is the answer to every problem. Fallen off your bicycle? Nice cup of tea. Your house has been destroyed by a meteorite? Nice cup of tea and a biscuit.

David Walliams, *Gangsta Granny*

Bullying

One school in Berkshire banned *Pokémon* after instances of bullying to obtain the rarer cards. The bullying has finally stopped, however, now that Mr Hunt the geography teacher has the complete set.

Angus Deayton, *Have I Got News for You*

Once I beat up the school bully with a baseball bat. Both his arms were completely broken, which gave me the courage.

Emo Philips

Constable Benton Fraser (Paul Gross): You know, we had a schoolyard bully in Tuktoyaktuk. Sometimes at night I can still remember him . . . coming into the classroom swinging that otter over his head. There was just no reasoning with him.
Det. Ray Vecchio (David Marciano): And I thought we had nothing in common!

Due South

I bought one of those anti-bullying wristbands when they first came out. I say 'bought', I actually stole it off a short, fat ginger kid.

Jack Whitehall

Business

I wonder sometimes if manufacturers of foolproof items keep a fool or two on their payroll to test things.

Alan Coren

Don't put all my eggs in one basket? Nice try, basket industry.

Dan Cronin, Twitter

Factories provide three things this country desperately needs: jobs, pride, and material for Bruce Springsteen songs.

Jack Donaghy (Alec Baldwin), *30 Rock*

I manufactured clown shoes, which was no small feat.

Stewart Francis

Most of my contemporaries at school entered the world of business, the logical destiny of bores.

Barry Humphries

(to brother): I see it as a combination of my business acumen and sales-manship and your ability to drive a three-wheeled van. Badly.

Del Trotter (David Jason), *Only Fools and Horses*

Camping

This guy asked me to go camping on vacation. Camping: that's the dumb-est vacation I ever heard of in my life. What, I'm gonna work all year so I can go out and pretend I'm homeless?

Alonzo Bodden

Make sure when you go camping that you have a groundsheet and a hammer . . . so you can dispose of the person who suggested going camping.

Jimmy Carr, *8 Out of 10 Cats*

You aren't allowed to have a party, you aren't allowed to have music, you aren't allowed to play ball games, you aren't allowed to have a camp fire, you have to park within two feet of a post, you have to keep quiet, you have to be in bed by eleven. This is not a holiday, it's a concentration camp.

Jeremy Clarkson

My fear of camping: I'm convinced bugs will crawl up my vagina and lay eggs. Isn't everyone?

Kathy Griffin

In a well-ordered universe, camping would take place indoors.

Morgan Matson, *Since You've Been Gone*

Mom, camping is not a date; it's an endurance test. If you can survive camping with someone, you should marry them on the way home.

Yvonne Prinz, *The Vinyl Princess*

Jews don't go camping. Life is hard enough as it is.

Carol Siskind

Canada

It's just a shame that for seven months of the year it is so cold that only Canadians would put up with it.

John Cleese, *So Anyway . . .*

Canada has just started building a wall.

Ricky Gervais, Twitter, the day after Donald Trump's election victory

Look at the Canadian flag. It's not a symbol of power, it's a leaf. Oh, don't screw with Canada, it'll dry up and blow away.

Jeremy Hotz

The Canadian version of Julius Caesar's memoirs? *I Came, I Saw, I Coped.*

Clive James

Canada is the perpetual wallflower that stands on the edge of the hall, waiting for someone to come and ask her for a dance.

Kevin Myers

I love Montreal. I heard if you can make it here, you can make it in Ottawa.

Amy Schumer, Just For Laughs, Canada

I don't trust any country that looks around a continent and says, 'Hey, I'll take the frozen part.'

Jon Stewart

Robin Scherbatsky (Cobie Smulders): How do you know the Canadian citizenship test is easy?

Barney Stinson (Neil Patrick Harris): It's Canada. Question one: Do you want to be Canadian? Question two: Really?

How I Met Your Mother

Canada is like a loft apartment over a really great party.

Robin Williams

Cannibalism

I'm not saying it's right. I'm just saying that every night millions of people go to bed hungry, and every day we bury perfectly good cuts of meat.

David Feldman

Every fight is a food fight when you're a cannibal.

Demetri Martin

Cats

I thought about buying a cat, but then I realised that buying a cat isn't going to make me any less lonely. It's just going to give my loneliness a mascot.

Simon Amstell

What evidence is there that cats are so smart anyway? Huh? What do they do? Because they're clean? I am sorry. My uncle Pete showers four times a day and he can't count to ten. So don't give me hygiene.

Elaine Benes (Julia Louis-Dreyfus), *Seinfeld*

When you yell at a dog, his tail will go between his legs and cover his genitals, his ears will go down. A dog is very easy to break, but cats make you work for their affection. They don't sell out the way dogs do.

Jack Byrnes (Robert De Niro), *Meet the Parents*

A new study says dogs feel genuine love for their owners. While cats just keep a journal of all the things they hate about you.

Jimmy Fallon

My nan had a cat with one eye. It walked into walls and tables. I used to think it was hilarious. It was a slapstick cat.

Noel Fielding

They say that cats are the only animals that can sit on your lap and ignore you. To which I say, 'You've never been to Spearmint Rhino.'

Dana Gould

Cats have a scam going. You buy the food, they eat the food, they go away; that's the deal.

Eddie Izzard

Dogs seem more photogenic than cats. In photos most cats look like sociopaths.

Demetri Martin

I think cats would have an even worse attitude if they found out how stupid their names were.

Demetri Martin

I recently bought a cat, but took it back a day later because our personalities clashed.

David Mitchell

A new report says that dogs can sniff out prostate cancer with almost ninety-eight per cent accuracy. The report also finds that cats can sniff it out with one hundred per cent accuracy but they prefer to watch you die.

Conan O'Brien

In ancient times cats were worshipped as gods; they have not forgotten this.

Sir Terry Pratchett

Cats will amusingly tolerate humans until someone comes up with a tin opener that can be operated with a paw.

Sir Terry Pratchett, *Men at Arms*

Every procedure for getting a cat to take a pill works fine – once.

Sir Terry Pratchett

So many cats, so few recipes.

Sandi Toksvig, *QI*

The main advantage of working at home is that you get to find out what cats really do all day.

Lynne Truss

Cats are smarter than dogs. You can't get eight cats to pull a sled through snow.

Jeff Valdez

Celebrities

Piers Morgan says that women send him knickers through the post. Presumably with the message: 'From one twat to another.'

Frankie Boyle, *Never Mind the Buzzcocks*

There's no shame in being second to Stephen Fry. Unless it's in a straight nose competition.

Russell Brand

Andrew Lloyd Webber is one of those odd, moth-like creatures who seem to combine extreme discomfort with the spotlight with an unstoppable compulsion to leap into it.

Craig Brown

I have no desire to be a celebrity. I've seen the job description.

Elaine Cassidy

Orlando Bloom apparently threw a punch at Justin Bieber last night during an argument at a nightclub. Orlando's hand was pretty sore today – you know, from all the high-fives he got.

Jimmy Fallon

Celebrity is a national drama whose characters' parts and plots are written by the tabloids, gossip columnists, websites and interactive buttons. The famous don't actually have to turn up to their own lives at all.

A.A. Gill

Paris Hilton is going on a goodwill mission to Rwanda. It's the first time an entire third world country will have to get immunisations for a visitor.

Chelsea Handler

Pete Waterman went down to Portsmouth once to visit the *Mary Rose* and was surprised to learn that it had sunk. *That's* how old he is.

Harry Hill, *Harry Hill's TV Burp*

Pete Waterman went on Friends Reunited and Moses got back in touch with him. *That's* how old he is.

Harry Hill, *Harry Hill's TV Burp*

Britney Spears told an interviewer if she weren't famous, she would be a teacher. So thank God she's famous.

Jay Leno

Margaret Meldrew (Annette Crosbie): Cilla Black's got a very infectious laugh.
Victor Meldrew (Richard Wilson): So has a hyena with anthrax.

One Foot in the Grave

I think you're the Tom Cruise for menopausal women. We're like putty in your hands.

Mrs Merton (Caroline Aherne) to Des Lynam, *The Mrs Merton Show*

You can't shame or humiliate modern celebrities. What used to be called shame and humiliation is now called publicity.

P.J. O'Rourke, *The Enemies List*

When I saw her sex tape, all I could think of were Paris Hilton's poor parents. The shame, the shame of the Hilton family. To have your daughter do a porno film . . . in a Marriott hotel.

Joan Rivers

Liz Hurley longs for the day when people stop pointing cameras at her. Speaking as someone who has seen all her films, I couldn't agree more.

Jonathan Ross

(at a comedy roast): I'm so glad Courtney Love is here; I left my crack in my other purse.

Sarah Silverman

Piers Morgan, who used to be editor of the *Mirror*. He's got a whole new career now as the bloke who used to be editor of the *Mirror*.

Linda Smith

Charity

A man knocked on my door and asked for a small donation towards the local swimming pool. I gave him a glass of water.

Anon

No wonder Bob Geldof is such an expert on famine. He's been dining out on 'I Don't Like Mondays' for thirty years.

Russell Brand

I saw a charity appeal in the *Guardian* the other day, and it read: 'Little Zuki has to walk thirteen miles a day just to fetch water.' And I couldn't help thinking, she should move.

Jimmy Carr

I did a sponsored walk once. In the end I raised so much money, I could afford a taxi.

Jimmy Carr

Rather than waste money on Christmas presents I paid for a goat to be sent to a village in Africa. He had a lovely time and wants to go again.

Gary Delaney, Twitter

Can we get on with this? I've got to do AIDS and Alzheimer's and land-mines this afternoon, and I want to get back for *Deal or No Deal*.

> Chris Martin waiting to do a charity spot, *Extras*

I can't give away my old clothes to the poor. They have enough to put up with without the added humiliation of wearing last season.

> Edina Monsoon (Jennifer Saunders), *Absolutely Fabulous*

I did a bit of charity work on my gap year. I went out and did volunteer work in a special needs school for children. Just playing games with them, football, tennis. And it does genuinely make you feel really good inside . . . because you always win.

> Jack Whitehall

Charm

Det. Kate Beckett (Stana Katic): Now Rick, be charming but not too charming.
Richard Castle (Nathan Fillion): That's like asking Superman not to be too super.

> *Castle*

(to Simon Cowell): You have the honesty of Abe Lincoln and the charm of the guy who shot him.

> Dane Cook

Inanimate objects fight me. They are not susceptible to persuasion or cajolery.

> Sir Terry Wogan

Chemistry

Bernard Black (Dylan Moran): You're my oldest friend. Don't you think it's about time we admitted how we feel about each other? Just for the summer.

Fran Katzenjammer (Tamsin Greig): No, I don't. I think we should wait.

Bernard: Until when?

Fran: Until at least one of us is dead.

Black Books

Patrick Maitland (Ben Miles): If I don't like a woman, if there's no chemistry, if I'm not attracted to her, then I don't lead her on. I just get out of there.

Sally Harper (Kate Isitt): Really?

Patrick: Every time, before she even wakes up.

Sally: So you do have sex with them, then?

Patrick: Well, there's no need to be cruel, is there?

Coupling

Chemistry can be a good and bad thing. Chemistry is good when you make love with it. Chemistry is bad when you make crack with it.

Adam Sandler

Monica Geller (Courteney Cox): Joey, did you even interview this woman before you asked her to move in?

Joey Tribbiani (Matt LeBlanc): Of course I did.

Monica Geller: What exactly did you ask her?

Joey Tribbiani: 'When can you move in?'

Friends

Chess

Tanya Peters (Anna Nicole Smith): What are you doing?

Lt. Frank Drebin (Leslie Nielsen): Oh! I was, uh, just conjugating my next move.

Tanya: Your bishop's exposed.

Lt. Drebin: It's these pants.

Naked Gun 33⅓: The Final Insult

This is considered a spectator sport? I've had more fun watching slush melt.

Dr Joel Fleischman (Rob Morrow), *Northern Exposure*

I got arrested for playing chess in the street. I said, 'It's because I'm black, isn't it?'

Milton Jones

I was playing chess with my friend and he said: 'Let's make this interesting.' So we stopped playing chess.

Matt Kirshen

Childhood

When I was a kid, my dad tried to think of ways to keep me occupied. His solution was to get my mum pregnant eight more times.

Stephen K Amos

Some of the happiest moments of my childhood were spent with my arm in packets of breakfast cereal, rooting around for a free gift.

Craig Brown

I had a wonderful childhood, which is tough because it's hard to adjust to a miserable adulthood.

Larry David

As a kid, I was made to walk the plank. We couldn't afford a dog.

Gary Delaney

I guess we were kinda poor when we were kids, but we didn't know it. That's because my dad always refused to let us look at the family's financial records.

Jack Handey, *Fuzzy Memories*

One of my earliest memories is seeing my mother's face through the oven window, as we played hide-and-seek and she said, 'You're getting warmer . . .'

Milton Jones

When I was a kid, I used to play doctor with this little girl in my neighbourhood and one day we got caught. Luckily it was a Wednesday and we were just playing golf.

Brian Kiley

I was raised as an only child, which really annoyed my sister.

Will Marsh

I was never a child. I was a menopausal woman within a child's body.

Tracey Ullman

I had a very anxious childhood. My mother never had time for me. You know, when you're the middle child in a family of five million, you don't get any attention.

Z (Woody Allen), *Antz*

Children

When you let a three-year-old dress herself, she always dresses like an east European prostitute – pink tights, pink dress, pink shoes, little plaits and bright-red lipstick.

David Baddiel

Living with kids is like living in a frat house. Everything's broken, nobody sleeps and there's a lot of throwing up.

> Ray Barone (Ray Romano), *Everybody Loves Raymond*

I got her a stool so that she can reach the chip pan. Well, when you've got kids, you've got to think safety first. That's why I make them wear yellow fluorescent jackets when I send them down the off licence late at night.

> Denise Best (Caroline Aherne), *The Royle Family*

Being a father is like doing drugs – you smell bad, get no sleep and spend all your money on them.

> Paul Bettany

It's impossible to hold an iPhone in the same hectare as a toddler without prompting an instant, bitter struggle for possession that makes the battle for Ukraine look dignified.

> Charlie Brooker

I don't think any of my kids would have a good word to say about me. I think they deny that they even know me. At school, they pretend they are Anton du Beke's kids.

> Rob Brydon

Learning to dislike children at an early age saves a lot of expense and aggravation later in life.

> Ed Byrne

Kids are like buckets of disease that live in your house.

> Louis C.K.

Of all the people in the world to have as a role model, our kid has to pick Eddie Munster.

> Roseanne Conner (Roseanne Barr), *Roseanne*

The only thing I've ever wanted for my kids is that they're happy and that they're out of the house. And I'll tell you what, happy ain't even that important.

> Roseanne Conner (Roseanne Barr), *Roseanne*

All my friends are always telling me how hard it is to have kids. 'Oh, David, it's so hard.' That's not hard. I'll tell you what hard is. Try talking your girlfriend into her third consecutive abortion. That takes finesse. You're just inconvenienced.

David Cross

Someday you'll have my children. In fact, they're in the car if you want them.

Roland T. Flakfizer (John Turturro), Brain Donors

I've learned that, as a parent, when you have sex your body emits a hormone that drifts down the hall into your child's room and makes them want a drink of water.

Jeff Foxworthy

It takes seven fewer muscles to smile than it does to frown. Save your energy, you're going to need it in your childbearing years.

Constable Benton Fraser (Paul Gross), Due South

Having kids means there's always someone around to blame your fart on.

Dana Gould

Toddlers are crap. They're too big to pick up but too small to send to the shop for fags.

Jeff Green

Hey, Mother, I come bearing a gift. I'll give you a hint. It's in my diaper and it's not a toaster.

Stewie Griffin (Seth MacFarlane), Family Guy

Kids: can't live with them, can't shoot them.

Grandpa Gustafson (Burgess Meredith), Grumpy Old Men

Kids are way too honest. They're like mini-alcoholics.

Gabriel Iglesias

I'd be the only dad keeping his kids home from school to teach me how to get to the next level on a videogame.

Clinton Jackson

Some kids in my neighbourhood were playing hide-and-seek and one of them ended up in an abandoned refrigerator. It's all anybody talked about for weeks. I said, 'Who cares? How many kids do you know get to die a winner?'

Anthony Jeselnik

The day my little boy was born, a friend of mine called me because his little girl was born the day before. He said, 'Who knows, maybe they'll end up getting married?' My little boy's a day old; his little girl's two days old. He's not going to marry someone twice his age!

Brian Kiley

The other day, my little boy talked back to my wife. She told him to do something and he said, 'No, I don't want to.' So I had to pull him aside and say, 'Listen, you got to teach me how to do that.'

Brian Kiley

Girls are complicated. The instruction manual that comes with girls is eight hundred pages, with chapters fourteen, nineteen, twenty-six and thirty-two missing and it's badly translated, hard to figure out.

Hugh Laurie

Malcolm (Frankie Muniz): Mom, I can't wear Reese's hand-me-downs. Look at this, Jell-O in the pockets, the fly's broken and it smells like wet dog.
Lois (Jane Kaczmarek): You should be glad he only wore it the one time.

Malcolm in the Middle

I've got two children. To be honest, I always wanted three children. Now I've got two, I only want one.

Lee Mack

My husband and I don't have children. We can't have children because we hate them.

Sarah Millican

I don't have a kid, but I think that I would be a good father, especially if my baby liked to go out drinking.

Eugene Mirman

What are children anyway? Midget drunks. They greet you in the morning by kneeing you in the face and talking gibberish. They can't even walk straight.

Dylan Moran

Children's parties aren't the same now. What's happened to running around, bleeding, torturing the simplest member of the group – simple childhood games?

Dylan Moran

Jack Donaghy (Alec Baldwin): What have children ever done for us?
Kenneth Parcell (Jack McBrayer): Well, they make our shoes and wallets.

30 Rock

I was having a fascinating conversation with the proud father of Norfolk's most suntanned child. Just passed his details on to social services.

Alan Partridge (Steve Coogan), *Alan Partridge: Alpha Papa*

Kids are like farts in that way. They never seem to bother the owner as much as they bother everyone else.

Karl Pilkington, *The Moaning of Life: The Worldly Wisdom of Karl Pilkington*

I say to my son, 'Don't do that, because if you do that, you're going to get hurt.' Then he does it and he doesn't get hurt. That pisses me off, because that is life telling him that I'm full of shit.

Romesh Ranganathan

Ideally they should give you a couple of practice kids before you have any for real. Sort of like bowling a few frames for free before you start keeping score. Let you warm up.

Paul Reiser

No book is going to make my daughter sad. Time to do what I do best: lie to a child.

Homer Simpson (Dan Castellaneta) *The Simpsons*

Earl Sinclair (Stuart Pankin): Lock him up and throw away the key.
Fran Sinclair (Jessica Walter): Earl, this is our child.
Earl: OK, you can keep the key.

Dinosaurs

Kids; it's the biggest decision you'll ever make, isn't it? That and whether to be a lager or a bitter drinker.

Tony Smart (Neil Morrissey), *Men Behaving Badly*

I can't have kids . . . because I have white couches.

Carrie Snow

Oh, kids ruin everything. I mean look at the stitching on this. You cannot trust a ten-year-old to do a good hidden button.

Karen Walker (Megan Mullally), *Will & Grace*

Am I ready [to father children]? They're not like a phone, are they? You can't get an upgrade. If you get a slow one, you're stuck with it.

Jack Whitehall

China

I find chopsticks frankly distressing. Am I alone in thinking it odd that a people ingenious enough to invent paper, gunpowder, kites and any number of other useful objects, and who have a noble history extending back three thousand years, haven't yet worked out that a pair of knitting needles is no way to capture food?

Bill Bryson, *Notes from a Small Island*

My sister has just married a Chinese billionaire . . . Cha Ching!

Stewart Francis

The Chinese food in China is not better than the Chinese food here, mostly because of differences of definitions of words that we have – like, for example, 'beef'.

Jake Johannsen

When it comes to Chinese food, I have always operated under the policy that the less known about the preparation the better. A wise diner who is invited to visit the kitchen replies by saying, as politely as possible, that he has a pressing engagement elsewhere.

Calvin Trillin

Christmas

Christmases were terrible, not like nowadays when kids get everything. My sister got a miniature set of perfumes called Ample. It was tiny, but even I could see where my dad had scraped off the 'S'.

Stephen K Amos

Christmas sweaters are only acceptable as a cry for help.

Andy Borowitz

You can return all the Christmas gifts you want, but you will never get back the time spent with your relatives.

Andy Borowitz

I bought myself a barge pole for Christmas. Thought I'd push the boat out.

Tony Cowards, Twitter

The advent calendar is a bar of rubbish chocolate smashed into bits and spread across a month of cardboard. It's a sort of strict one-a-day choco-late tablet diet to get you in shape for Christmas. And that shape is round.

Philomena Cunk (Diane Morgan)

I went to buy a Christmas tree and the guy asked, 'Are you going to put it up yourself?' I said, 'No, I was thinking the living room.'

Gary Delaney

That's the true spirit of Christmas; people being helped by people other than me.

Jerry (Jerry Seinfeld), *Seinfeld*

When it comes to Christmas presents, it's not the thought that counts, it's the receipt.

Miles Kington

I got the worst Christmas present ever. My sister gave me a grow-your-own-loofah kit. It was a clay pot, a bag of earth and five seeds. I think the clay pot hit her hardest.

Sean Lock, *QI*

Christmas presents: unwrapping proof that the people you love don't know you at all.

Sara Pascoe, Twitter

I love the holiday season. See ya in spring, toes!

Homer Simpson (Dan Castellaneta), *The Simpsons*

Brad Taylor (Zachery Ty Bryan): All I wanted was to be with my friends, Dad. A lot of people I like are going to be down there.
Tim Taylor (Tim Allen): Christmas is not about being with people you like. It's about being with your family.

Home Improvement

Class

You know you're working class when your TV is bigger than your bookcase.

Rob Beckett

The first day back at school after the summer holidays was when you found out which social class you were in. I was an in-between guy. I was never one of the rich kids that would come strolling in with a suntan and a new school bag but neither was I one of those who would come in with a black eye and a new second name.

Kevin Bridges

Posh people treat their money the same way they treat their children: send it away and when it comes back it's bigger.

Marcus Brigstocke, *The Now Show*

The upper class: keeps all the money, pays none of the taxes. The middle class: pays all of the taxes, does all of the work. The poor are there just to scare the shit out of the middle class.

George Carlin

I was born with a silver spoon in my mouth but I spat it out.

Kiera Chaplin, granddaughter of Charlie Chaplin

Like most liberals, I will do anything for the working classes, anything – apart from mix with them.

Kevin Day

I've worked out what ambience is. It's a night out without poor people, basically.

Micky Flanagan

You know I'm not a snob. I can get along with all kinds of people. I don't care which golf club they belong to.

Dorien Green (Lesley Joseph), *Birds of a Feather*

We had a crisis where I live. Everyone ran out of the same organic pesto at the same time.

Dylan Moran

I come from a perfectly ordinary, working-class family. I didn't really meet middle-class people until I went to university. It was quite a shock really. People were saying things like, 'Well, I was always going to end up doing English, because I was brought up surrounded by books,' and I'd think, 'Yes, so was I, but they were full of Green Shield Stamps.' I suppose we could have swapped them for books, but we had our eye on a twin-tub.

Linda Smith

I'm posh, but I don't take any stick for it. It's like I always say, 'Sticks and stones may break my bones, but fuck it, I'm with Bupa.'

Jack Whitehall

Clothes

It's not a dress in which you would want to walk the dog.

Alan Bennett, on Lady Gaga's costume made
entirely of meat, *Keeping On Keeping On*

Brian Topp (Mark Heap): Do you think I should lose the waistcoat?

Tim Bisley (Simon Pegg): I think you should burn it. Because if you lose it, you might find it again.

Spaced

I like my money where I can see it – hanging in my closet.

Carrie Bradshaw (Sarah Jessica Parker), *Sex and the City*

Like the firm handshake and looking people straight in the eye, the blazer had originally been a symbol of trust. Because of this, it had been purloined by the less-than-trustworthy and became their preferred disguise.

Craig Brown

Whenever I wear something expensive, it looks stolen.

Billy Connolly

If I wear too much tartan, I tend to look like a Thermos flask.

Ronnie Corbett

Trying on pants is one of the most humiliating things a man can suffer that doesn't involve a woman.

Larry David

There are five ages of swimwear: bikini, tankini, one-piece, one-piece with sarong and, finally, burying yourself to the neck in sand.

Jenny Eclair

I'm trying to think of a word to describe your outfit . . . affordable.

Dame Edna Everage (Barry Humphries), to audience member

(to Judy Finnigan): Tell me the story of that frock, Judy. It's obviously an old favourite. You were wise to remove the curtain rings.

Dame Edna Everage

Eventually I manage to cheer Mum up by allowing her to go through my wardrobe and criticise all my clothes.

Helen Fielding, *Bridget Jones's Diary*

Call me old-fashioned, but I did read in *Glamour* that one's shorts should always be longer than one's vagina.

Helen Fielding, *Bridget Jones: Mad About the Boy*

It's impossible to be unhappy in a poncho.

Noel Fielding

My belt holds my pants up, but the belt loops hold my belt up. I don't really know what's happening down there. Who is the real hero?

Mitch Hedberg

Wearing a turtleneck is like being strangled by a really weak guy, all day.

Mitch Hedberg

My suit is from the same tailor who made clothes for the PG Tips chimps. That's the ultimate fashion endorsement!

Harry Hill

Blimey, if that skirt was hitched any higher I could see what you had for breakfast.

DCI Gene Hunt (Philip Glenister), *Life on Mars*

Ray, you ever come into this office again dressed like a maths teacher, I'll paint your nuts the colour of hazelnuts and inform a bunch of squirrels that winter's coming!

DCI Gene Hunt, *Ashes to Ashes*

Some people arrange the clothes in their wardrobe according to colours; I arrange mine according to stains.

Sean Lock

One of my favourite clothing patterns is camouflage because when you're in the woods it makes you blend in, but when you're not it does just the opposite. It's like, 'Hey, there's an asshole.'

Demetri Martin

(of her wardrobe): Men are constantly trying to mentally undress me. I'm just trying to save them some time, that's all.

Ally McBeal (Calista Flockhart), *Ally McBeal*

Am I the only one who's always tempted to light the wick on top of a beret?

Paul Merton

(to daughter Saffy): Why does everything you wear look like it's bearing a grudge?

Edina Monsoon (Jennifer Saunders), *Absolutely Fabulous*

In her risqué, nude bodysuit, she looked like a splitting sack of over-ripe cantaloupes.

Camille Paglia, on Mariah Carey

Blanche Devereaux (Rue McClanahan): How does this dress look on me?
Sophia Petrillo (Estelle Getty): What's the difference? In half an hour it'll be crumpled up on the floor next to an empty bottle of Jack Daniel's.

The Golden Girls

Blanche: Do you think I'm dressed OK for the dog races?
Sophia: That depends. Are you competing?

The Golden Girls

I can't wear yellow anymore. It's too matchy-matchy with my catheter.

Joan Rivers

They say rubber's mainly for perverts. Don't know why. Think it's very practical actually. I mean, you spill anything on it and it just comes off. I suppose that could be why the perverts like it.

Scarlett (Charlotte Coleman), *Four Weddings and a Funeral*

You know the message you're sending out to the world with sweatpants? You're telling the world: 'I give up. I can't compete in normal society. I'm miserable, so I might as well be comfortable.'

Jerry Seinfeld

I'm sorry, Marc. I couldn't hear you over your loud shirt.

Betty Suarez (America Ferrera), *Ugly Betty*

Amy Townsend (Amy Schumer): Ooh, I like Tom's sweater. Does he teach computer in a church basement?

Kim Townsend (Brie Larson): Don't get all threatened just because you don't understand the concept of marriage!

Amy: You dress him like that so no one else wants to have sex with him? That's cool.

Trainwreck

In life there are two types of people: those who go to the shops in pyjama bottoms and flip-flops and people who aren't tools.

Jack Whitehall

Coffee

It is inhumane, in my opinion, to force people who have a genuine medical need for coffee to wait in line behind people who apparently view it as some kind of recreational activity.

Dave Barry

Coffee's out of the question. When I moved to California, I promised my mother that I wouldn't start doing drugs.

Sheldon Cooper (Jim Parsons), *The Big Bang Theory*

He doesn't have anyone to talk to. He spends all day with the trees and animals. This is what happens when you live too far away from franchised coffee outlets.

Mark Corrigan (David Mitchell), *Peep Show*

Starbucks is now banning smoking within twenty-five feet of its stores, which will get even worse for smokers once they realise every Starbucks is about twenty-five feet from another Starbucks.

Jimmy Fallon

I like my coffee the way I like my women: after waiting impatiently in a long line.

Dana Gould

Going to Starbucks for coffee is like going to prison for sex. You know you're going to get it, but it's going to be rough.

Adam Hills

The Starbucks staff at 4 a.m. are genetically closer to a moth.

Joe Lycett

I was in Starbucks and the person in front of me said: 'Can I have a tall, skinny, black Americano please?' I said, 'Are you ordering coffee or voting in the US elections?'

Michael McIntyre

Instant coffee is just old beans that have been cremated.

Edina Monsoon (Jennifer Saunders), *Absolutely Fabulous*

Starbucks say they are going to start putting religious quotes on cups. The very first one will say: 'Jesus! This cup is expensive!'

Conan O'Brien

I like my men like I like my coffee: making me anxious.

Sara Pascoe, Twitter

I had a cold and my doctor recommended coffee enemas. I can never go back to Starbucks.

Joan Rivers

Making a cup of coffee is like making love to a beautiful woman. It's got to be hot. You've got to take your time. You've got to stir . . . gently and firmly. You've got to grind your beans until they squeak. And then you put in the milk.

Swiss Toni (Charlie Higson), *The Fast Show*

Comedy

Am I the Irish comedian with half a finger? No, I'm the Irish comedian with nine and a half fingers.

Dave Allen

Three blind mice walk into a pub. But they are all unaware of their surroundings, so to derive humour from it would be exploitative.

Bill Bailey

It was a struggle for me at first. Nobody should be able to go for a curry after the show with the whole audience.

John Bishop

Being held hostage by an improv group. They're demanding ten thousand suggestions.

Josh Comers, Twitter

Analysing comedy is like dissecting a frog. Nobody laughs and the frog dies.

Barry Cryer

Trading lines with Robin [Williams] is, I imagine, like trading forehands with Ivan Lendl from three feet away.

Billy Crystal, *Absolutely Mahvelous*

Alternative comedy, because every other joke's funny.

Bob Fairchild (Ted Robbins), *Lead Balloon*

Who wants to see that again, really? A bunch of wrinkly old men trying to relive their youth and make a load of money.

Sir Mick Jagger's ironic take on the 2014 Monty Python reunion concerts

Eddie Izzard is talking about doing his act in German. Haven't the German people suffered enough?

Andy Kindler

Whitney Cummings has got the body of a crack whore, but she's got the razor-sharp wit . . . of a crack whore.

Seth MacFarlane

Comedy and sausages are the two things that, if you know how they're made, they affect the appetite.

Mike Myers

The truth is, we've always got on well. We just had different ideas about things like finances and how many wives you should have.

> Michael Palin on his fellow Monty Python members, with particular reference to John Cleese's four marriages

In a way, comedy is like sex; the more noise you hear, the better you think you're doing.

> Ray Romano

Comedy ages quicker than tragedy, to the extent that we can't know if the Ten Commandments may originally have been ten hilarious one-liners.

> Arthur Smith

I've never laughed a woman into bed, but I've laughed one out of bed many times.

> Jack Whitehall

Commercials

The key to eating healthy is not eating any food that has a TV commercial.

> Mike Birbiglia

In advertisements, there are just two types of women – wanton, gagging for it, or vacuous. We're either cumming on a window pane or laughing at salads.

> Bridget Christie

With Spotify if you want to hear adverts back to back for free, you have to put up with all this music. It sort of gets annoying after a while. I had to listen to Bananarama's full back catalogue just to get to my favourite double-glazing advert.

> Philomena Cunk (Diane Morgan)

Unlikely lines to hear in a TV commercial . . . itchy skin, dry flaking scalp? You disgust me!

> Hugh Dennis, *Mock the Week*

Some TV ads are irresponsible, like the one that goes, 'Hit me at thirty miles an hour and there's an eighty per cent chance I'll live.' Encouraging gambling! I mean, I like those odds but . . .

Ricky Gervais

I saw this commercial – it was for cat food – and at the end of it, it says: 'All natural food for your cat.' All natural food? But cat food's made out of horse meat. Yeah, that's the way it works in nature: the cat, right above the horse in the food chain.

Norm Macdonald

Oprah Winfrey's talk show is coming to an end. It's been revealed that a thirty-second ad for the final episode will cost one million dollars. In other words, the only person who can afford to buy an ad on Oprah's last show is Oprah.

Conan O'Brien

To my mind, no classical composer can really be considered a success until one of his pieces has been used on an aftershave advert.

Alan Partridge, *Nomad*

There are those terrible loan adverts. These awful, tragic, hollow-eyed wraiths come on, telling you these awful stories – 'I'm up to my eyes in debt, and, curiously, no reputable company would give me another loan! Then I discovered Dodgy Bastards. They've given me a million pounds and all they want in return are my kidneys.'

Linda Smith

Then there are the accident insurance adverts – 'where there's blame, there's a claim' – when people who've had these accidents come on like medieval beggars and wave their stumps at you for money with these outlandish stories. 'I slipped on a banana skin and successfully sued the Dominican Republic.'

Linda Smith

Common Sense

Common sense is so rare it should be considered a superpower nowadays.

Anon

Common sense and a sense of humour are the same thing, moving at different speeds. A sense of humour is just common sense, dancing.

Clive James

Common sense is like deodorant. The people who need it most never use it.

Bill Murray

Compassion

During the festive season, we must not forget those who are less fortunate than ourselves. The poor, for example. They may attempt to burgle your house while you are at church.

Mr Cholmondley-Warner (Jon Glover), *Harry Enfield's Television Programme*

My mother told me that life isn't always about pleasing yourself and that sometimes you have to do things for the sole benefit of another human being. I completely agreed with her, but reminded her that that was what blow jobs were for.

Chelsea Handler

Father Ted Crilly (Dermot Morgan): What was it Father Jack used to say about the needy? He had a term for them.
Father Dougal Maguire (Ardal O'Hanlon): 'A shower of bastards.'

Father Ted

If you're looking for sympathy, you'll find it between shit and syphilis in the dictionary.

David Sedaris, *Barrel Fever*

Compliments

If you are flattering a woman, it pays to be a little more subtle. You don't have to bother with men, they believe any compliment automatically.

Alan Ayckbourn

The worst compliment I ever had was when someone told me I had a nice eye. What about the other one?!

Roisin Conaty, *8 Out of 10 Cats*

The British are the Navratilovas of the backhanded compliment. This literary lioness I met at some soiree said to me, 'Oh, it's so tedious being beautiful, because men underestimate my intelligence. I wish I could make myself look less beautiful. Tell me, Kathy, how do you do it?'

Kathy Lette

If you want to get loads of compliments, always tell people you're ten or twenty years older than you are.

Sara Pascoe, Twitter

Compromise

Compromise is a stalling between two fools.

Stephen Fry

Confidence

Confidence is what you have before you understand the problem.

Woody Allen

Here's the deal. I'm the best there is, plain and simple. I wake up in the morning and I piss excellence.

Ricky Bobby (Will Ferrell), *Talladega Nights: The Ballad of Ricky Bobby*

One of life's sorest tragedies is that the people who brim with confidence are always the wrong people.

Charlie Brooker, *I Can Make You Hate*

Start thinking positively. You will notice a difference. Instead of, 'I think I'm a loser', try 'I definitely am a loser.'

Ellen DeGeneres, *The Funny Thing Is . . .*

Accept who you are. Unless you're a serial killer.

Ellen DeGeneres, *Seriously . . . I'm Kidding*

Confidence is ten per cent hard work and ninety per cent delusion.

Tina Fey

'Confidence is half the battle,' they say. I shouldn't imagine that's official military advice. 'Sorry, the guns have jammed and we've lost all our armour, but we still have positive body language; that ought to see us through some desert combat.'

Miles Jupp

Contraception

They've brought out a condom now for people with premature ejaculation and they've put an anaesthetic in the lining that makes you numb and you can last for longer. Or you can wear it inside out and you don't have to wake anybody up.

Frankie Boyle

I have always conducted my sex life according to three simple principles. One: if at all possible, ladies first. Two: it is easier to be forgiven than ask permission. And third, and most important: the ten seconds it takes to put on a condom beats the hell out of the ten years you have to pretend to like soccer.

Charlie Harper (Charlie Sheen), *Two and a Half Men*

Badly written love scenes are the ultimate in birth control. They are a literary contraceptive: read one and you'll never have sex again.

Kathy Lette

The thought of getting pregnant again is terrific birth control.

Bethany Lopez, *Indelible*

I got a new diaphragm – well, it's new to me.

Bonnie McFarlane

You have to pretend like you want to use a condom. When I bring it up, I like to say something fun, but honest. I'll be like, 'You're going to want to wear this, I've had a busy month.'

Amy Schumer

Trish Piedmont (Catherine Keener): Do you have protection?
Andy Stitzer (Steve Carell): I don't like guns.

The 40-Year-Old Virgin

Cookery

People say it's so easy to cook, but it's not as easy as *not* cooking.

Maria Bamford

Everton, let me explain things to you. In the world of cooking, I am Einstein. Lucinda is Isaac Newton. And you are a mud-dwelling unicellular bit of jelly with a predilection for consuming its own excrement.

Gareth Blackstock (Lenny Henry), *Chef!*

Becky Conner (Lecy Goranson): No one could eat this crud.
Dan Conner (John Goodman): Hey, if you don't finish your crud, you're not gonna get any crap for dessert.

Roseanne

The difference between a chef and a cook is the difference between a wife and a prostitute; cooks do meals for people they know and love, chefs do it anonymously for anyone who's got the price.

A.A. Gill

Women have been cooking for a thousand years and no one ever mentioned it. Men have been cooking for ten minutes and they never stop bloody going on about it.

Paul Heaton

I don't have a microwave oven, but I do have a clock that occasionally cooks shit.

Mitch Hedberg

This turkey is dry enough to choke a camel.

Blanche Hunt (Maggie Jones), *Coronation Street*

I am the world's worst cook. I can ruin anything. But I can do accents. I can serve the food with any accent you want.

Nicole Kidman

Victor Meldrew (Richard Wilson): I was just going to do a little bit of poached salmon for lunch. Nothing complicated, nothing that's going to smell.
Margaret Meldrew (Annette Crosbie): That's what you said about the squid in Stilton sauce, and they had half the road up outside looking for a gas leak.

One Foot in the Grave

I'm an appalling cook. I can just about create a glass of orange juice and a ham and cheese sandwich.

Dara O'Briain

Martha Stewart can lick my scrotum! Do I have a scrotum?

Sharon Osbourne, *The Osbournes*

Think palmier, think lattice, think pinwheel. But mainly, think massive horn.

Sue Perkins, delivering a pastries challenge, *The Great British Bake Off*

Susan Mayer (Teri Hatcher): Lynette?

Lynette Scavo (Felicity Huffman): I'm in.

Bree Van de Kamp (Marcia Cross): I'll make braised lamb steaks.

Lynette: I'm still in.

Desperate Housewives

Many Texas barbecue fanatics have a strong belief in the beneficial properties of accumulated grease.

Calvin Trillin

All you used to give me was TV dinners or convenience food; if it wasn't frozen or dehydrated we didn't eat it. If you'd been in charge of the Last Supper, it would have been a takeaway.

Rodney Trotter (Nicholas Lyndhurst) to brother Del, *Only Fools and Horses*

Why do men think they know how to cook outside when they haven't the smallest idea how to go about it indoors?

Sir Terry Wogan, on barbecues

Cosmetic Surgery

It looks as though the plastic surgery has left [David] Gest closely resembling the halfway point in a horror movie transformation sequence . . . If he didn't wear sunglasses all the time it'd be hard to know whether his face was on the right way up.

Charlie Brooker

Anne Robinson's face now appears so tight and Botoxed she seems to be pushing it through the taut skin of a tambourine.

Charlie Brooker

Most people who have plastic surgery are disappointed with the results, although they always look pleasantly surprised.

Jimmy Carr

I don't know much Anne Robinson spends on injecting her face with deadly poison, but it's not enough.

Sir Bruce Forsyth

I used to be a plastic surgeon, which raised a few eyebrows.

Stewart Francis

If God had wanted women to have giant, fake boobs, he'd be a lot like my brother.

Dana Gould

Cosmetic surgery is terrifying. It never looks good. Those women look weird. They look in the mirror and think they look great, but they don't see what we see. They scare small children.

Jerry Hall

For the first time ever, women are scoring higher than men on IQ tests. Scientists say it has something to do with breast implants – not that it makes the women smarter, it just makes the men dumber.

Jay Leno

A good rule to remember for life is that when it comes to plastic surgery and sushi, never be attracted by a bargain.

Graham Norton

Sylvester Stallone's mother's plastic surgery looks so bad it could have been bought through a mail-order catalogue.

Graham Norton

If anybody says their facelift doesn't hurt, they're lying. It was like I'd spent the night with an axe murderer.

Sharon Osbourne

My body is a temple, and my temple needs redecorating.

Joan Rivers

I wish I had a twin, so I could know what I'd look like without plastic surgery.

Joan Rivers

I've had so much plastic surgery, when I die they'll donate my body to Tupperware.

Joan Rivers

Norma Speakman (Liz Smith): Barbara, didn't Elsie next door have implants?
Barbara Royle (Sue Johnston): No, eggplants, Mam.

The Royle Family

She [Joan Rivers] looks like a Siamese cat walking into a gale.

Linda Smith

If you've dated a woman over five years and she wants a boob job, she ain't getting it for you. She is putting fresh meat on a new hook, that's all it is. She's trolling for idiot B because you have not lived up to her financial expectations. So she's gonna cast those double-Ds out into the dating pool.

Christopher Titus

I'd like to grow old with my face still moving.

Kate Winslet

Cricket

Diving stop there from Yuvraj [Singh], who can do no wrong at the moment. He could drop his trousers and still get a standing ovation.

Jonathan Agnew

It is not true that the English invented cricket as a way of making all other human endeavours look interesting and lively; that was merely an unintended side effect.

Bill Bryson, *Down Under: Travels in a Sunburned Country*

It is the only sport in which spectators burn as many calories as the players – more if they are moderately restless.

Bill Bryson, *Down Under: Travels in a Sunburned Country*

Any sport which goes on for so long that you might need a 'comfort break' is not a sport at all. It is merely a means of passing the time. Like reading.

Jeremy Clarkson, *The World According to Clarkson*

I lost my job as a cricket commentator for saying, 'I don't want to bore you with the details.'

Milton Jones

To the baffled outsider The Ashes competition has all the hallmarks of some kind of post-cremation entertainment in which rival family members vie for the remains of a particularly loved one.

Sandi Toksvig, *The Chain of Curiosity*

Crime

Ill-advised things to say in court: 'I would like to present my own defence . . . through the medium of dance!'

Frankie Boyle, *Mock the Week*

Murderers, stop murdering. Everyone will die eventually – just sit down and be patient.

Russell Brand

The Wilkinsons were burgled. On his income, I can't understand how they could afford to be burgled. Quite honestly, in their circumstances I think it's a mite pretentious of them to be burgled.

Hyacinth Bucket (Patricia Routledge), *Keeping Up Appearances*

Inspector Jacques Clouseau (Steve Martin): Don't you find it a little bit [of a] coincidence that the body fell *perfectly* within the chalk outline on the floor?
Ponton (Jean Reno): I think they drew the chalk outline later.
Inspector Clouseau: Ah!

The Pink Panther

A casino in South Dakota was robbed by a man dressed as a mummy. The police described the suspect as anywhere between twenty-five and eight thousand years old.

Craig Ferguson

DI Sam Tyler (John Simm): I want to talk to his family, his friends and his workmates. I want to find out if there was another motive.
DCI Gene Hunt (Philip Glenister): You do that, Sherlock, and if that doesn't work, try the butler.

Life on Mars

DI Tyler: I still think we need to entertain the possibility that this could be a racial killing.
DCI Hunt: Oh, well, let's entertain it, take it out for a prawn cocktail, a steak and a bottle of Liebfraumilch, then let's kick it into the gutter where it belongs.

Life on Mars

I've spent the past two years looking for my ex-girlfriend's killer . . . but no one will do it.

Anthony Jeselnik

I'd like to say to the man wearing camouflage gear and using crutches who stole my wallet at the weekend: 'You can hide, but you can't run.'

Milton Jones

Years ago, I used to supply filofaxes to the Mafia. Yes, I was involved in very organised crime.

Milton Jones

You can always tell when gas is expensive. You see street gangs doing walk-bys.

Larry the Cable Guy (Daniel Whitney)

I admire these phone hackers. I think they have a lot of patience. I can't even be bothered to check my own voicemails.

Andrew Lawrence

I've had a lot of stuff go missing since that keyhole surgeon moved in next door. Mostly small things, mind you.

Sean Lock

Things aren't right. If a burglar breaks into your home and you shoot him, he can sue you. For what, restraint of trade?

Bill Maher

I was arrested the other night, and for the one call I could make, I called a sex line. My wife was well mad. She hates it when I call her at work.

Lee Nelson (Simon Brodkin)

Toby Flenderson (Paul Lieberstein): Didn't you lose a lot of money on that other investment, the one from that email?
Michael Scott (Steve Carell): You know what, Toby? When the son of the deposed king of Nigeria emails you directly asking for help, you help. His father ran the freaking country, OK?

The Office (US)

Critics and Criticism

(reading out an album review): This pretentious ponderous collection of religious rock psalms is enough to prompt the question: 'What day did the Lord create Spinal Tap and couldn't he have rested on that day, too?'

Marty DiBergi (Rob Reiner), *This Is Spinal Tap*

Marty DiBergi: Let's talk about your reviews a little bit. Regarding *Intravenus De Milo*: 'This tasteless cover is a good indicator of the lack of musical invention within. The musical growth rate of this band cannot even be charted. They are treading water in a sea of retarded sexuality and bad poetry.'
Nigel Tufnel (Christopher Guest): That's . . . that's nitpicking, isn't it?

This Is Spinal Tap

A critic often has to play the role of coroner, dissecting a work to find out why it died.

David Edelstein

There is, perhaps, no more dangerous man in the world than the man with the sensibilities of an artist but without creative talent. With luck, such men make wonderful theatrical impresarios and interior decorators, or else they become mass murderers or critics.

Dame Edna Everage (Barry Humphries)

I have benefited greatly from criticism and at no time have I suffered a lack thereof.

Donald Rumsfeld

Looking for silliness in the writing of Russell Brand is like looking for hay in a haystack.

David Sexton, on Brand's political manifesto book, *Revolution*

Honest criticism is hard to take, particularly from a relative, a friend, an acquaintance or a stranger.

Daniel Tosh

Cyclists and Cycling

Trespassers in the motor car's domain, they [cyclists] do not pay road tax and therefore have no right to be on the road. Some of them even believe they are going fast enough not to be an obstruction. Run them down to prove them wrong!

Jeremy Clarkson

I'd change the law that allows people to ride around London on bicycles. They get in the way of limousines. Chiefly, my limousines. I have never mown a cyclist down, but not for want of trying.

Dame Edna Everage (Barry Humphries)

Combined bus and cycle lanes, what a crap idea that is! It would be like having a path in the jungle for walkers and lions.

Andy Parsons

I'm OK, just hit my head on the lamp-post, but I'm all right. The doctor asked me a few questions, my name and stuff. I said, 'I'm Chris Froome.'

Geraint Thomas, after a crash in the 2015 Tour de France

The day I notice a cyclist obey a stop sign is the day I'll stop enjoying watching them bounce off my hood.

Daniel Tosh

Cyclists: avoid getting a sore behind by simply placing a naan bread over your saddle. This will comfort your ride and when you return home, hey presto! A warm snack.

Top Tips, *Viz*

Why I'll never ride a bike in New York City . . . I don't want to spend money on an expensive bike lock that will end up getting stolen along with my bike.

Alex Watt

Dancing

If you'd said to me three months ago that I had an inner Beyoncé, I'd never have believed it. But I clearly did.

Ed Balls, on *Strictly Come Dancing*

When I dance, people think I'm looking for my keys.

Ray Barone (Ray Romano), *Everybody Loves Raymond*

John Sergeant retires from the *Strictly Come Dancing* competition . . . Having worked with Sergeant on a BBC comedy series in 1966, I can truthfully say that whatever he knows about rhythm and dance (i.e. nothing) he learned from me.

Alan Bennett, *Keeping On Keeping On*

I don't use pre-existing dance moves as they can be held up to a standard of proficiency that I don't think I possess. I let my dancing do the talking – to most people, it may resemble a spasm.

Russell Brand

Dancing makes me look like a coma victim being stood up and zapped with a cattle prod.

Mark Corrigan (David Mitchell), *Peep Show*

Morris dancing takes its name from the Moors, so maybe its origins are racist. Perhaps we could get it banned on those grounds. It's got to be worth a try.

Alan Davies

'Just because you can't dance doesn't mean you shouldn't dance'
– Alcohol.

Josh Hara, Twitter

I've only ever heckled once in my whole life: our Laura's tap recital. And it was for her own good, she was never going to make it and the classes were like eight pounds an hour.

Lilian (Paula Wilcox), *The Smoking Room*

You're an exception to the rule that anyone can learn to dance.

Craig Revel Horwood to Scott Mills, *Strictly Come Dancing*

I thought you were wriggling around like a slug in salt, actually.

Craig Revel Horwood to *Strictly Come Dancing* contestant Rachel Riley

Dancing is for people who can't communicate verbally.

Jon Richardson

Somebody just gave me a shower radio. Thanks a lot. Do you really want music in the shower? I guess there's no better place to dance than a slick surface next to a glass door.

Jerry Seinfeld

I'd be the world's worst lap dancer. I could not sit on a man's knee and not want to make 'giddy-up' noises.

Holly Walsh

Dating

I was on a date with this really hot model. Well, it wasn't really a date-date. We just ate dinner and saw a movie. Then the plane landed.

Dave Attell

I like psycho chicks. You hook up with a psycho, you're gonna learn something. First thing you learn is how to sleep with one eye open.

Alonzo Bodden

The problem with dating a model is they won't go out with you if your car's colour doesn't match their outfit.

Dane Cook

I am not crazy! I am dating a supermodel zoologist, whom I stole away from a professional football player and she is off to the Galapagos Islands to artificially inseminate iguanas. Now is that so hard to believe?!

Frasier Crane (Kelsey Grammer), *Frasier*

You don't proposition a woman like that on the first date! Last night after dinner, I dropped her home with nothing more than a courtly kiss on the wrist. Tonight may proceed to handholding. If all goes well, in two weeks, I shall storm the citadel of her womanhood.

Niles Crane (David Hyde Pierce), *Frasier*

I don't get what is so cool about dating DJs. That's like dating a valet because he drives a nice car.

Whitney Cummings

A date is an experience you have with another person that makes you appreciate being alone.

Larry David (himself), *Curb Your Enthusiasm*

Dating is great unless you don't like horrible awkwardness, lying and a deep foreboding sense of disappointment that never goes away.

Dov Davidoff

It's a bad sign when you see the person you're dating and get the same feeling as if you just saw police lights in your rear-view mirror.

Dov Davidoff

Danni Sullivan (Tara Reid): Do you even enjoy hanging out with me?
J.D. Dorian (Zach Braff): Enjoy is a strong word.

Scrubs

Nervous around the person you like? Sue them. They'll be forced to see you in court, well dressed and in control. Let the law be your wingman.

Mindy Furano, Twitter

Men don't realise that if we're sleeping with them on the first date, we're probably not interested in seeing them again either.

Chelsea Handler

You know how when you meet the right person, you know instantly? Why does it take a year and a half when it's the wrong one?

Phil Hanley

I've been single for so long now that when somebody says to me, 'Who are you with?', I automatically say, 'Vodafone.'

Miranda Hart

People on dates shouldn't even be allowed out in public.

Jerry (Jerry Seinfeld), *Seinfeld*

My girlfriend makes me want to be a better person . . . so I can get a better girlfriend.

Anthony Jeselnik

It's tough, but I try to wait until the second date before I bring up my dead girlfriends.

Anthony Jeselnik

Andy Stitzer (Steve Carell): I've been looking for that speed-dating card. Thank you so much for bringing it to me.
Jill (Erica Vittina Phillips): So you actually wrote that one girl looked like she was 'hurtin' for a squirtin'?

The 40-Year-Old Virgin

My eldest daughter brought a boy home the other day and I reacted quite badly. She came in and said, 'All right, Dad, this is Billy.' She went out of the room and I went up to this Billy and said, 'If you so much as touch her, I'll cut you!' This Billy starts crying. Still, that's seven-year-olds for you.

Phill Jupitus

Donna (Sharon Horgan): Billy? Are you insane? He tried to kill you!
Karen (Tanya Franks): Don't make out like that's negative. He was on ketamine.

Pulling

I'm still going on bad dates, when by now I should be in a bad marriage.

Laura Kightlinger

When you're single again, at the beginning you're very optimistic and you say, 'I want to meet someone who's really smart, really sweet, really sensitive.' Six months later, you're like, 'Lord, any mammal with a day job!'

Carol Leifer

According to a recent study, men on dating sites are more popular if they mention dancing or cooking. Because if there's one thing women love, it's a man who can lie.

Seth Meyers

I've always heard that women secretly want their father. So I used to walk around in a 1950s' business suit with a hat and a pipe. My opening line would be, 'You should be getting to bed now.'

Conan O'Brien

Max Bygraves (Peter Kay): I almost threw her out for being underage.
Paddy O'Shea (Paddy McGuinness): Underage? How old was she, you dirty dog?
Max: No, she was old enough, it was just she was . . . she was a kind of midget.
Paddy O'Shea: Ain't that a Queen song?

Max and Paddy's Road to Nowhere

Guys I've been meeting have the worst pick-up lines, like: 'Hey, what's your friend's name?'

Melanie Reno

I turned down a date once because I was looking for someone a little closer to the top of the food chain.

Judy Tenuta

We might go out, get to know each other a bit, you know. Might like each other, then – who knows – in time, maybe she might do some ironing for me.

Denzil Tulser (Paul Barber), *Only Fools and Horses*

George Williams (Roger Bart): It was nice talking with you, Dr Van de Kamp.

Dr Rex Van de Kamp (Steven Culp): Please, you're dating my wife! Call me Rex!

Desperate Housewives

Dating is interesting because often it ends up you've just been doing undercover research on your future enemy.

Bridger Winegar, Twitter

Deafness

How do deaf people tell the difference between yawns and screams?

Carl Donnelly

My grandfather is hard of hearing. He needs to read lips. I don't mind him reading lips, but he uses one of those yellow highlighters.

Brian Kiley

Lilian (Paula Wilcox): The deaf can't whistle, can they?
Len (Leslie Schofield): Not in tune.

The Smoking Room

My ex-wife was deaf. She left me for a deaf friend of hers. To be honest, I should have seen the signs.

Tim Vine

Death

I don't think I will ever die doing something that I love, because what I love is not dying.

Chris Bennett

I think about death. I don't want to die with clothes in the cleaners.

Elayne Boosler

Winnie McGoogan (Eilish O'Carroll): Have you been out for your evening walk?
Grandad Brown (Dermot O'Neill): Aye, up at the graveyard.
Winnie: Awch, who's dead?
Grandad: The whole fecking lot of them!

Mrs Brown's Boys

When someone close to you dies, move seats.

Jimmy Carr

If you love sleep, you'll really enjoy death.

Dov Davidoff

My wife and I just took out life insurance policies on one another, so now it's just a waiting game. Who's going to be the first to experience certainly tremendous sorrow, coupled with a sweet chunk of change?

Bil Dwyer

Alan Garner (Zach Galifianakis): I was so upset when my grandpa died.
Phil Wenneck (Bradley Cooper): How'd he die?
Alan: World War Two.
Phil: Died in battle?
Alan: No, he was skiing in Vermont, it was just during World War Two.

The Hangover

I hope when they die, cartoon characters have to answer for their sins.

Jack Handey

I hope that after I die, people will say of me, 'That guy sure owed me a lot of money.'

Jack Handey

I don't get this fashion for happy funerals. This is a very fashionable idea that, when you die, it's supposed to be a celebration and joyous and everyone laughing, but I want people's lives torn apart when I go. I want to be embalmed and brought out when we have guests.

Jeremy Hardy

DC Chris Skelton (Marshall Lancaster): Think he drowned then?
DCI Gene Hunt (Philip Glenister): No, Christopher. I think he tried to drink the entire river for a bet and failed!

Ashes to Ashes

The world's oldest woman passed away at 116. They keep dying. I think that title may be cursed.

David Letterman

At a cemetery, looking for my name on tombstones. This is the goth version of googling yourself.

Todd Levin, Twitter

You can't really do smiley faces on death certificates. Does look a little bit insensitive.

Dr 'Mac' Macartney (Julian Rhind-Tutt), *Green Wing*

Death is a funny thing. Not funny-haha, like a Woody Allen movie but funny strange, like a Woody Allen marriage.

Norm Macdonald, *Based on a True Story*

I saw a sign on the side of the road the other day that said, 'Tiredness can kill'. I didn't know that. Last Saturday, I stayed up all night watching movies. I could have died!

Ardal O'Hanlon

(of the late Graham Chapman): He always regarded death as highly overrated.

Michael Palin

Robert Adler, the co-inventor of the TV remote, died this week at the age of ninety-three. In accordance with his wishes, he will be buried between two enormous sofa cushions.

Amy Poehler, *Saturday Night Live*

It is my wish to die of unique causes, perhaps in a high-speed tricycle crash, a bizarre stapling incident or as a result of inadvertently sucking my brains out through my ear while trying to untwist the vacuum hose.

Paula Poundstone, *There's Nothing in This Book That I Meant to Say*

Jack Lawrence (Billy Crystal): You're a tragic hero. You're Lou Gehrig.
Dale Putley (Robin Williams): Who?
Jack: Lou Gehrig. Everybody knows Lou Gehrig. The baseball player. He died of Lou Gehrig's Disease.
Dale: Wow, what are the odds on that?

Fathers' Day

Denise Best (Caroline Aherne): Can we not talk about Nana dying?
Jim Royle (Ricky Tomlinson): Yeah, have some respect. Wait till she's out the door.

The Royle Family

I don't want to die before my parents die, especially my mother, because I don't want her to get the chance to pick out what I'm going to wear for eternity.

Jon Stewart

Democracy

Bernard Woolley (Derek Fowlds): But surely the citizens of a democracy have a right to know.

Sir Humphrey Appleby (Nigel Hawthorne): No, they have a right to be ignorant. Knowledge only means complicity in guilt; ignorance has a certain dignity.

Yes, Minister

Democracy is being allowed to vote for the candidate you dislike least.

Ed Byrne

I believe democracy is our greatest export. At least until China figures out a way to stamp it out of plastic for three cents a unit.

Stephen Colbert

Democracy consists of choosing your dictators, after they've told you what you think it is you want to hear.

Alan Coren

Democracy is very different in US-and-A from Kazakhstan. In America, woman can vote, but horse cannot!

Borat Sagdiyev (Sacha Baron Cohen), *Borat: Cultural Learnings of America for Make Benefit Glorious Nation of Kazakhstan*

What's the point of having a democracy if everybody's going to vote wrong?

Dick Solomon (John Lithgow), *3rd Rock from the Sun*

Depression

I've never really thought of myself as depressed as much as paralysed by hope.

Maria Bamford

You can't reason yourself back into cheerfulness any more than you can reason yourself into an extra six inches in height.

Stephen Fry

The Grand Old Duke of York, he was a manic depressive. Well, when he was up, he was up . . .

Milton Jones

Richard Karinsky (Malcolm Gets): Oh God, I hate Mondays.
Caroline Duffy (Lea Thompson): It's Tuesday, Richard.
Richard: I know. I'm still trying to get over yesterday.

Caroline in the City

A new study found that people who are depressed have a greater risk of a stroke. Well, that should cheer them up.

Jay Leno

The only difference between disappointment and depression is your level of commitment.

Marc Maron

My dad is actually a manic depressive, which is very exciting half the time.

Marc Maron

Ernie 'Coach' Pantusso (Nicholas Colasanto): How's life treating you, Norm?
Norm Peterson (George Wendt): Like it caught me in bed with its wife.

Cheers

Sometimes when I'm feeling down because nothing seems to be going right, I like to take a home pregnancy test. Then I can say, 'Hey, at least I'm not pregnant!'

Daniel Tosh

I am depressed because of the state of my life at the moment. I've got this horrible feeling that if there is such a thing as reincarnation, knowing my luck I'll come back as me.

Rodney Trotter (Nicholas Lyndhurst), *Only Fools and Horses*

Dialect

A Geordie said to me, 'Are yous looking at us?' How many mistakes can you make in one sentence?

Michael McIntyre

My mum and dad are Scottish but they moved down to Wolverhampton when I was two 'cause they wanted me to sound like a twat.

Susan Murray

You must learn the northern tongue. 'Owt' is any, 'nowt' is none, 'ta' is thanks, 'mint' is good, 'tea' is supper, 'dinner' is lunch, a 'barm cake' is a sort of bap, a 'bap' is a tit and a 'tit' . . . is a tit.

Jonathan 'JP' Pembersley (Jack Whitehall), *Fresh Meat*

Dieting

I'm on the mirror diet. You eat all your food in front of a mirror in the nude. It works pretty good, though some of the fancier restaurants don't go for it.

Roseanne Barr

I don't need a diet pill. I need something that gives you an electric shock when you reach for food.

Joy Behar

I'm on this new diet. I don't eat anything, and when I feel like I'm about to faint I eat a cube of cheese. I'm just one stomach flu away from my goal weight.

Emily Charlton (Emily Blunt), *The Devil Wears Prada*

I'm sick of listening to otherwise intelligent people moaning about being faint with hunger when they're on some ridiculous, self-inflicted, five-hundred-calorie-a-day diet. Yes, you're hungry; you're also very boring. So, shut up about it, or open the biscuits.

Jenny Eclair

Dieting on New Year's Day isn't a good idea as you can't eat rationally but really need to be free to consume whatever is necessary, moment by moment, in order to ease your hangover. I think it would be much more sensible if resolutions began generally on January 2nd.

Helen Fielding, *Bridget Jones's Diary*

I realise it has become too easy to find a diet to fit in with whatever you happen to feel like eating and that diets are not there to be picked and mixed but picked and stuck to, which is exactly what I shall begin to do once I've eaten this chocolate croissant.

Helen Fielding, *Bridget Jones's Diary*

I have written the only diet book that I believe needs to exist, and here it is – chapter one: Eat a bit less. Chapter two: Move about a bit more. The end.

Miranda Hart, *Is It Just Me?*

Disability

If I need directions, I ask a man with one leg, 'cause he definitely knows the easiest way to get there.

Dave Attell

There are things that I'll never laugh at. The handicapped. Because there's nothing funny about them. Or any deformity. It's like when you see some-one look at a little handicapped and go, 'Ooh, look at him, he's not able-bodied. I am, I'm prejudiced.' Yeah, well at least the little handicapped fella is able-minded. Unless he's not. It's difficult to tell with the wheel-chair ones.

David Brent (Ricky Gervais), *The Office*

I've got nothing against disabled people – I've even got one of their stickers on my car.

Damian Callinan

Disabled toilets: ironically the only toilets big enough to run around in.

Jimmy Carr

Bonnie Swanson (Jennifer Tilly): Somebody save him, he can't swim!
Peter Griffin (Seth MacFarlane): Oh, he's not even kicking. Kick, Joe, kick!
Lois Griffin (Alex Borstein): Peter, he's a paraplegic!
Peter: That doesn't mean he can't hear. Kick, Joe, kick!

Family Guy

I had someone ask me, when I said I had an artificial right leg, 'Can you still have sex?' I said: 'Yeah. What does your husband do? Take a run-up?'

Adam Hills

I always hid my foot when I was a kid because I didn't know anyone who looked cool with a prosthetic [leg]. Then finally I got a blade and I thought, I'm going to look cool. But then Oscar Pistorius ruined it for all of us.

Adam Hills

Are you saying that you think disabled access is a Dalek conspiracy?

David Mitchell, *QI*

I've ridden the lisp gravy train for quite some time. But on the scale of disabilities, it falls somewhere between a lazy eye and irritable bowel syndrome.

Nikki Payne

I learned that people in wheelchairs are allowed to have marathons . . . which, to me, seems like cheating, but what are you gonna say?

Sarah Silverman

(to a disabled man): I have to walk in heels all day long. You get to sit in a chair and roll.

Gabrielle Solis (Eva Longoria), *Desperate Housewives*

Disapproval

Homosexuals and single women in their thirties have natural bonding, both being accustomed to disappointing their parents and being treated as freaks by society.

Helen Fielding, *Bridget Jones's Diary*

You'll have to excuse my gran. I swear she could suck the fun out of a bouncy castle.

Bethany Platt (Lucy Fallon), *Coronation Street*

It's not worth doing something unless someone, somewhere, would much rather you weren't doing it.

Sir Terry Pratchett

Divorce

In my day, when two people broke up you were mad, you were angry, you hated each other. Whatever happened to the sanctity of divorce?

Martin Crane (John Mahoney), *Frasier*

One minute you're newlyweds , making love on the floor of Concorde. Then, before you know it, your lawyers are arguing over who gets to keep the box your dog defecates in.

Jack Donaghy (Alec Baldwin), *30 Rock*

It's pretty scary when even Angelina Jolie and Brad Pitt are like, 'I can do better.'

Jimmy Fallon

Some people have their marriages annulled, which means they never existed. Boy, talk about denial! What do you say when people see your wedding album? 'Oh, that was just some play I was in.'

Carol Leifer

Clowns divorce. Custardy battle.

Simon Munnery

My dad survived five divorces and the women he married cleaned him out every time. I used to think my dad got divorced because he wanted new furniture.

Christopher Titus

I lost twenty-eight pounds in my divorce, because that's what a soul weighs.

Christopher Titus

Jane divorced her husband. Apparently she came home from work unexpectedly one morning and found him in bed with the milkman. Honest to God, the milkman! But from that day forward I've noticed she never takes milk in her tea.

Shirley Valentine (Pauline Collins), *Shirley Valentine*

I've got two daughters and I was divorced when they were young – four and two. They took it bad, because I told them it was their fault.

Rich Vos

Doctors

Marianne Walker (Doreen Mantle): Am I your first official patient?
Dr Martin Ellingham (Martin Clunes): You are indeed. Collect a thousand loyalty points and you get a free coffin.

Doc Martin

Bert, it's been a long day. Take two aspirin and insult me in the morning.

Dr Martin Ellingham, *Doc Martin*

My doctor was quite a large man. He looked like the only thing he'd ever cured was pork.

James Farmer

An apple a day keeps the doctor away but in my experience so does an air rifle and an open bedroom window.

Harry Hill

There should be no embarrassing bending over at the doctor's office in this day and age. We're in the age of laser eye surgery. They perform surgery on your eye with a laser! Prostate exam? Finger in the ass.

Mario Joyner

The last time I had a pap smear, the guy needed leather gloves and an oyster shucker.

Magda (Lin Shaye), *There's Something About Mary*

Things you don't want to hear from your surgeon: 'Good morning, Mrs A . . . No? Oh, sorry, it seems you've got MRSA.'

Andy Parsons, *Mock the Week*

Wow! You do look like your sister.

Gynaecologist Dr Pellagrino (Tim Bagley) during a vaginal examination, *Knocked Up*

As time goes on, the more I value doctors and plumbers. Doctors a little more. I can fix my own toilet but I still can't operate on myself.

Bob Saget

I hate gynaecologists! A man who can look you in the vagina, but never in the eye.

Patsy Stone (Joanna Lumley), *Absolutely Fabulous*

Dogs

They say that dogs lick their genitalia because they can. But I think it's at least partially because they don't have the internet.

Scott Adams

The owners of a dog which swallowed a diamond worth twelve thousand pounds had to wait three days until it re-emerged. With a bit of planning it could have been a nice way to propose.

Frankie Boyle

Pitbulls are like a gun you can pet.

Bill Burr

Dad wanted a big dog, a 'man dog', a dog that, if it was human, would enjoy a pint and stare at the barmaid's arse.

Alan Carr

I never leave a dog alone in a car on a hot day. I make sure it's with an elderly person holding a baby.

Dane Cook

Harry Dunne (Jeff Daniels): One time, we successfully mated a bulldog with a shih tzu.
Mary Swanson (Lauren Holly): Really? That's weird.
Harry: Yeah, we called it a bullshit.

Dumb and Dumber

Why are all the dogs at dog shows really nice dogs? You never see a pitbull with a ribbon around its head going, 'If you say one word . . .'

Lee Evans

People always want to compare their dogs to having kids. That's insulting. First of all, nobody has a dog because they were too drunk to pull out.

Greg Giraldo

Chihuahuas are the perfect pet if you don't have a person in your life who screams and shits their pants every time there's a noise.

Dana Gould

I love it when dogs yawn. Especially when it's in the middle of another dog's speech.

Dana Gould

Our dog just wanders around the house with a concerned look on his face. Dogs are just people who can't find their phone.

Dana Gould

As anyone who's ever adopted a dog will tell you, there's always the fear that one day the birth parents will come scratching at the door.

Dana Gould

People teach their dogs to sit; it's a trick. I've been sitting my whole life and a dog has never looked at me as though he thought I was tricky.

Mitch Hedberg

The vet says the dog will not lick the salve because the salve tastes bad to the dog . . . Hello? He's already licking his ass.

Jake Johannsen

I love this dog! We totally bonded. We just sat there together in the park. He checked out butts. I checked out butts.

Jack McFarland (Sean Hayes), Will & Grace

I'm suspicious of people who don't like dogs, but I trust a dog when it doesn't like a person.

Bill Murray

Get a good dog. We have not picked up food in the kitchen for fifteen years.

Paul Reiser

I don't get it when you compliment a dog and their owner says, 'Thank you'. Like, mate, I'm addressing the dog, don't make this about you.

@rubyetc via Twitter

Dogs have no money. They're broke their entire lives. But they get through. You know why dogs have no money? No pockets.

Jerry Seinfeld

A dog will stay stupid. That's why we love them so much. The entire time we know them, they're idiots. Think of your dog: every time you come home, he thinks it's amazing. He has no idea how you accomplish this every day. You walk in the door: the joy of this experience overwhelms him. He looks at you. 'He's back. It's that guy, that same guy . . . Another can of food? I don't believe it!'

Jerry Seinfeld

After I ask a stranger if I can pet their dog and they say, 'Yes', I like to respond, 'I'll keep that in mind,' and walk off.

Bridger Winegar, Twitter

Dreams

Belinda Carlisle sang, 'We dream the same dream.' But I can't believe that every night Belinda Carlisle has a wet dream about Wilma Flintstone.

David Baddiel

Ray Barone (Ray Romano): Do you remember me having any dreams when I was a kid?
Frank Barone (Peter Boyle): I remember you wetting the bed.
Ray: No, I mean, do you remember what I wanted to be?
Frank: Dry.

Everybody Loves Raymond

Had my dream again where I'm making love, and the Olympic judges are watching. I got a 9.8 from the Canadians, a perfect 10 from the Americans and my mother, disguised as an East German judge, gave me a 5.6. Must have been the dismount.

Harry Burns (Billy Crystal), *When Harry Met Sally . . .*

Thankfully, dreams can change. If we had all stuck with our first dream, the world would be overrun with cowboys and princesses.

Stephen Colbert

Last night I dreamed I secretly added gluten to everything in Gwyneth Paltrow's refrigerator.

Dave Hill, Twitter

DI Sam Tyler (John Simm): I was just dreaming.
DCI Gene Hunt (Philip Glenister): What I call a dream involves Diana Dors and a bottle of chip oil.

Life on Mars

Chris Stevens (John Corbett): It's like Jung says, 'The unconscious is revealed through the imagery of our dreams, which express our innermost fears and desires.'
Bernard Stevens (Richard Cummings Jr): Jung said that?
Chris: Yeah, I think it was Jung. Or maybe Vincent Price.

Northern Exposure

Driving

Europeans, like some Americans, drive on the right side of the road, except in England, where they drive on both sides of the road; Italy, where they drive on the sidewalk and France where, if necessary, they will follow you right into the hotel lobby.

Dave Barry

I don't even bother to honk at motorists who almost kill me. Generally, it's a bad idea to honk down here anyway, inasmuch as the south Florida motoring public is as heavily armed as Iraq, but not as peace-loving.

Dave Barry

I am the one in the family who does all the driving, because my husband never learned to drive . . . in my opinion.

Jo Brand

There are many rules for the elderly in the *Highway Code*. I have one too and here it is: get a bloody move on.

Jeremy Clarkson

I only passed my driving test at fifty-six. My children were vile – every time they got into the car, they crossed themselves like Portuguese footballers.

Jilly Cooper

Misleading etiquette . . . If, when driving, a police car flashes you from behind, it means you're not going fast enough.

Jack Dee, *I'm Sorry I Haven't a Clue*

Steve Punt: Speed humps don't really work at all, especially the ones that only cover part of the road, where there's three of them, because that only encourages you to head for the middle one, get one wheel either side of the hump and crash into the car doing exactly the same thing in the opposite direction.

Hugh Dennis: It's like the modern equivalent of jousting.

The Now Show

How did you do? Well, let's just see, shall we? You can't park, you can't change lanes, you can't make right-hand turns, you damaged private property and you almost killed someone. Offhand, I'd say you failed.

Driving test examiner (Ron Orbach), *Clueless*

Don't ever get your speedometer confused with your clock, like I did once, because the faster you go, the later you think you are.

Jack Handey

You know, you drive almost slow enough to drive Miss Daisy.

Det. Sgt. Mike Lowrey (Will Smith), *Bad Boys*

A friend of mine said, 'You become a driver on the day you first confidently apply mascara while going round Hyde Park Corner.'

Victoria Coren Mitchell

I can't swim. I can't drive, either. I was going to learn to drive but then I thought, 'Well, what if I crash into a lake?'

Dylan Moran

Once I was so out of it I nodded off during my driving test. I woke up and found a note saying, 'You've failed.'

Ozzy Osbourne

I'm the only person I know who's ever been pulled over for attempted speeding.

Paula Poundstone

Driving on the left (or the right or, in parts of Europe, on the left and the right as the mood takes you) is a rule which works, since following it means you're more likely to reach your intended rather than your final destination.

Sir Terry Pratchett

Marge Simpson (Julie Kavner): Homer! Don't drink and drive.
Homer Simpson (Dan Castellaneta): Fine. I'll drive between sips.

The Simpsons

Drugs

Marijuana? It's harmless really, unless you fashion it into a club and beat somebody over the head with it.

Bill Bailey

Can't we give Lance Armstrong a break? I tried riding a bike once on drugs. If anything it was a lot harder. I was in a hedge within seconds.

Tim Burgess

Darlene Conner (Sara Gilbert): Oh, come on, Dad, do you really think what I did was that bad?
Dan Conner (John Goodman): Yes.
Darlene: Give me a break. You grew up in the sixties, I've seen the photo albums. I mean, those clothes had to have some pharmaceutical explanation.

Roseanne

They'll never win a war on drugs. It's hard enough to win a war even when you're not on drugs.

Paul Bassett Davies, Twitter

I haven't tried heroin, but I imagine the rush is like remembering I have pie in the fridge.

Amy Dillon, Twitter

If you want to buy marijuana, press the hash key.

Clement Freud

So drug dealers don't find it funny when you ask for a receipt?

Gary Gulman

Drugs, eh? What's the point? They make you forget, make you talk funny, make you see things that aren't there. My old grandma got all that for free when she had a stroke.

DCI Gene Hunt (Philip Glenister), *Life on Mars*

If you've never seen an elephant ski, you've never been on acid.

Eddie Izzard

I think I was once given cocaine but I sneezed, so it didn't go up my nose. In fact, it may have been icing sugar.

Boris Johnson

Hiya, kids. Here is an important message from your uncle Bill. Don't buy drugs. Become a pop star and they give you them for free!

Billy Mack (Bill Nighy), *Love Actually*

Don't do drugs, kids. There's a time and place for everything. It's called college.

Jerome 'Chef' McElroy (Isaac Hayes), *South Park*

I don't do drugs. If I want a rush, I get out of the chair when I'm not expecting it.

Dylan Moran

A man in Colorado wants marijuana to be classified as a vegetable. That is an ingenious way to get Americans to stop smoking pot.

Conan O'Brien

A ballot will allow Californians to vote on whether to legalise recreational marijuana. They will have the option of voting either 'Yes' or 'Hell, yes'.

Conan O'Brien

The best way to smuggle drugs into a country is to place them carefully in a dog's bottom, because at the airport, if the sniffer dog suspects anything, the officials will think they're just being frisky – unless, of course, your dog wears sunglasses and sweats a lot.

Ardal O'Hanlon

My son Jack just got out of rehab. He's seventeen years old and he got hooked on OxyContin, and I'm just a little pissed off that he never gave me a few.

Ozzy Osbourne, 2003

There's only two types of people who are against drugs: the people who have never done drugs and the people who really sucked at doing drugs.

Doug Stanhope

I've never understood the point of ecstasy. I think if I wanted to get dehydrated and jump about with a load of people I've never met before, I could go to a Methodist barn dance.

Victoria Wood

Drunkenness

Never get drunk when you're wearing a hooded sweatshirt, because eventually you'll think there's someone right behind you.

Dave Attell

People will blame anything but the booze on their upset stomach. They'll say: 'For some reason, when I got in I was sick as a pig – it must have been something I ate.' And you say: 'I bet it was that packet of crisps you had between pints nine and ten.'

Jack Dee

You know you have a drinking problem when the bartender knows your name – and you've never been to that bar before.

Zach Galifianakis

Lois Griffin (Alex Borstein): You're drunk again.

Peter Griffin (Seth MacFarlane): No, I'm just exhausted 'cause I've been up all night drinking.

Family Guy

I got so drunk last night I found myself dancing in a cheesy bar . . . or, as some people prefer to call it, a delicatessen.

Sean Hughes

I got my dog when I was drunk in a pet store. We had nine cats at the time. The cats started hiding the alcohol after that.

Paula Poundstone

Nothing good ever happens in a blackout. I've never woken up and been like, 'What is this pilates mat doing out?'

Amy Schumer

Dyslexia

Matchmaking is hard. I texted my dyslexic friend asking if she fancied Alan and she got all upset for some reason.

Gary Delaney, Twitter

Scrabble was invented by the Nazis to piss off kids with dyslexia.

Eddie Izzard

Dyslexia, for me, is rather like being a six-fingered typist on LSD.

Stephen Richards

My boyfriend had a sex manual, but he was dyslexic. I was lying there and he was looking for my vinegar.

Victoria Wood

The Economy

I had no idea about the global financial crisis. Watching it unfold was like watching my father being molested by a clown. I knew it was going to affect me, I just wasn't entirely sure how.

Adam Hills

The economy is so bad that bedbugs are now infesting sleeping bags and tents because they can't afford to stay in hotels any more.

Jay Leno

The economy is so bad, in Beverly Hills I saw a woman tanning . . . using the sun.

Jay Leno

Are you sick and tired of hearing the term 'fiscal cliff'? People don't understand it. It doesn't tell you how serious the situation is. They need more colourful metaphors. Here's how to explain it: 'It's 4 a.m. for our economy and Lindsay Lohan is behind the wheel . . .'

Jay Leno

As City markets crashed and flew off, the government tried to stabilise the economy with an emergency currency based on the Queen's eggs, several thousand of which were removed from her ovaries in 1953 and held in reserve.

Chris Morris, *The Day Today*

Education

I think I'm learning a lot from my creative writing classes. The entire experience is just indescribable.

Stewart Francis

Education is the sum of what students teach each other between lectures and seminars.

Stephen Fry

My parents said they had to make a lot of sacrifices to pay for my education . . . because they were both druids.

Milton Jones

You've always been the same, even at school. Nothing but books, learning, education – that's why you're no good at snooker.

Del Trotter (David Jason) to brother Rodney, *Only Fools and Horses*

Embarrassment

Woody Boyd (Woody Harrelson): I feel so ashamed. Promise not to tell my mother?
Diane Chambers (Shelley Long): Mum's the word.
Woody Boyd: Promise not to tell my mum?

Cheers

My life is just a series of embarrassing incidents strung together by telling people about those embarrassing incidents.

Russell Brand, *My Booky Wook*

Who hasn't, in the moment awaiting a toddler to meet your hand in a high-five, thought, My self-esteem depends on what happens next?

Carrie Brownstein, Twitter

Watching sex on telly with your parents – that's embarrassing. I didn't even know they knew how to use the camcorder.

Jimmy Carr

Because I am an Englishman I've spent most of my life in a state of embarrassment.

Colin Firth

I know when I grow up my kids will be embarrassed of me. Because no matter how cool your parents are, you're always gonna be embarrassed of them. Do you think Jesus was embarrassed of his dad? He'd be like, 'Yeah, my dad created the world, but he's not *that* cool.'

Jim Gaffigan

Why do I always meet women as I'm leaving the dog park with a big bag of poop? And it's always on the day I forgot my dog.

Dana Gould

One of the most awkward things that can happen in a pub is when your pint-to-toilet cycle gets synchronised with a complete stranger.

Peter Kay

If someone says to you, 'That's a bit embarrassing,' it immediately is, even if it previously wasn't.

David Mitchell

My dad still has this knack of embarrassing me. I have this dream that I'm at Buckingham Palace collecting my MBE from the Queen for being a smashing guy and he says, 'Do you know he didn't have a proper girlfriend till he was nineteen?'

Gary Strang (Martin Clunes), *Men Behaving Badly*

Emotion

I've had a good snivel . . . and you do feel a bit better afterwards, like a radiator that has been bled.

Julie Burchill

Goody, you are supposed to fix me with a steady manly stare, not snivel like a Frenchman who's caught his baguette in his bicycle spokes.

Insp. Raymond Fowler (Rowan Atkinson), *The Thin Blue Line*

Este told me I looked like Larry David today, and I cried because that might be the nicest thing she's ever said to me.

Alana Haim, on feeling the love from her sister

Feelings are like your mother's breasts. You know they're there, but they're better left unfelt.

> Charlie Harper (Charlie Sheen), *Two and a Half Men*

Sports are an acceptable way for men to show emotion. A guy who won't hug his kid will slip a guy a tongue in a sports bar when his team wins.

> Richard Jeni

I haven't cried this hard since *Toy Story 3*.

> Raj Koothrappali (Kunal Nayyar), *The Big Bang Theory*

If you see someone crying, ask if it's because of their haircut.

> Keply Pentland, Twitter

Men do cry, but only when assembling furniture.

> Rita Rudner

Son, feelings are what women have. They come from their ovaries.

> Stan Smith (Seth MacFarlane), *American Dad!*

I'm against having emotions, not against using them.

> Harvey Specter (Gabriel Macht), *Suits*

Crying would be much more fun if tears screamed 'Weeeeee!' as they rolled down our faces.

> Amber Tozer, Twitter

England

English cuisine has received a lot of unfair criticism over the years, but the truth is that it can be a very pleasant surprise to the connoisseur of severely overcooked livestock organs served in lukewarm puddles of congealed grease.

> Dave Barry

Southend is like Las Vegas. It's the only other place in the world where you can pay for sex with chips.

> Rob Beckett

If you live to be ninety in England and can still eat a boiled egg, they think you deserve the Nobel Prize.

Alan Bennett, *An Englishman Abroad*

I've lived in Manchester since my twenties and I've only been in three fights, not a bad average.

John Bishop

I've been to Liverpool, and never walking alone is actually pretty good advice.

Frankie Boyle

Anyone from Norwich? Gimme six!

Marcus Brigstocke

English is full of booby traps for the unwary foreigner. Any language where the unassuming word 'fly' signifies an annoying insect, a means of travel and a critical part of a gentleman's apparel is clearly asking to be mangled.

Bill Bryson, *The Mother Tongue*

I grew up in Slough in the 1970s. If you want to know what Slough was like in the 1970s, go there now.

Jimmy Carr

On the seventh day God didn't rest. He looked at what he had created and thought, Oh damn it, England's gone all wrong. The sea is washing silt off the coastlines in the north and depositing it in an ugly bulbous lump near Kent. Today we call this unholy place East Anglia.

Jeremy Clarkson

(of the Isle of Wight): All the clocks stopped in 1952.

Alan Davies

These are sophisticated people – they live in Kent for God's sake!

Celia Dawson (Anne Reid), *Last Tango in Halifax*

They say what happens in Manchester today happens in the rest of the world tomorrow. So listen up, rest of the world: tomorrow it's going to drizzle.

Jack Dee, *I'm Sorry I Haven't a Clue*

I went to a pub quiz in Liverpool, had a few too many drinks, so wasn't much use. Just for a laugh I wrote 'The Beatles' or 'Steven Gerrard' for every answer. Came second.

Will Duggan

Some people say Birmingham looks great in the summer. I reckon it looks better in the rear-view mirror.

Stewart Francis

A cut-glass English accent can fool unsuspecting Americans into detecting a brilliance that isn't there.

Stephen Fry

The biggest influence Stafford had on me was it made me want to leave Stafford.

Dave Gorman

Some people in England only have their wheelie bins collected once a fortnight. Their suffering is unimaginable.

Russell Howard

Ping pong was invented on the dining tables of England in the nineteenth century and it was called whiff whaff. And there, I think, you have the difference between us and the rest of the world. Other nations, the French, looked at a dining table and saw an opportunity to have dinner; we looked at it and saw an opportunity to play whiff whaff.

Boris Johnson

Keep Britain tidy: chop off Norfolk and Cornwall.

Milton Jones

This guy said he wanted to understand my culture. I said, 'Well, I'm from Ealing. What are you going to do? Memorise the Central Line?'

Shappi Khorsandi

Do you have any idea what it's like being English? Being so correct all the time, being so stifled by this dread of doing the wrong thing, of saying to someone, 'Are you married?' and hearing, 'My wife left me this morning', or saying, 'Do you have children?', and being told they all burned to death on Wednesday. We're all terrified of embarrassment. That's why we're so . . . dead. Most of my friends are dead, you know. We have these piles of corpses to dinner.

> Archie Leach (John Cleese), *A Fish Called Wanda*

I speak as your native guide to the mysterious tribe called the English. Dress code is everything. You can be a card-carrying Nazi, you can pay gigolos to eat gnocchi out of your navel and you won't be pilloried – as long as you never, ever wear linen with tweed.

> Kathy Lette

Eat in most restaurants in England and pretty soon your head will no longer be on speaking terms with your stomach.

> Kathy Lette

The English don't speak English, they speak euphemisms. So when they'd say to me, 'Oh, you Australians are so refreshing,' I thought that meant they really liked me. It took me a while to realise that meant, 'Rack off you loudmouth colonial nymphomaniac!'

> Kathy Lette

Newcastle people are so hard up, they hold in their piss until they go on holiday.

> Sean Lock

It's well documented in official records that the city's original name was 'Snottingham' or 'Home of Snots', but when the Normans came they couldn't pronounce the letter 'S', so decreed the town be called 'Nottingham' or the 'Home of Notts'. It's easy to understand why this change was resisted so fiercely by the people of Scunthorpe.

> Humphrey Lyttelton, *I'm Sorry I Haven't a Clue*

I'm from Wigan and people say to me, quite seriously, 'You travel all over the world. I bet you're always glad to get home to God's own country.' Well, if God prefers Rotherham to Bath, he's got an extraordinary way of showing it.

Stuart Maconie, on the north/south divide

When the 7/7 bombings happened, the city reacted in a phenomenally 'London' way. They went: 'Oh, my God! There's a bomb on the Piccadilly line. Well, I can get the Victoria line and change at Euston.'

Dara O'Briain

Go to London. I guarantee you'll either be mugged or not appreciated. Catch the train to London, stopping at Rejection, Disappointment, Backstabbing Central and Shattered Dreams Parkway.

Alan Partridge (Steve Coogan), *I'm Alan Partridge*

When sneery city people apply the word 'culture' to Norfolk, they usually prefix it with 'agri', 'horti' or 'it doesn't have any'.

Alan Partridge, *Nomad*

Croydon: less of a place, more of a punchline.

Sue Perkins

In north London, they erect blue plaques in honour of famous entertainers; in south London, they put up yellow signs, saying, 'Did anyone see this murder?'

Arthur Smith

One thing is certain about the Angel of the North statue. It is definitely northern because it is out there day and night, all weathers, freezing cold, and it hasn't got a coat. In fact, not even a T-shirt!

Linda Smith

Do you know that if you hold a shellsuit up to your ear you can hear Romford?

Linda Smith

(My home town) Erith isn't twinned with anywhere but it does have a suicide pact with Dagenham.

Linda Smith

There is nothing more English than bad sex, so on behalf of the entire nation, I thank you.

> Novelist Rowan Somerville, who won the 2010 Bad Sex in Fiction prize for a scene in his book *The Shape of Her*

George (Ian Lindsay): You know, I think marriage is tremendous.
Gary Strang (Martin Clunes): I hate to be cynical, George, but you think Croydon is tremendous.

> *Men Behaving Badly*

Brighton looks as though it is a town helping the police with their enquiries.

> Keith Waterhouse

I've never seen the point of East Anglia. I thought it was just designed to stop the people of Hull doing their shopping in London.

> Victoria Wood

Environment

We dictators aren't all bad. While western countries continue to ravage our planet's resources, we preserve our land and conserve it by burying thousands of bones in single mass eco-graves.

> Admiral General Aladeen (Sacha Baron Cohen), *The Dictator*

Bernard Black (Dylan Moran): Anyway, you had your chance with her. What did you talk about?
Manny Bianco (Bill Bailey): Offshore wind farms. I couldn't think of anything else.

> *Black Books*

In Scotland we have mixed feelings about global warming because we will get to sit on the mountains and watch the English drown.

> Frankie Boyle

Hippies. They're everywhere. They wanna save the Earth, but all they do is smoke pot and smell bad.

Eric Cartman (Trey Parker), *South Park*

A big blizzard proves there's no global warming in the same way being out of milk proves there's no such thing as cows.

Dana Gould

The global warming scenario is pretty grim. I'm not sure I like the idea of polar bears under a palm tree.

Lenny Henry

President George W. Bush has a plan to fight global warming. He says that if we need to, we can lower the temperature dramatically just by switching from fahrenheit to celsius.

Jimmy Kimmel

Al Gore said that global warming is more serious than terrorism; unless the terrorist is on your plane – then that extra half a degree doesn't bother you so much.

Jay Leno

One very dramatic scene in the Al Gore global warming movie [*An Inconvenient Truth*] is when a glacier melts and they find more Al Gore ballots from the election.

David Letterman

Experts say this global warming is serious, and they are predicting now that by the year 2050 we will be out of party ice.

David Letterman

Scientists in Alaska have found a gap between the horizon and the Earth. The gap, which is nine miles across, is believed to have been caused by recent storms which tore the horizon from its moorings. A team of civil engineers have set out to lash the horizon down with steel.

Rosie May (Rebecca Front), *The Day Today*

Serving meat and dairy products at an event to combat climate change is like selling pistols at a gun-control rally.

Morrissey

A group of scientists warned that, because of global warming, sea levels will rise so much that parts of New Jersey will be under water. The bad news? Parts of New Jersey won't be under water.

Conan O'Brien

Al Gore met with Donald Trump to discuss climate change. To try to explain it in terms Trump would understand, Gore said, 'The planet is getting hotter than your daughter Ivanka.'

Conan O'Brien

Green protesters are our best passengers. They're always flying off to their demonstrations.

Ryanair boss Michael O'Leary

Envy

(to Buzz Aldrin): Are you upset that Michael Jackson gets all the credit for the moonwalk but you were the first geezer to actually do it?

Ali G (Sacha Baron Cohen), *Da Ali G Show*

Jealous? Of the Irish? The only reason, love, I can think to be jealous of the Irish is that they're further away than us from France.

Guv (Al Murray), *Time Gentlemen Please*

I could tell by their audible gasps that the people on the beach were jealous of me when I found five shark's teeth. Locating them wasn't really the problem, but pulling them out of my leg was.

Jarod Kintz, *It Occurred to Me*

Why does everything have to go right for her? I wish sometimes her dad would get caught with child porn, just to knock the smug out of her.

Sharon Morris (Sharon Horgan) about her friend Fran, *Catastrophe*

Every time a friend's child succeeds, I feel something so unpleasant there isn't a word for it, not even in German.

Judith Woods

Ethnicity and Racism

I feel sorry for Obama because he's still got to fight the innate racism of Americans. Did you see his first speech, when he got made President and they put all that bullet-proof glass in front of him? I think that shows you how racist America still is. Just because he's black doesn't mean he's going to shoot anybody!

Frankie Boyle

In Barack Obama, America has now elected its first openly black President.

Rory Bremner

There are two types of people I hate: racists and Norwegians.

Stewart Francis

I wish I was ethnic; I'm nothing. 'Cause if you're Hispanic and get angry, people are like: 'He's got a Latin temper.' But if you're a white guy and you get angry, people are like, 'That guy's a jerk.'

Jim Gaffigan

Just read an article saying the cast of 12 Years a Slave should clean up at the Oscars –
awful that people still think like that in 2014.

@kerihw via Twitter

In many ways racism is like cricket: invented here, but perfected in Australia.

Nish Kumar

I think racism is a terrible thing. I think we should all learn to hate each other on an individual basis.

Cathy Ladman

You can only vote within your race or your group. Just pretend it's the 1950s. It makes it easier to understand.

Prison inmate Nicky Nichols (Natasha Lyonne), *Orange is the New Black*

You have to work a bit harder to offend me because I'm from the home of some of the best racism in the world. I'm a snob when it comes to racism.

South African comedian Trevor Noah

Exercise

I belong to a gym now. Well, let me rephrase that: I don't belong there at all, but I go.

Ted Alexandro

In my experience, the best way to turn happy children into shrieking monsters is to mention the phrase 'lovely long walk'.

Craig Brown

I went to a gym, and they offered me free membership for life if I posed for a 'Don't let this happen to you' poster.

Lenny Clarke

I'm so unfamiliar with the gym, I call it James.

Ellen DeGeneres

I'm actually pretty athletic. I have to work out just to look fat.

Will Ferrell

The more women walk around in sweatpants, the harder it is to tell who's out jogging and who's running away from a mugger.

Dana Gould

There is no such thing as a fun run as, even if you are dressed as an elephant, you still have to run.

Miranda Hart, *Is It Just Me?*

Today I did seven press-ups: not in a row.

Daniel Kitson

According to a new study, fifty per cent of Americans are not getting enough exercise. We hear this all the time. You want Americans to exercise more, make the remote heavier.

Jay Leno

I go running when I have to: when the ice cream van is doing sixty.

Wendy Liebman

Hiking is just walking where it's OK to pee.

Demetri Martin

A friend of mine runs marathons. He always talks about this 'runner's high'. But he has to go twenty-six miles for it. That's why I smoke and drink. I get the same feeling from a flight of stairs.

Larry Miller

I'm on a strict running programme. I started yesterday. I've only missed one day so far.

Kevin Nealon

Running is never fun. Running is something that you do when there's a man chasing you with a knife.

Ardal O'Hanlon

My favourite machine at the gym is the vending machine.

Caroline Rhea

The best activities for your health are pumping and humping.

Arnold Schwarzenegger

I try to keep fit. I've got these parallel bars at home. I run at them and try to buy a drink from both of them.

Arthur Smith

I phoned the local ramblers club today, and this bloke just went on and on.

Tim Vine

Eyes and Eyesight

I saw a twinkle in her eye I have not seen since the neighbours' children discovered our new electric fence.

> Niles Crane (David Hyde Pierce), *Frasier*

I've just noticed: your eyes match the spinach in your teeth.

> Barry Cryer, *I'm Sorry I Haven't a Clue*

The only advantage to wearing glasses is you can do that dramatic removal.

> Jim Gaffigan

The good thing is that as you get older and your looks go, your eyesight deteriorates, too.

> Rupert Graves

When I worked in a cosmetics shop, a woman came in looking for something to bring out her bright blue eyes. I gave her meat skewers.

> Hattie Hayridge

I wear glasses myself – as an affectation, as a badge of high intellect, and to see with.

> Simon Munnery

The first thing men notice about a woman is her eyes. Then, when her eyes aren't looking, they notice her breasts.

> Conan O'Brien

The skin under your eyes is starting to look like Hugh Hefner's ball sack.

> Jacob Palmer (Ryan Gosling), *Crazy, Stupid, Love*

My eye doctor told me 'Do you know you have one eye set higher than the other eye? It's no big deal. It doesn't affect your vision or anything. I just thought you'd like to be self-conscious for the rest of your life.'

> Brian Regan

Failure

Failure is just success rounded down.

Ryan North

Scott Andrews (Charlie Hofheimer): I feel like such a loser.
Dale Putley (Robin Williams): Come on, Scott, you're still young! Being a true loser takes years of ineptitude.

Fathers' Day

It was a pretty disappointing day. It was kind of a slap in the face to realise that I wasn't as important as I thought I was to a certain young executive. Who I had cared about. But you know, I'm not going to cry about it. I did that on the way home.

Michael Scott (Steve Carell), *The Office* (US)

I don't fail. I succeed in finding what doesn't work.

Christopher Titus

Fame

It's a strange sight, I guess, this thing that was contained in a rectangle in their living room, now floating freely in Asda. They look at you as if there's been a spillage.

Richard Ayoade, on being recognised

Any idiot can get laid when they're famous. That's easy. It's getting laid when you're broke and unknown that takes some talent.

Kevin Bacon

I want to be so famous that drag queens will dress like me in parades when I'm dead.

Laura Kightlinger

One great benefit of not being on TV every week is that people will be a lot less interested in what I have in my supermarket basket. I could even un-tint my car windows – or at least opt for a lighter shade.

Hugh Laurie

Before the competition, people wouldn't piss on me if I was on fire. Now I believe they would.

Geraldine McQueen (Peter Kay), Britain's Got the Pop Factor . . . and
Possibly a New Celebrity Jesus Christ Soapstar Superstar Strictly on Ice

I got briefly mistaken for someone who might be good in bed which was very, very good.

Bill Nighy

The downside of fame? I can't walk out of a nice restaurant without immediately getting harassed and hounded by a waiter holding the bill.

Conan O'Brien

I live in Notting Hill; you live in Beverly Hills. Everyone in the world knows who you are; my mother has trouble remembering my name.

Will Thacker (Hugh Grant), Notting Hill

The price of fame? Who in their right mind would want to pay it?

Sir Terry Wogan

Families

Peggy Bundy (Katey Sagal): You haven't been very nice to my family.
Al Bundy (Ed O'Neill): Neither has nature. Go bother it!

Married . . . with Children

If most people have a family tree, we have family tumbleweed . . . it just keeps rolling along picking up dirt and debris.

Camilla Cleese, daughter of four times married John Cleese

Frasier Crane (Kelsey Grammer): That's my brother, Niles. He's a little . . . how would you describe Niles, Dad?

Martin Crane (John Mahoney): I usually just change the subject.

Frasier

I come from a very traditional family. When I was seven, my uncle Terry hanged himself on Christmas Eve. My family didn't take his body down until the sixth of January.

Nick Doody

I remember when Grandpa's memory started to go. It was the day I caught him urinating with the door open, which is not a huge deal but it's annoying when I'm trying to drive.

Jon Dore

On life's list of fun things to do, visiting my in-laws comes in somewhere below sitting in a tub full of scissors.

Jeff Foxworthy

I come from a very large family: nine parents.

Jim Gaffigan

Give me a burger, onion rings and a list of people who killed their parents and got away with it. I need some heroes.

Lorelai Gilmore (Lauren Graham), *Gilmore Girls*

I never saw my granddad while I was growing up because he was excellent at hiding.

Harry Hill

My granddad would never throw anything away. He was killed by a hand grenade.

Milton Jones

My other grandfather was a peeping tom. He used to drill holes in the floor and spy on the people in the flat below. He died recently but I kind of like thinking about him up there sometimes . . . looking down on us.

Milton Jones

Blood may be thicker than water, but it's certainly not as thick as ketchup. Nor does it go as well with French fries.

Jarod Kintz, *This Book is Not for Sale*

I had a buddy of mine call up the other day, all upset 'cause he slept with his third cousin. I'm like, 'Man, if it upsets you that much, quit countin' them!'

Larry the Cable Guy (Daniel Whitney)

I'll be spending the holidays with my family; nothing special, just some light bickering and biting sarcasm.

Ray Romano

I come from a long line of fighters. My maternal grandfather was the toughest guy I ever knew. World War Two veteran. Killed twenty men, then spent the rest of the war in an Allied prison camp. My father . . . battled blood pressure and obesity all his life. Different kind of fight.

Dwight Schrute (Rainn Wilson), *The Office* (US)

Nothing in life is fun for the whole family. There are no massage parlours with ice cream and free jewellery.

Jerry Seinfeld

I can't wait till Sunday. I'm gonna see my favourite niece, and my other niece . . .

Sarah Silverman

I have nephews. They love spending time with us. They love it because we let them do whatever they want to do – they're not our kids, we don't care. 'Only thing I have to do is keep you alive, that's it.'

Wanda Sykes

Personally, I think any more than two or three kids is not a family, it's a litter.

Tracey Ullman

I'm related to people I don't relate to.

Bill Watterson, *Calvin and Hobbes*

Fans

It's been twenty-six years since I was last here. Before, my fans were all taking drugs; this time they're all taking medication.

Bette Midler at a 2005 concert in Brisbane, Australia

I used to get young girls hanging around the stage door, now it's women in their sixties and seventies. You have to walk quite slowly when you're being stalked these days.

Paul Nicholas, 2017

Violet Crosby (Frances de la Tour): Will there be a lot of single men?
Freddie Thornhill (Sir Ian McKellen): It's a science-fiction fan club event – they'll be single but they'll be disgusting.

Vicious

Fantasy

Fantasy is an exercise bicycle for the mind. It might not take you anywhere, but it tones up the muscles that can.

Sir Terry Pratchett

Sad old blokes, I'm told, now dream of me with a whip in hand.

Anne Robinson

Fate

Providence dictates that objects that are too large to lose, such as houses, always come with tiny keys, specially designed to give you the slip.

Craig Brown

Fate is just what you call it when you don't know the name of the person screwing you over.

Lois (Jane Kaczmarek), Malcolm in the Middle

Fathers

Pte. Baldrick (Tony Robinson): You know my dad was a nun.
Capt. Edmund Blackadder (Rowan Atkinson): No, he wasn't.
Baldrick: He was too, sir. 'Cause whenever he was up in court and the judge asked 'Occupation?', he'd say, 'None'.

Blackadder Goes Forth

I was raised by just my mom. See, my father died when I was eight years old. At least, that's what he told us in the letter.

Drew Carey

I was entrusted with the task of being a single father for two days and, frankly, I'd have been better off doing underwater knitting. I made a complete hash of it. When my wife arrived home on Sunday evening, way past the kids' bedtime, one child was bleeding profusely, one had left home and the other was stuck up a tree.

Jeremy Clarkson, The World According to Clarkson

My father was a magician. Well, not really. He just disappeared a lot.

Alex Edelman

I love my dad. He used to be a professional wrestler in Mexico. So when he hit us, he didn't really hit us.

Felipe Esparza

My dad used to collect empty beer bottles, which is a nice way of saying he was an alcoholic.

Stewart Francis

And even though I'm proud my father invented the rear-view mirror, we're not as close as we appear.

Stewart Francis

My relationship with my father had been on the slide since the time I was fifteen and called the police to report him for child molesting. He had never molested me, but I wanted to have a party that weekend and needed him out of the house.

Chelsea Handler

My father used to like my mother to get dressed up as a nurse. Then he used to like her to go out to work . . . as a nurse. Brought in some extra money.

Harry Hill

I grew up in the seventies when dads weren't hands-on but entertainers were.

Adam Hills

You know how you look up to your dad when you're a little kid like he's got some special dad knowledge. And then you find out all he really knows is how to have sex with your mom.

Jake Johannsen

You know you're a dad when you discover that not only have you developed an opinion about crib bumpers, but you have actually uttered it aloud.

Steve Johnson

You know you're a dad when, for the first time in your life, the vomit you are covered in is not of your own making.

Steve Johnson

My wife just told me the good news – I'm going to be a dad for the first time. The bad news is we already have two kids.

Brian Kiley

Now that I'm a dad, I call my dad and ask him for advice. He always says the same thing: 'How did you get this number?!'

Brian Kiley

If you ever want to torture my dad, tie him up and, right in front of him, refold a road map incorrectly.

Cathy Ladman

My stepfather doesn't like it when I call him my 'fake-dad'. He prefers 'faux-pa'.

> Glenn Moore

Fatherhood has changed my life. I can't just leave my little boy at home, go clubbing, bosh some pills, bang a bird, come back to the flat two days later. These days I'm a dad; I got to take him with me.

> Lee Nelson (Simon Brodkin)

Someone told me I should tell my dad I love him before he dies, but what if I get the timing wrong and he lives for another twenty years? I don't think either of us could deal with the embarrassment. I'd have to kill him!

> Ardal O'Hanlon

My father always said I would do something big one day. 'I've got a feeling about you, John Osbourne,' he'd tell me, after he'd had a few beers. 'You're either going to do something very special or you're going to go to prison.' And he was right, my old man. I was in prison before my eighteenth birthday.

> Ozzy Osbourne, *I Am Ozzy*

My daughter is appalled by it at all times, but you know you have to appal your fourteen-year-old daughter otherwise you're not doing your job as a father.

> Richard Osman, on the marriage proposals he receives as co-host of TV game show *Pointless*

The most challenging part of being a dad is trying to postpone the moment when they realise you don't know anything.

> Paul Reiser

Homer Simpson (Dan Castellaneta): Just remember, if your mother asks, I took you to a wine tasting.
Lisa Simpson (Yeardley Smith): That's a terrible thing for a father to do.
Homer: That's why she'll believe it.

> *The Simpsons*

Robbie Sinclair (Jason Willinger): Every day it's the same thing. He comes home and says, 'Franny, get me a beer.' And then he yells at me.
Earl Sinclair (Stuart Pankin): Not true. Sometimes I yell at you first.

Dinosaurs

The belt was his favourite child development tool.

Tony Soprano Sr (James Gandolfini), *The Sopranos*

Fatherhood is great because you can ruin someone from scratch.

Jon Stewart

My father, too, had a weekly column in a Sunday newspaper and I am aware that I am the third generation in my family to sit earning a living in this way. It makes me wonder how things might have transpired if Papa had been, say, a chiropodist instead. Even now I might be bent over someone's foot declaring, 'Heavens, that fungus has spread.'

Sandi Toksvig

Dad, you were like a father to me.

Ethan Tremblay (Zach Galifianakis), *Due Date*

My father said, 'Always leave them wanting more.' Ironically, that's how he lost his job in disaster relief.

Mark Watson

I'm sure wherever my father is, he would be looking down on us. He's not dead, just very condescending.

Jack Whitehall

Fear

My biggest fear is that when I die, my wife will sell my bicycles for what I told her they cost.

Anon

A fear of heights is illogical. A fear of falling, on the other hand, is prudent and evolutionary.

> Sheldon Cooper (Jim Parsons), *The Big Bang Theory*

I am brave. Rollercoasters? Love 'em. Scary movies? I've seen *Ghostbusters*, like, seven times. I regularly drive through neighbourhoods that have only recently been gentrified. So yeah, I'm pretty much not afraid of anything . . . except for clowns.

> Phil Dunphy (Ty Burrell), *Modern Family*

The best part of chronic head lice is it takes away your fear of dying alone.

> Dana Gould

I don't like heights. That's why I stopped growing at fifth grade.

> Sammy Kamin (Billy Crystal), *My Giant*

They say that if you're afraid of homosexuals, it means that deep down inside you're actually a homosexual yourself. That worries me, because I'm afraid of dogs.

> Norm Macdonald

Feminism

Feminism is not a fad. It's not like *Angry Birds*. Although it does involve a lot of angry birds. Bad example.

> Bridget Christie

I don't think feminists realise that by keeping their name after marriage they are jeopardising their future children's banking security.

> Gary Delaney

We need to stop asking famous women which inspiring woman made her into a feminist and start asking her which act by a mediocre man did.

> Alana Massey, Twitter

There's no such thing as a feminist – just women who pay for their own breast implants.

Bonnie McFarlane

Tell me, Germaine, what's the difference between being sexually liberated in the sixties and an old slapper now?

Mrs Merton (Caroline Aherne) to Germaine Greer, *The Mrs Merton Show*

Without feminism, you wouldn't be allowed to have a debate on women's place in society. You'd be too busy giving birth on the kitchen floor – biting down on a wooden spoon, so as not to disturb the men's card game – before going back to quickliming the dunny.

Caitlin Moran, *How To Be a Woman*

(to TV historian Mary Beard): Generally speaking, as a woman, I'm a big admirer of your work, because before you, it was all either men or Simon Schama.

Tracey Pritchard (Monica Dolan), *W1A*

Fishing

Advice to anglers: don't take advice from people with missing fingers.

Henry Beard, *Fishing*

The formal term for a collection of fishermen is an exaggeration of anglers.

Henry Beard, *Fishing*

As a rule of thumb, I would say the smaller the pond, the more belligerent the fish.

Craig Brown

Whoever came up with ice fishing must have had the worst marriage on the planet.

Jeff Cesario

I am aware, of course, that many men do hate the sight of their wife and children. Doctors even have a name for these people: anglers.

Jeremy Clarkson

I love fishing. It's like transcendental meditation with a punchline.

Billy Connolly

I used to love going fishing. I think it was really about the clothes. Nothing says real man like a vest with thirty-eight pockets and a mesh hat with hooks in it.

Craig Ferguson

They say, 'Give a man a fish and he'll eat for a day, but teach a man to fish and he'll get his own show on the Discovery Channel.'

Craig Ferguson

They should call fishing what it really is: tricking and killing.

Demetri Martin

Fish deserve to be caught because they are lazy. Two million years of evolution and they still haven't got out of the water.

Simon Munnery

I just want to get the work over as soon as possible so I can do some fishing. Fishing relaxes me. It's like yoga except I still get to kill something.

Ron Swanson (Nick Offerman), *Parks and Recreation*

Flatulence

I hate dates. I sit home all day and I don't fart once. I go on a date and I've got twenty in the bank straight away.

Carl Barron

The rooms were small and airless and cramped. To make matters worse, somebody in our group was making the most dreadful silent farts. Fortunately, it was me, so I wasn't nearly as bothered as the others.

Bill Bryson, *The Road to Little Dribbling: More Notes from a Small Island*

Terry Hoitz (Mark Wahlberg): Your farts aren't manly.

Allen Gamble (Will Ferrell): Are you serious?

Terry: They sound like a baby blowing out birthday candles.

The Other Guys

Before we got engaged, he never farted. Now it's a second language.

Caroline Rhea

Flirting

Blanche Devereaux (Rue McClanahan): Girls. Do you see that man over there staring at me? He's undressing me with his eyes.

Rose Nylund (Betty White): Do you want to move to another table?

Blanche: Not yet. He's only half done.

The Golden Girls

There are times not to flirt. When you're sick, when you're with children, when you're on the witness stand.

Joyce Jillson

All right! I met him in a bar! He flirted with me, thought I was a whore. Made me feel . . . I don't know, special.

Karen Walker (Megan Mullally), *Will & Grace*

Flowers

If you think squash is a competitive activity, try flower arranging.

Alan Bennett

I love the way garages leave black buckets outside for your dead flowers.

Jack Dee

Foxgloves: worn by foxes to avoid leaving fingerprints when killing chickens.

Eddie Izzard

Why do people give each other flowers? To celebrate various important occasions, they're killing living creatures. Why restrict it to plants? 'Sweetheart, let's make up. Have this deceased squirrel.'

Jerry Seinfeld

Hey, somebody got flowers! Or as I like to call them, poor people jewellery.

Karen Walker (Megan Mullally), *Will & Grace*

Food and Drink

I bought some ready-to-eat apricots the other day. They say you are what you eat, which is true. Because as soon as I bought these ready-to-eat apricots, I was ready to eat apricots.

James Acaster

What's the two things they tell you are healthiest to eat? Chicken and fish. You know what you should do? Combine them – eat a penguin.

Dave Attell

There isn't a problem on this earth that a doughnut cannot make better.

Roseanne Barr

Eating rice cakes is like chewing on a foam coffee cup, only less filling.

Dave Barry

I'm a big fan of pastries the size of a baby that contain enough calories for a year. That seems like an effective use of time.

Mike Birbiglia, *Sleepwalk With Me and Other Painfully True Stories*

Invent a drink called Responsibly and your advertising is set forever.

Emmy Blotnick, Twitter

If you took all the money that we in the west spend on food in one week, you could feed the third world for one year. I'm not sure about you, but I think we're being overcharged on groceries.

Jimmy Carr

It's impossible to eat a Toblerone without hurting yourself.

Billy Connolly

I read that just half a glass of wine a day can add seven hours to your life. I've worked out that I'm going to live to 179.

Joseph Connolly

Brussels sprouts are what happens when a pea and a cabbage get married and have a fat baby.

Philomena Cunk (Diane Morgan)

Health food would seem healthier if the people who sold it looked less unhealthy.

Dov Davidoff

Unlike European mustards that bring out the subtle flavours of food, English mustard makes your nose bleed.

Jack Dee

It doesn't matter what day it is, Father, there is always time for a nice cup of tea. Sure, didn't our Lord himself on the cross pause for a nice cup of tea before giving himself up for the world?

Mrs Doyle (Pauline McLynn), *Father Ted*

You see a butcher unloading a delivery van, and he gets out a side of a cow. Where's the other side? Is there a cow still grazing in a field with a side missing?

Lee Evans

Last week a group of chefs baked the world's largest pizza, which is gluten-free and contains nine thousand pounds of cheese. Or, as Americans put it, 'You had me at "world's largest pizza", you lost me at "gluten-free", then you won me back with "nine thousand pounds of cheese".'

Jimmy Fallon

I never do any television without chocolate. That's my motto and I live by it. Quite often I write the scripts and I make sure there are chocolate scenes.

Dawn French

I saw a recipe for guilt-free pizza. The only reason you should ever feel guilty after eating a pizza is if you killed the delivery boy.

Ed Gamble

Have you ever noticed nobody has ever ordered a grapefruit the size of a tumour? There's no reciprocity.

Janeane Garofalo

Peach flavour yoghurt tastes best on the way back up.

Brüno Gehard (Sacha Baron Cohen)

A burrito is a sleeping bag for ground beef.

Mitch Hedberg

You ever dip your biscuit in your tea and it breaks? I swear, you never get used to that. Rich Teas should be called one-dips. Hobnobs are like Marines. They're like the bloody SAS of the biscuit world, Hobnobs. You dip a Hobnob, it's like, 'Again! Again! Dip me again! I'm going nowhere me, son, dip me! Is that all you've got? Come on!'

Peter Kay

Twinkies are the only food that has a longer shelf life than the life of the average shelf.

Jay Leno

I wouldn't touch a hot dog unless you put a condom on it. You realise that the job of a hot dog is to use parts of the animal that the Chinese can't figure out how to make into a belt?

Bill Maher

At the stroke of midnight, Neil wept softly, cradling the sour cream as it expired.

@Leemanish, Twitter

(of turkey): I can't stand the stuff. My grandmother said to me when I was about twelve, 'Never eat anything that's ugly when it's alive. It's not going to taste any prettier when it's cooked.'

James Martin

I'll never forget my first experience of swede. It was at school and I thought I was getting mashed potato. I've never got over it.

Paul Merton

Healthy things are delicious if either a) they're deep-fried or b) there's nothing else to eat. Couscous salad is much better than no food at all but, on the modern culinary battlefield, it's a mere flint-headed arrow to the state-of-the-art cruise missile that is a fried egg sandwich.

David Mitchell

It's a sad day when your child looks at you and asks, 'Daddy, is this organic?' Organic? I grew up on Angel Delight! We didn't have anything in the house if it wasn't neon!

Dylan Moran

Eggs. They're not a food, they belong in no group. They're just farts clothed in substance.

Dylan Moran

Putting a damp spoon back in the [sugar] bowl is the tea-drinking equivalent of sharing a needle.

Alan Partridge, *I, Partridge: We Need to Talk About Alan*

Does it have apples in it? No. What about pine? No pine either. Perfect, we'll call it a pineapple.

@peeznuts, Twitter

Tea without sugar is just vegetable soup.

Lance Slater (Toby Jones), *Detectorists*

I couldn't really see the point of having lunch unless it started at one o'clock and ended a week later in Monte Carlo.

Arthur Smith

Marty (Sean Power): I can't eat your cereal. That muesli you buy, it's grey. It's like dust with bits in it. It should come in an urn. You don't pour it, you scatter it around.

Rick Spleen (Jack Dee): Do you want some fruit? Oh no, you're American, aren't you?

Lead Balloon

The first time I tried organic wheat bread, I thought I was chewing on roofing material.

Robin Williams

I love nachos. I wish more foods simulated digging through the garbage.

Bridger Winegar, Twitter

Calm down, spikes on pineapple. You're protecting a decent-tasting fruit. Not a bank with lots of money.

Michelle Wolf, Twitter

If I need a buzz, I have a piccalilli sandwich with Worcester sauce. That takes your mind off your bunions, believe me.

Victoria Wood

Football (American)

My wife calls me 'Much Maligned'. She thinks that's my first name. Every time she reads a story about me, that's always in front of my name.

Chris Bahr

Denver Broncos won the Super Bowl in 2016. I'm not saying American football is boring but they had Coldplay to liven it up halfway through.

Jimmy Carr, *8 Out of 10 Cats*

Just because one paedophile is a football coach, please don't turn against all paedophiles.

Dana Gould

I knew Rocket Ismail was fast, but I never knew how fast until I saw him playing tennis by himself.

Lou Holtz

The man who complains about the way the ball bounces is likely the one who dropped it.

Lou Holtz

You've got a better chance of completing a pass to the Venus de Milo.

Vance Johnson

On eBay, a group of four Super Bowl tickets is going for fifty-one thousand dollars. Although to be fair, that price includes a full-body rubdown from stadium security.

Jimmy Kimmel

I wanted to have a career in sports when I was young, but I had to give it up. I'm only six feet tall, so I couldn't play basketball. I'm only one hundred and ninety pounds, so I couldn't play football. And I have twenty-twenty vision, so I couldn't be a referee.

Jay Leno

According to a *Sports Illustrated* poll, thirty per cent of male readers said they would rather watch a big play-off game than have sex. The other seventy said, 'Hey, that's why they have half-time.'

Jay Leno

Most football teams are temperamental. That's ninety per cent temper and ten per cent mental.

Doug Plank

If God wanted women to understand men, football would never have been created.

Roger Simon

France

I took an estimated two thousand years of high school French and, when I finally got to France, I discovered that I didn't know one single phrase that was actually useful in a real-life French situation.

Dave Barry

Escargot is French for 'fat crawling bag of phlegm'.

Dave Barry

Let's face it, the French army couldn't beat a girls' hockey team.
Bill Bryson, *Neither Here Nor There: Travels in Europe*

Calais is an interesting place that exists solely for the purpose of giving English people in shellsuits somewhere to go for the day.
Bill Bryson, *Notes from a Small Island*

I ran out of deodorant in Paris and had to go all the way to London to buy a new stick.

Dave Chappelle

The French hate anything that is ugly. If they see an animal that is ugly, they immediately eat it.

Jeremy Clarkson

I can have a go at the French because I'm half-French, half-English with a stupid name like Gervais. I've got qualities of both, French and English, which is good. I'm crap in bed, but at least I've got bad breath.

Ricky Gervais

(to a Frenchman): You see, the thing about the Germans is it's all above board, they're perfectly clear about what their ambition is; it's world domination – by any means possible. They're up to something, but they're telling us about it. Not like you lot, sneaking around. I mean look at the words that the French have given the English: espionage, sabotage, camouflage, fromage . . .

Guv (Al Murray), *Time Gentlemen Please*

Is French kissing in France just called 'kissing'?

Peter Kay

When I was in high school, I was in the French club. We didn't really do anything. Every once in a while, we'd surrender to the German club.

Brian Kiley

The French will eat anything. Over here, My Little Pony is a toy; over there, it's a starter.

Paul Merton

Italians manifestly enjoy life, but a Frenchman on holiday is Eeyore with cancer.

Tim Moore, *Geronimo!: Riding the Very Terrible 1914 Tour of Italy*

I don't know why we don't grow a big hedge up the English Channel. Spoil their light.

Al Murray, The Pub Landlord

We shouldn't insult the French, of course, because they're not here to defend themselves. And we know how good they are at that.

Al Murray

The French have launched their own version of Google, called Quaero. You just type in the subject you're interested in, and Quaero refuses to look it up for you.

Amy Poehler, *Saturday Night Live*, 2006

Friendship

It's got to the point where I think my friends would rather hang out with their own kids than hang out with me. I'm, like, 'Where's the loyalty, man? I've known you for twenty-five years. How long have you known your baby? A month?'

Arj Barker

My second husband believed I had such a fickle attitude to friendship that each Friday he would update the list of my Top 10 friends in the manner of a *Top of the Pops* chart countdown.

Julie Burchill

Friends should always tell you the truth. But please don't.

Louis C.K.

One good reason to maintain only a small circle of friends is that three out of four murders are committed by people who know the victim.

George Carlin

Friendship's more lasting than love, and more legal than stalking.

Jane Christie (Gina Bellman), *Coupling*

What exactly does that expression mean, 'friends with benefits'? Does he provide her with health insurance?

Sheldon Cooper (Jim Parsons), *The Big Bang Theory*

Borrowing money from a friend is like having sex. It just completely changes the relationship.

George Costanza (Jason Alexander), *Seinfeld*

A true friend will go with the Instagram filter that flatters you.

Whitney Cummings

Why can't you be happy for me and then go home and talk about me behind my back like a normal person?

Lillian Donovan (Maya Rudolph), *Bridesmaids*

Friends – they spend years trying to find you a boyfriend, but the moment you get one, they instantly tell you to dump him!

Bridget Jones (Renée Zellweger), *Bridget Jones: The Edge of Reason*

Can't a guy just buy some bagels for his friends so they'll owe him a favour, which he can use to get someone fired who stole a co-manager position from him, anymore? Jeez. When did everyone get so cynical?

Dwight Schrute (Rainn Wilson), *The Office* (US)

In every group of girlfriends, there's that one who is the sluttiest; if you don't have that friend, *you're* that friend.

Amy Schumer

I hate when your friends quit drinking on you. It's sad. I've lost more friends to AA than Liberace did to the virus.

Doug Stanhope

A lot of people say, 'A stranger is just a friend you haven't met yet.' But I've been mugged four times and I haven't kept in touch with any of them.

Chris Stokes

Friends are just enemies who don't have enough guts to kill you.

Judy Tenuta

I'm good friends with twenty-five letters of the alphabet . . . I don't know why.

Chris Turner

Funerals

If we bury you ass up, I've got a place to park my bike.

Patch Adams (Robin Williams), *Patch Adams*

At funerals, I like to pass around sponges instead of tissues, then at the end I squeeze the tears into tubes to see who grieved the most.

Aisling Bea, Twitter

I went to a funeral recently and they handed out Kleenex before the funeral. Which I thought was cocky.

Mike Birbiglia

Rob Brydon (himself): You know, when someone dies, and they go to the funeral and they say, 'We should have done this when he was alive! He would have loved this!'
Steve Coogan (himself): What, cremated him?

The Trip

Misleading etiquette . . . At a funeral, don't forget to throw an old mattress in the hole for luck.

Barry Cryer, *I'm Sorry I Haven't a Clue*

A friend of mine drowned. So at the funeral we got him a wreath in the shape of a lifebelt. Well, it's what he would have wanted.

Gary Delaney

Hopefully, my funeral is a long way off. I'm approaching seventy – unfortunately, from the wrong direction. When it finally comes, I'd like to be carried into the church to the sound of Queen's 'We Are The Champions', a suitably low-key number for such a solemn event.

Dame Edna Everage (Barry Humphries)

I want to write my own eulogy, and I want to write it in Latin. It seems only fitting to read a dead language at my funeral.

Jarod Kintz, *I Want*

Nana Moon (Hilda Braid): Alfie, I've decided I want to be cremated.
Alfie Moon (Shane Richie): Come on then, get your coat.

EastEnders

Gash Nesbitt (Andrew Fairlie): My brother was burnt to a crisp in a joyride.
Rab C. Nesbitt (Gregor Fisher): Aye, looking back it was overkill getting him cremated.

Rab C. Nesbitt

Funerals are insane. The chicks are so horny, it's not even fair. It's like fishing with dynamite!

Chazz Reinhold (Will Ferrell), *Wedding Crashers*

At my funeral, I want Meryl Streep crying in five different accents.

Joan Rivers

The Future

I believe in making the world safe for our children, but not our children's children, because I don't think children should be having sex.

Jack Handey

Today is tomorrow's tadpole of opportunity.

Gus Hedges (Robert Duncan), *Drop the Dead Donkey*

Garlic bread, it's the future. I've tasted it.

Brian Potter (Peter Kay), *Peter Kay's Phoenix Nights*

Ice cream with cookie dough! Unnecessarily big TVs! Thursday night football! And the globe feels so warm. I am in awe of the future!

Homer Simpson (Dan Castellaneta), *The Simpsons*

Dr Lilith Sternin-Crane (Bebe Neuwirth): Well, I'm off. I don't know what the future holds. Whatever happens, I only hope I can realise my full potential. To acquire things the old Lilith never had.
Carla Tortelli (Rhea Perlman): Like a body temperature?

Cheers

When I think of the future, I think of doing my washing so I've something to wear tomorrow.

Julie Walters

Gambling

Last year, people won more than one billion dollars playing poker. And casinos made twenty-seven billion just by being around those people.

Samantha Bee

I used to buy lottery tickets every week until I realised you could watch it on TV for nothing.

Jimmy Carr

They call gambling a disease, but it's the only disease where you can win a bunch of money.

Norm Macdonald

Isn't it funny that you get James Bond in his dinner jacket, with his Martini, being super-sophisticated and glamorous – and bingo being a bit tragic. Yet roulette and bingo are the same thing in the end: games of chance for money. You'd never get a film called *Gala Bingo Royale*. It's a class thing.

Stuart Maconie

Henry Davenport (David Swift): Filling in these lottery tickets is harder than I thought. I was going to use the number of times I had sex last month, but the ticket only goes up to forty-nine!
Joy Merryweather (Susannah Doyle): Try limiting it to the number of times there was someone else there.

Drop the Dead Donkey

Cliff Clavin (John Ratzenberger): How come black seventeen, Norm?
Norm Peterson (George Wendt): Ah, well seventeen is because Vera and I were married on the seventeenth. And black is because Vera and I were married on the seventeenth.

Cheers

Playing poker online is like being mugged without the company.

Lucy Porter

Gosh, I just love gambling here in Vegas. Sure, I may lose one hundred thousand dollars, but the drinks are free so it evens out!

Karen Walker (Megan Mullally), *Will & Grace*

In Vegas, I got into a long argument with the man at the roulette wheel over what I considered to be an odd number.

Steven Wright

Games

Everyone must know by now that the aim of Scrabble is to gain the moral high ground, the loser being the first player to slam the board shut and upset all the letters over the floor.

Craig Brown

Monopoly may also end in tears, but its tensions are cruder, lacking the infinitely subtle shadings of irritation and acrimony provided by Scrabble.

Craig Brown

Lois Griffin (Alex Borstein): What's going on down here?
Stewie Griffin (Seth MacFarlane): Oh, we're playing house.
Lois: That boy's all tied up.
Stewie: Roman Polanski's house.

Family Guy

Reese Witherspoon is my favourite actress that sounds like the answer to a Cluedo game.

Andrea Mann, Twitter

Gardening

Americans would rather live next to a pervert, heroin-addict, communist pornographer than a person with an unkempt lawn.

Dave Barry

Bulb: potential flower buried in autumn, never to be seen again.

Henry Beard, Gardening

Hoeing: a manual method of severing roots from stems of newly planted flowers and vegetables.

Henry Beard, Gardening

How dare you! Murdered my wife and buried her in the garden? I have never been so insulted in my life. You know how much I've spent on that garden. You think I'm going to dig a hole in it?

Boycie (John Challis), *Only Fools and Horses*

Sssh, Richard! *If* we can't afford a gardener, that's all the more reason why we should look as though we *can* afford a gardener. So in future, could you look like someone who enjoys doing his own gardening but could afford a gardener if he wanted to.

Hyacinth Bucket (Patricia Routledge), *Keeping Up Appearances*

I don't have the patience for growing things. Yes, I realise there's nothing quite as satisfying as eating food that you've pulled up from the ground and that's why, at the height of the planting season, I bury cans of tomato soup in my backyard and dig them up in late spring.

Ellen DeGeneres, *The Funny Thing Is . . .*

If you water it and it dies, it's a plant; if you pull it out and it grows back, it's a weed.

Gallagher

I got a cactus in my bathroom, but we've got nothing to say to each other.

Max Goldman (Walter Matthau), on talking to one's plants, *Grumpier Old Men*

My fake plants died because I did not pretend to water them.

Mitch Hedberg

Honey, what's the point of being in the suburbs if you're not going to fuck a gardener?

Samantha Jones (Kim Cattrall), *Sex and the City*

I'm really glad we arrived back to find this half-eaten double whopper with cheese lying in my front rose bed. Some people put manure in theirs, but I'll have none of it. A double whopper with cheese is the thing. Harry Wheatcroft swears by them!

Victor Meldrew (Richard Wilson), *One Foot in the Grave*

I tell you what often gets overlooked; garden fences.

Tim Vine

Gay and Lesbian

Jack McFarland (Sean Hayes): She doesn't know I'm gay.
Grace Adler (Debra Messing): Has she *met* you?

Will & Grace

Larry Sanders (Garry Shandling): What if she's not a lesbian? Did you guys ever think of that?
Stevie Grant (Bob Odenkirk): She's a lesbian. I can tell, right? I've had sex with a lesbian.
Artie (Rip Torn): So you had sex with a lesbian. You gotta have sex with *two* lesbians, that's the whole point.

The Larry Sanders Show

Mitt Romney has come out strongly against gay marriage, because as a committed Mormon he believes that marriage is a sacred covenant between a man and no more than four women.

Richard Bacon, *Have I Got News for You*

I thank God for gay men. Because if it wasn't for them, us fat women would have no one to dance with.

Roseanne Barr

I felt like a man trapped in a woman's body. Then I was born.

Chris Bliss

My brother is gay and my parents don't care, as long as he marries a doctor.

Elayne Boosler

I would have loved to have had a gay dad. Do you remember at school, there were always kids saying, 'My dad's bigger than your dad. My dad will batter your dad!' So what? 'My dad will shag your dad. And your dad will enjoy it!'

Frankie Boyle

I say no to gay marriage. It'll end up leading to gay divorce, and that'll be bitchy.

Jimmy Carr

I'm homophobic in the sense that I'm arachnophobic. I'm not scared of spiders, I'm not scared of gays – but if I saw one in my bath, I would probably scream.

Jimmy Carr

Lesbians love whale-watching. It's any sea mammal really – whales, manatees, dolphins. They go crazy for dolphins. I don't know what it is – I think it's the blowhole.

Margaret Cho

I think the best part of being gay is when you're done, you could turn over and talk about football.

Andrew Dice Clay

I'm a sex machine to both genders. It's all very exhausting. I need a lot of sleep.

Rupert Everett

I was a lesbian once at school, but only for about fifteen minutes.

Fiona (Kristin Scott Thomas), *Four Weddings and a Funeral*

Gays don't vomit. They're a very clean people. And they have been ever since they came to this country from France.

Peter Griffin (Seth MacFarlane), *Family Guy*

If there were gays in the army, *Saving Private Ryan* would have been a hell of a lot shorter film. There is no way it would take gay men three hours to find Matt Damon.

Adam Hills

The Bible says gays aren't natural. What, and a talking snake is?!

Russell Howard

It's ridiculous that some people feel superior to the gay minority. They're the only couples you'll ever find poking around for ceramics and candle holders in the winery gift shop and both parties really want to be there.

Richard Jeni

Gay men understand what's important: clothes, compliments and cocks.

Samantha Jones (Kim Cattrall), *Sex and the City*

That's one reason why gays shouldn't be allowed into the army. Because if we're in battle, is he going to be looking at me and going, 'Ooh, he looks tasty in a uniform'? And I'm not homophobic, all right? Come round, look at my CDs. You'll see Queen, George Michael, Pet Shop Boys. They're all bummers.

Gareth Keenan (Mackenzie Crook), *The Office*

I suddenly had this really mad desire to have an affair with a woman. I was divorced. I was childless. I figured there's got to be one more way to really tick off my mom.

Carol Leifer

Gays are now allowed to serve openly in the military. So maybe our next war could be a musical.

David Letterman

Years ago, if you were gay, your only options were the clergy or suicide. Or presenting a game show.

Lilian (Paula Wilcox), *The Smoking Room*

Rev. Pat Robertson says that if more states legalise gay marriage, God will destroy America. He did say that afterwards, gays will come in and do a beautiful renovation.

Conan O'Brien

In my mind, God made Adam and Eve, he didn't make Adam and Steve.

Alan Partridge (Steve Coogan), *I'm Alan Partridge*

I can't believe Liberace was gay. I mean, women loved him! I didn't see that one coming.

Austin Powers (Mike Myers), *Austin Powers: International Man of Mystery*

Well, I'd like to say a nice big thank you to Emma for putting to one side all our doubts about our Antony being a sausage jockey.

Jim Royle (Ricky Tomlinson), *The Royle Family*

Stuart Bixby (Sir Derek Jacobi): I hoped she [my mother] would have figured out our situation by now. I have been dropping little clues.
Freddie Thornhill (Sir Ian McKellen): Yes. Like living with a man for forty-eight years.

Vicious

God doesn't hate gay people, he's just mad they found a loophole in the system.

Daniel Tosh

Genes

I'm just sitting here thinking, what if my kid gets Rick's nose and my ears and eyes? Throw in my grandfather's third nipple, I might as well pitch a tent and charge admission.

Roz Doyle (Peri Gilpin), *Frasier*

You can inherit male-pattern baldness from your mother's father, but not a tendency to fight in World War One.

Jeremy Hardy, *The News Quiz*

Aside from the need for corrective lenses and the tendency to be abducted by extraterrestrials involved in an international governmental conspiracy, the Mulder family passes genetic muster.

Fox Mulder (David Duchovny), *The X-Files*

Genitalia

You have Christ between your thighs . . . only with a shorter beard.

Darald Braden (Jack McBrayer), *Forgetting Sarah Marshall*

The scrotum is a design fault, excess elbow skin put in between men's legs to keep their balls so they don't have to hold them in their hand . . . although it didn't work!

Billy Connolly

Why do all balls look like they're one-hundred-and-fifty years old?

Whitney Cummings

If you're a guy and you pull your pants down and the girl you're with immediately starts text messaging her friends, you have a small penis.

Chelsea Handler

If female genitalia could speak, it would sound exactly like Enya.

Dylan Moran

I don't consider myself beautiful or famous, but my vagina certainly is. Everyone knows this. I have the Angelina Jolie of vaginas.

Amy Poehler, *Yes Please*

Office worker (Paul Roache): Hey, Fletcher, how's it hanging?
Fletcher Reede (Jim Carrey): Short, shrivelled, and always to the left.

Liar Liar

My vagina is like Newark; men know it's there but they don't want to visit.

Joan Rivers

Germany

If you go to Germany and get drunk, at some point you will try to look up Hitler in the phone book.

Dave Attell

It should have been written into the armistice treaty that the Germans would be required to lay down their accordions along with their arms.

Bill Bryson, *Neither Here Nor There: Travels in Europe*

Jeff Greene (Jeff Garlin): You really love that [German shepherd] dog.
Larry David (himself): It's nice to be affectionate to something German.
You don't get the opportunity that often, you know.

Curb Your Enthusiasm

The Germans are a cruel race. Their operas last for six hours and they
have no word for fluffy.

Ben Elton

We have a saying in Germany, 'Don't blame the fish.' But then we have
other sayings too, mostly involving genocide.

Klaus Heissler (Dee Bradley Baker), *American Dad!*

According to a new book about Adolf Hitler, he suffered from chronic gas.
Apparently he had chronic gas so often that he would constantly leave a
room if he had a problem. You know Hitler: he didn't want to offend
anyone.

Jay Leno

The German language sounds like typewriters eating tinfoil being kicked
down the stairs.

Dylan Moran

I respect the Germans. They tried twice.

Al Murray, The Pub Landlord

Death? It's like being on holiday with a group of Germans.

Arnold Rimmer (Chris Barrie), *Red Dwarf*

German is a language that has the unfortunate effect on the English ear
and eye of seeming to contain nothing but orders.

Sandi Toksvig

I just deleted all the German names off my phone. It's Hans-free.

Darren Walsh

Germans talk straight because we want to make sure we come across clearly. The British disease of saying 'Sorry' and 'Thank you' when you don't mean it and showering everyone with faint praise such as 'Good effort', 'That was interesting' and 'How was it for you?' helps no one and is certainly not an indication of politeness.

Henning Wehn

In Britain, what you have to do is bloody swearing. In Germany, we don't have to swear. Reason being, things work.

Henning Wehn

Gifts

Never buy a man a plasma TV until you're married. A lot of men once they have a plasma TV, they don't need a girlfriend.

Greg Behrendt

A couple of months ago, I gave my girlfriend some fancy lingerie and she actually got mad at me. She said, 'Anthony, I think this is more of a gift for you than it is for me.' And I said, 'If you want to get technical, it was originally a gift for my last girlfriend.'

Anthony Jeselnik

My girlfriend bought me a collared shirt for my birthday, mainly so I don't get too far ahead of her when she takes me for a walk.

Jarod Kintz, *This Book is Not for Sale*

My husband wanted one of those big-screen TVs for his birthday. So I just moved his chair closer to the one we have already.

Wendy Liebman

I bought her this handkerchief, and I didn't even know her size.

Larry Lipton (Woody Allen), *Manhattan Murder Mystery*

I bought my wife a beautiful diamond ring and I even had it engraved – with the price.

Michael McIntyre

He was a great dad. Every year he got so mad when Santa didn't bring me presents.

Homer Simpson (Dan Castellaneta), The Simpsons

I like to take back a gift for my partner if I've been away and I tend to get them at the airport. The look on her face when she says, 'Oh, Frank, another European plug adapter' really moves me.

Frank Skinner, Room 101

Beware of geeks bearing gifts.

Steven Wright

Gluttony

To an American the whole purpose of living, the one constant confirmation of continued existence, is to cram as much sensual pleasure as possible into one's mouth more or less continually. Gratification, instant and lavish, is a birthright.

Bill Bryson, Notes from a Small Island

I don't stop eating when I'm full. The meal isn't over when I'm full. It's over when I hate myself.

Louis C.K.

Make sure you order dessert because I was reading in Cosmo where it says that a healthy appetite is considered sexy nowadays. I was so far ahead of my time.

Roseanne Conner (Roseanne Barr), Roseanne

I just ate twenty-four of these cookies, but they're fat-free so it's OK.

Caroline Duffy (Lea Thompson), Caroline in the City

I'm allergic to sushi. Every time I eat more than eighty pieces, I throw up.

Andy Dwyer (Chris Pratt), Parks and Recreation

There is absolutely no one, apart from yourself, who can prevent you, in the middle of the night, from sneaking down to tidy up the edges of that hunk of cheese at the back of the fridge.

Boris Johnson

A woman set a new world record for eating one hundred and eighty-three buffalo wings. I don't think there will be a second date.

David Letterman

I constantly walk into a room and don't remember why. But for some reason I think there's going to be a clue in the fridge.

Caroline Rhea

God

Unlikely lines to read in the Bible . . . And Samson cried, 'Lord, why have you given me all my strength in my hair?' And the Lord replied, 'Because you're worth it.'

Frankie Boyle, *Mock the Week*

If God had meant us to go metric, why did he give Christ twelve apostles?

Gyles Brandreth

Tell people that there's an invisible man in the sky who created the universe and the vast majority will believe you. Tell them the paint is wet, and they have to touch it to be sure.

George Carlin

I bet when *Godzilla* first came out, God was like, 'Damn, that name's way cooler.'

@ElleOhHell, Twitter

If there is a God, why did he make me an atheist? That was his first mistake. Well, the talking snake was his first mistake.

Ricky Gervais

They say when God closes a door, he opens a window. Sounds to me like he's on the toilet.

Dana Gould

If there is a God, his plan is very similar to someone not having a plan.

Eddie Izzard

I'll tell you what's unnatural in the eyes of God: contact lenses.

Zoe Lyons

If we were truly created by God, why do we occasionally bite the insides of our mouths?

Dara O'Briain

Thirty-six per cent of Americans say that they've heard the voice of God. It's not clear how many of those are mistaking the voice of God for the voice of Morgan Freeman. That's an easy mistake to make.

John Oliver

There is a rumour going around that I have found God. I think this is unlikely because I have enough difficulty finding my keys, and there is empirical evidence that they exist.

Sir Terry Pratchett

For someone so concerned with marriage licences, God sure was focused on dinosaurs for a hundred and eighty million years.

Ari Scott, Twitter

Do you think God gets stoned? I think so. Look at the platypus.

Robin Williams

Golf

I don't enjoy playing videogame golf because there is nothing to throw.

Paul Azinger

There was never much said on the course when I played with Nick [Faldo]. I probably knew him twenty years before I heard him complete a sentence.

Paul Azinger

John Daly's driving is unbelievable. I don't go that far on my holidays.

Ian Baker-Finch

Fairway: a narrow strip of mown grass that separates two groups of golfers looking for lost balls in the rough.

Henry Beard, *Golfing: A Duffer's Dictionary*

Follow through: the part of the swing that takes place after the ball has been hit but before the club has been thrown.

Henry Beard, *Golfing: A Duffer's Dictionary*

A tap-in is a putt that is short enough to be missed one-handed.

Henry Beard, *Golfing: A Duffer's Dictionary*

Personally, I belong to the speedy school of golf. If it were left up to me, I would introduce a new rule that said every golf ball has to stay in motion from the moment it leaves the tee to the moment it plops into the hole, thus obliging each player to run along after his ball and give it another whack before it stops rolling.

Craig Brown

If God had wanted man to play golf, He would have given him an elbow-less left arm, short asymmetrical legs with side-hinged knees and a trapezoid rib cage from which diagonally jutted a two-foot neck topped by a three-eyed head.

Alan Coren

John Daly's divots go further than my drives.

David Feherty

Colin Montgomerie has a face like a warthog that has been stung by a wasp. He is a few French fries short of a Happy Meal.

David Feherty

Jim Furyk has a swing like a man trying to kill a snake in a phone booth.

David Feherty

That one is so far right Michael Moore could make a documentary about it.

David Feherty, on a wayward drive

I am sorry Nick Faldo couldn't be here this week. He is attending the birth of his next wife.

David Feherty

The average golfer's handicap is his IQ. Girls, believe me, if your hubby keeps golfing, he will soon have the brain frequency of a lower primate.

Kathy Lette

What's the penalty for killing a photographer – one stroke or two?

Davis Love III

I think golf is a waste of time and a waste of a sunny afternoon. I also stink at it. I have never found anything, including divorce and a sexual harassment suit, more frustrating.

Jay Mohr

Another woman has been linked to Tiger Woods and this one is forty-eight years old. Or, as Tiger refers to her, 'my senior tour'.

Conan O'Brien

In my retirement I go for a short swim at least once or twice every day. It's either that or buy a new golf ball.

Gene Perret

The last thing you want to do is shoot eighty wearing tartan trousers.

Ian Poulter

Why am I using a new putter? Because the last one didn't float too well.

Craig Stadler

My kids used to come up to me and say, 'Daddy, did you win?' Now they say, 'Daddy, did you make the cut?'

Tom Watson

The intensity of Tiger Woods's life is just ridiculous. He says the reason he loves scuba diving so much is because the fish don't recognise him.

Lee Westwood

They say if you are stuck behind one on a golf course, that a tree is ninety per cent air. How come, then, that you invariably send your ball crashing into the remaining ten per cent?

Sir Terry Wogan

Guilt

Leonard Hofstadter (Johnny Galecki): I did a bad thing.
Sheldon Cooper (Jim Parsons): Does it affect me?
Leonard: No.
Sheldon: Then suffer in silence.

The Big Bang Theory

I feel guilty about everything, from the pollution caused by Chinese industrialisation to not wearing some pairs of boxers as much as others. I'm sorry, stripy blue – you're just too tight.

Mark Corrigan (David Mitchell), *Peep Show*

Dr Alan Harper (Jon Cryer): What kind of man chooses sex with an insatiably hot stranger over quality time with his little boy?
Charlie Harper (Charlie Sheen): Oh, I don't know – the kind of man who's been married for twelve years and had sex twelve times?

Two and a Half Men

In a courtroom, reasonable doubt can get you off for murder. In an engagement, it makes you feel like a bad person.

Miranda Hobbes (Cynthia Nixon), *Sex and the City*

If I have an orgasm, I feel that I have to give six weeks of community service to various charities.

Richard Lewis

If you've had the right kind of education, it's amazing how many things you can find to feel guilty about.

Pete McCarthy, *McCarthy's Bar*

I'll have the worst day of my life with a side order of guilt, please!

Bruce Nolan (Jim Carrey), *Bruce Almighty*

Sometimes stuff just happens and there's nothing you can do about it. For example, Lisa Peterson hasn't talked to me since the eleventh grade because no matter how much you apologise, you can't go back and un-dry-hump someone's boyfriend.

Penny (Kaley Cuoco), *The Big Bang Theory*

There's no problem so awful that you can't add some guilt to it and make it even worse.

Bill Watterson, *The Complete Calvin and Hobbes*

Hair

I'm not bald; I'm just taller than my hair.

Clive Anderson

The simple truth is that balding African-American men look cool when they shave their heads, whereas balding white men look like giant thumbs.

Dave Barry

You know what you are? You're a beard with an idiot hanging off it.

Bernard Black (Dylan Moran), *Black Books*

A decent beard has long been the number one must-have fashion item for any fugitive from justice.

Craig Brown

What am I supposed to do if I go bald? Get a wig? Fat, goofy, gay, wig. I might as well get a piano and start an Elton John tribute act.

Alan Carr

Lanie Parish (Tamala Jones): I also recovered some blue hairs on her neck, left by the attacker.

Richard Castle (Nathan Fillion): Blue hairs . . . So she was killed by a little old lady or Katy Perry.

Castle

I hate having long hair. It's like walking around with a dead koala on your back.

Russell Crowe

(of comedian Frankie Howerd's toupee): He used to scratch the back of his head when he was talking to you sometimes and the hairpiece would go up and down like a pedal bin.

Barry Cryer

Anyone can be confident with a full head of hair. But a confident bald man – there's your diamond in the rough.

Larry David

I do have hair; the hair is just not everywhere. I realise it's really just at the holes: my nose, my ears, my butt. I'm like a tub: just sheer white porcelain and then a clump of hair at the drain.

Greg Fitzsimmons

My son actually said to me once, 'You should get your hair cut like Gary Barlow.' I've shunned him since; he now lives in the shed.

Noel Gallagher

Look at the evil people in the world: Saddam Hussein, Hitler, Stalin. What do they all have in common? Moustaches!

Brüno Gehard (Sacha Baron Cohen), *Brüno*

Victor Melling (Michael Caine): Your hair should make a statement.

Gracie Hart (Sandra Bullock): As long as it doesn't say, 'Thank you very much for the Country Music Award!'

Miss Congeniality

Michael Fabricant's hair looks so peculiar that everyone assumes that it is a wig. On the other hand, nobody would conceivably buy a wig which looked like that. It is strawberry-blond and has a shiny plastic sheen. Overall, it looks as if My Little Pony had been in a terrible accident and its tail had been draped over Mr Fabricant's head.

Simon Hoggart

George Costanza (Jason Alexander): When do you start to worry about ear hair?
Jerry (Jerry Seinfeld): When you hear like a soft rustling.

Seinfeld

Conditioner adverts tell you that coconut oil is really good for your hair. Well, it doesn't seem to work that well for coconuts.

Lloyd Langford

I usually find that women with long grey hair have twelve cats and a history of mental illness.

Frank Skinner

I don't trust a man with curly hair. I can't help picturing small birds laying sulphurous eggs in there.

Sue Sylvester (Jane Lynch), *Glee*

Knowing your hairdresser could shave off your eyebrows and remove an ear and you'd still say, 'That's great, thanks.'

Rob Temple, *Very British Problems*

Halloween

(dressed as Charlie Chaplin) So apparently no one dresses up for Halloween here. I wish I had known that before I used grease paint for my moustache. And I can't even take off my hat because then I'm Hitler.

Pam Beesly (Jenna Fischer), *The Office* (US)

Abi Harper (Siobhan Hayes): Don't you like Halloween then?

Ben Harper (Robert Lindsay): I've nothing against devil worship per se. Just the enforced jollity that comes with it.

My Family

Halloween is just a made up holiday, created by the razor-blade industry.

Anthony Jeselnik

Halloween is the beginning of the holiday shopping season. That's for women. The beginning of the holiday shopping season for men is Christmas Eve.

David Letterman

Hangovers

You know you're hungover when you brush your teeth with your sunglasses on.

Anna Kendrick, Twitter

I can't think of anything worse after a night of drinking than waking up next to someone and not being able to remember their name or how you met or why they're dead.

Laura Kightlinger

A kid once said to me, 'Do you get hangovers?' I said, 'To get hangovers, you have to stop drinking.'

Lemmy

Vyvyan (Adrian Edmondson): What's a good thing for a hangover?

Mike (Christopher Ryan): Drinking heavily the night before.

The Young Ones

Happiness

Contentment is knowing you're right. Happiness is knowing someone else is wrong.

Bill Bailey

All rational people agree it's a truth self-evident that it's impossible to have a good time on New Year's Eve. The pressure's too immense.

Mark Corrigan (David Mitchell), *Peep Show*

Living one's life with unguarded vulnerability is one of the keys to happiness. It's also one of the keys to getting mugged.

Dov Davidoff

There is a new survey out about the happiest professions. I think the whole premise is flawed. You're supposed to find true happiness outside of work – from friends, family and YouTube videos of old people falling down.

Craig Ferguson

Ladies, your happiness is very important to us. You have to understand that. Because when you're happy, you let us touch you.

Adam Ferrara

(of Gail Platt): Never happy unless she's got someone's hands around her throat.

Blanche Hunt (Maggie Jones), *Coronation Street*

(to DI Alex Drake): Looking very chirpy, Bolls. You've been sitting on the washing machine again?

DCI Gene Hunt (Philip Glenister), *Ashes to Ashes*

I truly believe that happiness is possible even when you're thirty-three and have a bottom the size of two bowling balls.

Bridget Jones (Renée Zellweger), *Bridget Jones: The Edge of Reason*

Happiness is the twinkle in your grandmother's eye as you reverse the tractor off her legs.

Hugh Laurie

Tears streamed down my face. I was so happy I wanted to shout it from the rooftop. But at the same time I knew that that afternoon's downpour would have made the slate tiles so slippery that achieving any kind of purchase would have been impossible.

Alan Partridge, *I, Partridge: We Need to Talk About Alan*

Health

Mrs Overall can't have gone far. That's one of the blessings of osteoporosis.

Miss Babs (Celia Imrie), *Acorn Antiques: The Musical*

Since I had my gastric bypass surgery in 1998, I eat like a bird. Unfortunately, that bird is a California condor.

Roseanne Barr

Laughter is the best medicine, though it tends not to work in the case of impotence.

Jo Brand

Norm Peterson (George Wendt): Hey, Frasier, you're a doctor. What happens to old, dead skin?
Frasier Crane (Kelsey Grammer): Apparently it sits on barstools and drinks beer all day.

Cheers

If it wasn't for the rectal probe, I'd have no sex life at all.

Barry Cryer

The only time it's cool to yell, 'I have diarrhoea!' is when you're playing Scrabble.

Zach Galifianakis

Remember, what happens in Vegas stays in Vegas. Except for herpes.

Sid Garner (Jeffrey Tambor), *The Hangover*

My dad suggested I register for a donor card – he's a man after my own heart.

Masai Graham

John Gustafson (Jack Lemmon): Pop, I wish you'd try the low-fat bacon.
Grandpa Gustafson (Burgess Meredith): Well, you can wish in one hand and crap in the other and see which gets filled first.

Grumpier Old Men

Fun fact: did you know that HIV is actually Roman for 'high five'? Pass it on –or, rather, don't.

Rhys James

As a child I had a medical condition that meant I had to eat soil three times a day in order to survive. Lucky my older brother told me about it really.

Milton Jones

Recently I had bird flu, but it's all relative, isn't it? If I had rabies and you offered me bird flu, I'd bite your hand off.

Milton Jones

I got a postcard from my gynaecologist. It said, 'Did you know it's time for your annual check-up?' No, but now my mailman does.

Cathy Ladman

My whole family is lactose intolerant. When we take pictures, we can't say 'Cheese'.

Jay London

The worst time to have a heart attack is during a game of charades.

Demetri Martin

Unlikely greetings cards . . . Get well soon. P. S. I know it's terminal, but they didn't have a card for that.

Andy Parsons, *Mock the Week*

Took the batteries out of the carbon monoxide alarm because the loud beeping was giving me a headache and making me feel sick and dizzy.

Ruthe Phoenix, Twitter

I like colonic irrigation because sometimes you find old jewellery.

Joan Rivers

I went to my doctor and told him, 'My penis is burning.' He said, 'That means somebody is talking about it.'

Garry Shandling

Seasickness comes in two stages. In the first you think you are going to die, and in the second you are afraid you are not going to.

Sandi Toksvig, *The Chain of Curiosity*

Scientists say that being fat can lead to dementia. I have decided, however, to throw caution to the winds and proceed with my all-cream-cake regime. It seems to me that the fatter I get, the fewer places I will go and so the less I will have to remember.

Sandi Toksvig, *The Chain of Curiosity*

I hope we find a cure for every major disease because I'm sick of walking 5K. I'm pretty sure I don't have to walk to cure cancer. I'll just write a cheque.

Daniel Tosh

Linda, you know my feelings on asthma. Take a deep breath and get over it.

Jill Tyrell (Julia Davis), *Nighty Night*

(examining the sore on her lip) Grace Adler (Debra Messing): It's not herpes! It's not even close to herpes!
Karen Walker (Megan Mullally): Well, it's close enough to get invited to the herpes family picnic.

Will & Grace

I think hiccup cures were really invented for the amusement of the patient's friends.

Bill Watterson, *Calvin and Hobbes*

When I told jokes about cystitis, people would write in and say, 'I've got cystitis and it isn't funny.' So I would reply, 'Well, send it back and ask for one that is.'

Victoria Wood

I'm addicted to placebos. I'd give them up, but it wouldn't make any difference.

Steven Wright

My nephew has HDADD. He has trouble focusing but when he does it's unbelievably clear.

Steven Wright

Heaven and Hell

It's the only thing that worries me about going to heaven: would I ever get used to the height?

Norman Clegg (Peter Sallis), *Last of the Summer Wine*

Harry Block (Woody Allen): You're air-conditioned here?
The Devil (Billy Crystal): Sure! Fucks up the ozone layer.

Deconstructing Harry

Do you know, when I'm in bed with Clare it's like I've died and gone to heaven? In fact, it's probably better than heaven 'cause I shouldn't think you're allowed to do it doggy-fashion in heaven, are you?

Martin Henson (Matthew Cottle), *Game On*

Some con-men sell life insurance. The church sells afterlife insurance. It's brilliant! Everyone thinks you might need it, and no one can prove you don't.

Brian Hope (Eric Idle), *Nuns on the Run*

Heaven: the biggest waste of time we ever invented, outside jigsaws.

Caitlin Moran

I hope God speaks English. If I get up to heaven and have to point at a menu, I'm gonna be pissed off.

Daniel Tosh

I doubt there's a heaven. I think the people from hell have probably bought it for a timeshare.

Victoria Wood

Hecklers

Don't get your tits out!

Heckler to Jo Brand

I deliberately keep my weight up so that a tosser like you won't fancy me.

Jo Brand, after a heckler called her 'fat'

I, sir, am heterosexual, and one day I will show you the statistics and make you weep.

Russell Brand

I've done a gig in a prison before. A guy got up ten minutes into my set and went back to his cell. *That*'s a heckle.

Kevin Bridges

Hey Mike Pence! You call that being booed? Try doing a gig for some chartered surveyors and accidentally calling them quantity surveyors.

Ed Byrne, Twitter, after US Vice President-elect Pence was booed on Broadway, 2016

Did your mother never tell you not to drink on an empty head?

Billy Connolly

Well, it's a night out for him, isn't it? And for his family it's a night off.

Jack Dee

Why don't you go into that corner and finish evolving?

Russell Kane

Get off, you bastard! . . . Has he gone yet?

Blind heckler to Frank Skinner

Look, it's all right to donate your brain to science, but shouldn't you have waited till you died?

Arthur Smith

Heckler at a gig at Warrington University: I came here for comedy.
Jack Whitehall: No, mate, you came here because you screwed up your A-Levels.

Herbal Remedies

'(They say) herbal medicine's been around for thousands of years.' Indeed it has, and then we tested it all and the stuff that worked became 'medicine'. And the rest of it is just a nice bowl of soup and some potpourri.

Dara O'Briain

Rick Spleen (Jack Dee): I want proper medicine – stuff that was made by scientists and tested on animals, not something you went out and found under a hedge.
Pharmacist (Christopher Douglas): You have a very interesting view of homeopathy.
Rick: Yeah, well my wife just wants to kick the flu. She doesn't want to dance around a fire until she goes into a trance and contacts her ancestors.

Lead Balloon

History

There is no better way of forgetting something than by commemorating it.

Alan Bennett, *The History Boys*

What did Richard III ever contribute to Britain? He reigned for two years, had his arse kicked at the Battle of Bosworth Field and spent the next fifty-two decades . . . relaxing in the ground, enjoying an indulgent rot in his VIP car park. Just because you qualify for a disabled bay doesn't mean you get to hog it for five hundred years.

Charlie Brooker

Historians are the consummate hairdressers of the literary world: cooing in public, catty in private.

Craig Brown

My great uncle Arthur died at the Battle of the Little Bighorn. But he wasn't involved in the fighting. He was camping in a nearby field and popped over to complain about the noise.

Rob Brydon

Revisionist historians now claim that far from being mad, Joan of Arc may have been a victim of food poisoning. Makes sense, I can't tell you the number of times I've eaten a few dodgy prawns and ended up commanding the French army.

Angus Deayton, *Have I Got News for You*

The history of the world would have been very different if, when the serpent gave the apple to Eve, Eve had sat down and deduced gravity from it.

Miles Kington

In a town as old as Pawnee, there's a lot of history in every acre. This wooded area is the site of the – er – murder, actually, of Nathaniel Bixby Mark. He was a pioneer who was killed by a tribe of Wamapoke Indians after he traded them a baby for what is now Indianapolis. They cut his face off . . . and they made it into a dreamcatcher. And they made his legs into rainsticks. And that's the great thing about Indians back then – they used every part of the pioneer.

Leslie Knope (Amy Poehler), *Parks and Recreation*

You know, with Hitler, the more I learn about that guy, the more I don't care for him.

Norm Macdonald

History began on 4 July 1776. Everything that happened before that was a mistake.

Ron Swanson (Nick Offerman), Parks and Recreation

Hobbies

Norm Peterson (George Wendt): I wish I had time for a hobby.
Cliff Clavin (John Ratzenberger): Norm, you've got time to make your own coal!

Cheers

Recently I've been attending meetings of Eavesdroppers Anonymous – not that they know.

Milton Jones

Astronomers, like burglars and jazz musicians, operate best at night.

Miles Kington

Hollywood

Hollywood is a cross between a health farm, a recreation centre and an insane asylum.

Sir Michael Caine

It's nice to finally get scripts offered to me that aren't the ones Tom Hanks wipes his butt with.

Jim Carrey

Hollywood movies are designed for fifteen-year-old youths from North Dakota who, intellectually speaking, are on equal terms with a British zoo animal.

Jeremy Clarkson

I hate the way Hollywood always changes everything. For instance, *Twister* the movie is nothing like the board game.

Tony Cowards, Twitter

The film industry is like Anne Robinson: always on the lookout for a new face.

Jack Dee

Typical Hollywood crowd – all the kids are on drugs and all the adults are on rollerskates.

Eric Idle

In Hollywood, there is another name for a woman's fortieth birthday party; it's a retirement party.

Artie Lange

In Hollywood, a romantic man is one who talks to you after sex.

Kathy Lette

(receiving an American Film Institute Life Achievement Award in 2015): *Saturday Night Live* producer Lorne Michaels is really responsible for me being here tonight; Lorne, thank you for driving.

Steve Martin

Right now, my job is that I'm like an ambulance chaser. I've got to look for movies with white guys falling out of them.

Chris Rock

Hollywood: it's either people who are unhappy or soon will be.

Jonathan Ross

Home Improvement

I do like a bit of DIY. I put some shelves up – did it properly, nice and straight. Then some idiot goes and puts something on them.

Jack Dee

A man I met recently had employed a builder to screw a wine rack to the wall. How he could bear the shame of standing by while another man drilled four holes in some brickwork and inserted some rawlplugs! He can regard himself as little more than a receptacle for keeping sperm at the right temperature until it's needed.

James May, *Notes From The Hard Shoulder*

I do have a fantasy life in which I can grout bathrooms.

Will Self

Tim Taylor (Tim Allen): This is my house, that is my dishwasher, and I will rewire it if I want to.
Jill Taylor (Patricia Richardson): No! You will not rewire it and screw it up like you did the blender.
Tim: What is your problem with the blender? It's the only blender on the block that can puree a brick!

Home Improvement

Getting out your toolbox and causing hundreds of pounds worth of damage to your house because it's bank holiday Monday.

Rob Temple, *Very British Problems*

Victor Meldrew (Richard Wilson): Surely you can't change a light bulb if you've only got one arm?
Mrs Warboys (Doreen Mantle): You can if you've still got the receipt.

One Foot in the Grave

Homelessness

People say, 'Don't give homeless people money. They'll only spend it on beer and cigarettes.' I'd always assumed that they were. I've never given money to a homeless guy and thought, 'I hope he's putting that into his ISA.'

Frankie Boyle

No matter how much you give a homeless person for tea, you never get that tea.

Jimmy Carr

I once did a gig in the US for the homeless. It was nice to see so many bums on seats.

Jimmy Carr

Birds do it, bees do it, even educated fleas do it. Let's do it. Let's live in a homeless man's beard.

Mary Charlene, Twitter

I saw this homeless guy and this homeless girl and they were making out. At one point, this guy walked by and yelled, 'Get a box!'

Dane Cook

I did a charity gig recently for *The Big Issue*. While playing bingo for people who live on the streets, it's always difficult to shout, 'House!'

Ross Noble

Honesty

If you absolutely have to tell her the truth, at least wait until the timing's right . . . and that's what deathbeds are for.

Chandler Bing (Matthew Perry), *Friends*

If there is any dirty trick I cannot stand, it is honesty.

Amy Brookheimer (Anna Chlumsky), *Veep*

I believe in honesty with my kids. When they say, 'Daddy, what will I be when I grow up?', I tell them, 'Disappointed.'

Hal Cruttenden

Whenever I'm on my computer, I don't type 'lol', I type 'lqtm' – 'laugh quietly to myself'. It's more honest.

Demetri Martin

I've seen honest faces before. They usually come attached to liars.

Homer Simpson (Dan Castellaneta), *The Simpsons*

My dad doesn't like lies. He says it hurts people in the long run. He prefers the truth. That hurts them instantly.

Christopher Titus

Honeymoon

We're going on honeymoon to India next month and I wanted to know what the weather was going to be like. So I phoned my bank.

Shappi Khorsandi

The honeymoon is an odd tradition. You've just taken the vows when you rush off to some vacation hideaway, where you spend every second of every day with the very person to whom you pledged your entire life. Two weeks apart would make more sense. You've got the rest of your lives to get sick of each other. Why rush it?

Jeff Stilson

Horse Racing

Jockeys are three-foot high hobbits in a pimp's outfit.

Lee Evans

You could remove the brains from ninety per cent of jockeys and they would weigh the same.

John Francome

Owning a racehorse is probably the most expensive way of getting on to a racecourse for nothing.

Clement Freud

It's the 6.30 Queen Henry Stakes, which is generally regarded as the litmus test for Derby form. Jockey folklore says that if you cock up the Queen Henry, you might as well ride the Derby on a cow.

Alan Partridge (Steve Coogan), *The Day Today*

The sandwiches at Teesside Park were definitely on the firm side of good.

Ian Watkinson

Hospitals

I don't want to say the wait was long, but the guy in front of me was being treated for a musket wound.

Nick Di Paolo

On a Friday night, it's like a field hospital in the Battle of the Somme. There's blokes with blood coming out of their heads and Bacardi Breezer bottles stuck in their necks.

John O'Farrell, on A&E departments

A minor operation is one performed on somebody else.

Victoria Wood

Hotels

A spa hotel is like a normal hotel, only in reception there's a picture of a pebble.

Rhod Gilbert

She knows what she's talking about. Mom's been on more hotel pillows than a chocolate mint.

Charlie Harper (Charlie Sheen), *Two and a Half Men*

I'm staying in a strange hotel. I called room service for a sandwich and they sent up two hookers.

Bill Maher

Posh hotels have a turn-down service. I had never heard of this and there was a knock at the door and a woman said, 'I've come to turn down your bed.' To which I said, 'Well, many women have in the past. Why should you be any different?'

Michael McIntyre

A hotel is the only place in the world where you walk in and the first thing you do is steal everything before you take your coat off.

Dylan Moran

I checked in to a hotel the other day and the woman behind the desk said to me, 'Do you have a floor preference?' I said, 'Yeah, I would like a floor.' Apparently, they can just suspend you from the ceiling now.

Paula Poundstone

I like staying in hotels. I like their tiny soap. I like to pretend it's regular-sized and my muscles are huge.

Jerry Seinfeld

I stayed in a really old hotel last night. They sent me a wake-up letter.

Steven Wright

Housework

Have you noticed that if you leave the laundry in the hamper long enough, it's ready to wear again?

Elayne Boosler

All these programmes on TV about women being domestic goddesses are just not true. I'd like to have a programme that truly represented how women approach housework. And if I did, it would be called *Fuck It, That'll Do*.

Jo Brand

The act, when vacuuming, of running over a string at least a dozen times, reaching over and picking it up, examining it, then putting it back down to give the vacuum one more chance.

Rich Hall

I am allergic to domestic goddesses. Men would prefer a woman with a dirty mind to a clean house.

Kathy Lette

No wife ever shot a husband while he was vacuuming.

Kathy Lette

Now, where's my flannel got to? I leave it in the rail, and she has to put it away 'so we know where things are'. Well, it doesn't work, does it, because I bloody well don't know where it is. The riddle of the Bermuda Triangle was finally solved today when it was revealed that Mrs Margaret Meldrew of 19 Riverbank had for the past fifty years been putting all the ships and planes away so we'd know where they were.

Victor Meldrew (Richard Wilson), *One Foot in the Grave*

The hardest thing about having visitors is saying, 'Sorry about the mess', when you know this is the cleanest the house has been in weeks.

Ruthe Phoenix, Twitter

I decided to sell my Hoover – well, it was just collecting dust.

Tim Vine

Hunting

If you permed a fox, I think it'd look a bit like Mick Hucknall. I actually think it'd be kinder to perm them than hunt them. And they'd be too embarrassed to go out and bother the sheep.

Sean Lock

Hunting is not a sport. In a sport, both sides should know they're in the game.

Paul Rodriguez

Husbands

I look at husbands the same way I look at tattoos. I want one but I can't decide what I want and I don't want to be stuck with one I'm just going to grow to hate and have to have surgically removed later.

Margaret Cho

Ex-husbands are like Crosby, Stills and Nash. They keep coming back – older and fatter.

Grace Kelly (Brett Butler), *Grace Under Fire*

Had two husbands, one was too short, one was gay. Still, sweetie, if you want to know how to peck a dwarf on the cheek as he's walking out of the house to the disco in your dress, then I'm your girl!

Edina Monsoon (Jennifer Saunders), *Absolutely Fabulous*

Being a good husband is like being a good stand-up comic. You need ten years before you can even call yourself a beginner.

Jerry Seinfeld

Julie Christie was absolutely amazing in *Away From Her*. Brilliant movie. It was the moving story of a woman who forgets her own husband. Hillary Clinton calls it the feel-good movie of the year.

Jon Stewart, 2007

Husbands are like sofas; both sag in the end.

Janet Street-Porter

Hygiene

Joan Bell (Lorraine Cheshire): I've just been on the toilet, Eddie.

Eddie Bell (Mark Benton): Number one or number two, Joan?

Joan: Number two.

Eddie: Why not? It's our anniversary. Treat yourself.

Early Doors

This place smells worse than a pair of armoured trousers after the Hundred Years War. Baldrick, have you been eating dung again?

Edmund Blackadder (Rowan Atkinson), *Blackadder II*

I wish you wouldn't raise your arms like that, Richard. Not when you're overheated. It's very common out-of-doors. If you have to perspire, I wish you'd go into the *back* garden.

Hyacinth Bucket (Patricia Routledge), *Keeping Up Appearances*

The missus has bought scented toilet paper. So I've been walking about with an arse smelling of cinnamon.

Danny Dyer

If it's yellow let it mellow, if it's brown flush it down.

Bernie Focker (Dustin Hoffman), *Meet the Fockers*

Brave is the man who brushes the lavatory clean, but braver still the man who cleans the lavatory brush.

Miles Kington

My idea of getting lucky in the men's room is when the motion sensor works on the faucet.

David Letterman

Mr Bastard (Roger Sloman): Where's your toilet?
Neil (Nigel Planer): Oh, upstairs. Just follow your nose.

The Young Ones

Showering with a partner is not sexy – it is taking it in turns being cold.

Celia Pacquola

There are just four pieces of toilet paper left. If I've judged this right, that should be just enough to clean my backside after what I hope will be a straightforward ablution. And it is – the texture of stool exactly as firm and dry as I'd hoped. I could probably have done it in three.

Alan Partridge, *Nomad*

Soap-on-a-rope: that comes in handy – a lot of times in the shower I want to hang myself.

Jerry Seinfeld

If you take a shower with your boyfriend, I guarantee by the time you step out of that shower, your breasts will be sparkling clean.

Sarah Silverman

We used to have newspaper for toilet roll. We were low on hygiene, but high on current affairs.

Frank Skinner, *Room 101*

Misleading etiquette . . . British men consider you rude if you don't share their urinal.

Sandi Toksvig, *I'm Sorry I Haven't a Clue*

Ideas

———

There is no idea so bad that it cannot be made to look brilliant with the proper application of fonts and colour.

Scott Adams, *Dilbert's Guide to the Rest of Your Life: Dispatches from Cubicleland*

An original idea. That can't be too hard. The library must be full of them.

Stephen Fry, *The Liar*

I've got an idea – an idea so smart that my head would explode if I even began to know what I'm talking about.

Peter Griffin (Seth MacFarlane), *Family Guy*

I'd just like you to stir-fry a few ideas in my think-wok.

Gus Hedges (Robert Duncan), *Drop the Dead Donkey*

The problem is that the people with the most ridiculous ideas are always the people who are most certain of them.

Bill Maher

It's an idea, I don't know. Who knows where it fucking came from? Isaac Newton invented gravity because some asshole hit him with an apple.

Christopher Moltisanti (Michael Imperioli), *The Sopranos*

I'll be more enthusiastic about thinking outside the box when there's evidence of any thinking going on inside it.

Sir Terry Pratchett

'Blue-sky thinking' is thinking that isn't clouded by thought.

Steve Punt, *The Now Show*

Incest

You know, even if this DNA test does come out positive, it only makes us half-brother and sister. So if we did it twenty times, it was only wrong ten.

Amanda Tanen (Becki Newton), *Ugly Betty*

Infidelity

If diamonds are a girl's best friend, does that mean my ex is going to sleep with them too?

Sarah Beattie via Twitter

My girlfriend worries about me cheating on a night out, but I always try to reassure her and say to her, 'Why would I go out and have a burger when I have steak at home?' The only problem is, when you are drunk, burgers are well nice.

Rob Beckett

My girlfriend asked me if I was having sex behind her back. I replied: 'Yes, who did you think it was?'

Jimmy Carr

Nancy Bartlett (Sandra Bernhard): Dan, did he tell you anything? Is there another woman?
Dan Conner (John Goodman): No offence, Nancy, but it's a miracle there's one.

Roseanne

Monogamy is God's way of making death seem like a more reasonable option.

Dov Davidoff

Yes, I'm married. But my wife understands that a good politician has to be appealing to the ladies. The fact that I haven't even got close to cheating on her is a disappointment to both of us.

Tom Haverford (Aziz Ansari), *Parks and Recreation*

Men cheat for the same reason that dogs lick their balls . . . because they can.

Samantha Jones (Kim Cattrall), *Sex and the City*

I think I have monogamy! I caught it from you people.

Samantha Jones (Kim Cattrall), *Sex and the City*

I think my husband is having an affair with his secretary, because I would find lipstick on his shirt covered with white-out.

Wendy Liebman

Beverly Lincoln (Tamsin Greig): So, when you're having affairs with these married men, is there any sense of . . . ?
Carol Rance (Kathleen Rose Perkins): Danger.
Beverly: I was going to say remorse.

Episodes

My wife and I both made a list of five people we could sleep with. She read hers out: 'One, George Clooney; two, Brad Pitt; three, Justin Timberlake; four, Jake Gyllenhaal; five, Johnny Depp.' I thought, I've got the better deal here. 'One, your sister . . .'

Michael McIntyre

Peggy Olson (Elisabeth Moss): I have a boyfriend.
Joyce Ramsay (Zosia Mamet): He doesn't own your vagina.
Peggy: No, but he's renting it.

Mad Men

Women are like the police; they could have all the evidence in the world, but they still want the confession.

Chris Rock

Philanderers: avoid the embarrassment of shouting out the wrong name in bed by having flings only with girls who have the same name as your wife.

Top Tips, *Viz*

Insects

Surely fruit flies have got to be healthier than normal flies.

Carl Barron

I am perfectly willing to share the room with a fly, as long as he is patrolling that portion of the room I don't occupy. But if he starts that smart-ass fly shit, buzzing my head and repeatedly landing on my arm, he is engaging in high-risk behaviour.

George Carlin, *Brain Droppings*

It isn't fair: the caterpillar does all the work, and the butterfly gets all the glory.

George Carlin

The only thing with eight legs I want to see in my house is a KFC bucket.

Jimmy Carr, *8 Out of 10 Cats*

Raj Koothrappali (Kunal Nayyar): I don't like bugs, OK. They freak me out.
Sheldon Cooper (Jim Parsons): Interesting. You're afraid of insects and women. Ladybugs must render you catatonic.

The Big Bang Theory

My dad kept bees – not for the honey, no: the fur.

Harry Hill

Victor Meldrew (Richard Wilson): There's a wasp in the middle of this ice cube!

Mrs Warboys (Doreen Mantle): I know. It was the only one left; I didn't think you were all that fussy.

Victor: Didn't think I was all that fussy?! I'll have a slice of dead rat in it as well if you've got one, please, and a dog turd on a cocktail stick!

One Foot in the Grave

Bees: they're very much a one-recipe species, aren't they?

David Mitchell, *QI*

Insults

After divorcing his first wife, Mark Thatcher has married again. And who's the lucky lady? Well, the first wife, obviously.

Clive Anderson

You're a pea-brained, prat-faced, talentless, pillock-headed cretin. If you took an intensive course of intelligence injections and studied till you drop, then one day you might make it to moron third-class failed.

Gareth Blackstock (Lenny Henry), *Chef!*

I've never been so insulted. Outside my marriage, that is.

Norris Cole (Malcolm Hebden), *Coronation Street*

Your mother's ashamed of you. Your daughter barely knows you. Your donor kidney would reject you if it could.

Hayley Cropper (Julie Hesmondhalgh) to Tracy Barlow, *Coronation Street*

You know, you're about as annoying as a condom filled with fire ants.

Roger Furlong (Dan Bakkedahl), *Veep*

Alistair Deacon (Philip Bretherton): Mike Barbosa stepped off a plane this morning.

Lionel Hardcastle (Geoffrey Palmer): Is it too much to hope that it was in midair at the time?

As Time Goes By

Look at you all grown up and back living with Mom. How good do you feel about yourself right now on a scale from one to . . . two?

> Charlie Harper (Charlie Sheen), *Two and a Half Men*

Dr Alan Statham (Mark Heap): Do you want me to report you for that earring?

Dr 'Mac' Macartney (Julian Rhind-Tutt): Only if I can report you for that moustache.

Dr Statham: Most women find male body piercing repugnant. I, thankfully, am completely intact.

Dr Macartney: Well, even I draw the line at piercing arseholes.

> *Green Wing*

The easiest time to add insult to injury is when you're signing somebody's cast.

> Demetri Martin

Cliff Clavin (John Ratzenberger): I didn't tell you guys 'cause I didn't want you to think any less of me.

Norm Peterson (George Wendt): I don't think that's possible, Cliff.

> *Cheers*

Jane (Cheri Oteri): Do you like my new dress?

Fletcher Reede (Jim Carrey): Whatever takes the focus off your head!

> *Liar Liar*

Look, I think we've all got something we can bring to this discussion. But I think from now on the thing you should bring is silence.

> Arnold Rimmer (Chris Barrie), *Red Dwarf*

Veronica Mars (Kristen Bell): You wrote 'slut' on my car last year at Shelly's party. Why?

Madison Sinclair (Amanda Noret): Because 'whore' had too many letters.

> *Veronica Mars*

Fred Flintstone (John Goodman): I've got half a mind . . .

Pearl Slaghoople (Elizabeth Taylor): Oh, don't flatter yourself!

> *The Flintstones*

Diane Chambers (Shelley Long): I'm having a bad day. Aren't I allowed to have a bad day?

Carla Tortelli (Rhea Perlman): Sure, you've given us plenty. Keep one for yourself.

Cheers

Do you know ninety per cent of household dust is made of dead human skin? That's what you are to me.

Malcolm Tucker (Peter Capaldi), *The Thick of It*

You're worse than dead meat. I don't know what you're laughing at. You're too toxic to even feed to the vultures.

Malcolm Tucker (Peter Capaldi), *The Thick of It*

How did you hurt your back? Running away from good taste?

Karen Walker (Megan Mullally), *Will & Grace*

Intelligence

I was going to go on *Mastermind* but I can't sit on leather.

Babs (Kate Robbins), *dinnerladies*

Lloyd Christmas (Jim Carrey): Flying somewhere?

Mary Swanson (Lauren Holly): How'd you guess?

Lloyd: I saw your luggage. Then when I noticed the airline ticket, I put two and two together.

Dumb and Dumber

I'm exceedingly smart. I graduated college at fourteen. While my brother was getting an STD, I was getting a Ph.D. Penicillin can't take this away.

Sheldon Cooper (Jim Parsons), *The Big Bang Theory*

Whenever I meet a pretty girl, the first thing I look for is intelligence, because if she doesn't have that, then she's mine.

Anthony Jeselnik

Intelligence is like four-wheel drive. It only allows you to get stuck in more remote places.

Garrison Keillor

Why do men like intelligent women? Because opposites attract.

Kathy Lette

Where would we be without the agitators of the world to attach the electrodes of knowledge to the nipples of ignorance?

Dick Solomon (John Lithgow), *3rd Rock from the Sun*

I can always guess how many jelly beans are in a jelly bean jar, even if I'm wrong.

Brick Tamland (Steve Carell), *Anchorman 2: The Legend Continues*

Internet

The internet. Can we trust in that? Of course not. Give it six months and we'll probably discover Google's sewn together by orphans in sweatshops. Or that wifi does something horrible to your brain, like eating your fondest memories and replacing them with drawings of cross-eyed bats and a strong smell of puke.

Charlie Brooker

They call it 'surfing' the net. It's not surfing; it's typing in your bedroom.

Jack Dee

Before you marry a person, you should first make them use a computer with slow internet service to see who they really are.

Will Ferrell

The internet's a creepy thing, especially if you have kids. It's very creepy that I use the same machine to masturbate with as I use to teach my kid the alphabet.

Greg Giraldo

The internet contains everything in the whole wide world ever. I don't know about you, but I find everything in the whole wide world ever to be a bit distracting.

Dave Gorman

I needed a password eight characters long, so I picked *Snow White and the Seven Dwarfs*.

Nick Helm

A lot of bloggers seem to be socially inadequate, pimpled, single, slightly seedy, bald, cauliflower-nosed young men sitting in their mother's basements and ranting.

Andrew Marr

Edina Monsoon (Jennifer Saunders): Mother, are you still on the computer?
Mother (June Whitfield): Yes, dear. Sometimes you get into a porn loop and just can't get out.

Absolutely Fabulous

There's something fishy about Google's motto, 'Don't be evil'. I'm not saying it's controversial but it makes you think, Why bring that up? Why have you suddenly put the subject of being evil on the agenda? It's suspicious in the same way as UKIP constantly pointing out how racist they're not.

David Mitchell, *Thinking About It Only Makes It Worse*

Egypt has responded to hundreds of thousands of protesters by shutting down the internet. Just a word of advice: if you want people to stay at home and do nothing, you should turn the internet back on.

Conan O'Brien

Wikipedia is the best thing ever. Anyone in the world can write anything they want about any subject. So you know you are getting the best possible information.

Michael Scott (Steve Carell), *The Office* (US)

The internet is just the world passing notes around a classroom.

Jon Stewart

Blogs are for anoraks who couldn't get published any other way.

Janet Street-Porter

Google has caused a lot of problems in my relationship. I share a computer with my girlfriend, and she would look up anything. 'I'm going to look up apples today.' She just hits 'A'. It's 'Asian ass porn' instantly. Google, all I ask is that you let her type three letters before you jump to such a bold conclusion. It's bad enough that I'm clearing my history every three hours.

Daniel Tosh

Trigger with a computer? Do me a favour, he's still struggling with light switches.

Rodney Trotter (Nicholas Lyndhurst), *Only Fools and Horses*

Conjunctivitis.com – that's a site for sore eyes.

Tim Vine

Intuition

Diane Chambers (Shelley Long): Do you believe in intuition?
Woody Boyd (Woody Harrelson): No, but I have the strange feeling that someday I will.

Cheers

Inventions

Before the invention of the alphabet, filing was impossible. Or very easy.

Chris Addison

If the Nobel Prize was awarded by a woman, it would go to the inventor of the dimmer switch.

Kathy Lette

You can now buy bacon-scented candles because we've all wondered what it would smell like if Miss Piggy perished in a house fire.

Frank Skinner, *Room 101*

Ireland

We don't have anything as urgent as *mañana* in Ireland.

Stuart Banks

An eighties bar has opened in Belfast. Of all the major cities where you don't want to go and celebrate the eighties, Belfast is up there.

Kevin Bridges

Just to clear misconceptions, we Irish are not drunk all the time. Sometimes we are asleep.

Dave Callan

Irish people love Muslims. They have taken a lot of the heat off us. Before, we were 'the terrorists' but now we're 'the *Riverdance* people'.

Andrew Maxwell

Many people die of thirst but the Irish are born with one.

Spike Milligan

The Irish. They're a sidecar to our motorbike: going nowhere without us.

Al Murray, The Pub Landlord

If you can't go into an Irish bar and get into a conversation, that's like a special needs kid going to summer holiday camp and not getting a hug.

Phil Nichol

You think things are all legal or illegal in this country. In Ireland that's not the way we do it. We've got a greater appreciation of the greyness of the human condition, between the white and the black. There are three states of legality in Irish law. All the stuff which comes under, 'That's grand', then it moves into, 'Ah, now, don't push it', and finally it moves into, 'Right, you're taking the piss'. That's when the police sweep in.

Dara O'Briain

This is the first time that Irish people go: 'You're going to England? Sure it's full of terrorists. Come to Ireland. We've no terrorists. They're all play-wrights now.'

Dara O'Briain

In Ireland, when you get a prescription for antibiotics, you don't say. 'Will it work? Will there be any side-effects?' No, it's, 'Will I be able to drink with these?'

Ardal O'Hanlon

An Irish satnav has a yearly update and the immortal phrases, 'Straight on, you can't miss it' and, 'Jaysis, I told you that already.' Though really you'd probably just get all the directions in one go at the start.

Tommy Tiernan

Italy

The Italians park the way I would if I had just spilled a beaker of hydrochloric acid in my lap.

Bill Bryson, *Neither Here Nor There: Travels in Europe*

In Italy, even the policemen look like they've just come off a catwalk. One I found, standing on a rostrum in the middle of a Roman square, was immaculate, as was his routine. Each wave of the hand, each toot of the whistle and each twist of the body was Pan's People perfect. Never mind that the traffic was completely ignoring him, he looked good, and that's what mattered. Looking good in Italy is even more important than looking where you're going.

Jeremy Clarkson, *Motorworld*

In Italy, you sometimes get the impression they'd be happier to lose the Pope than lose their right to drive like maniacs.

Jeremy Clarkson, *Motorworld*

You have to be careful in my country because we have bad cars and good wine, a dangerous combination.

Francesco De Carlo

I don't speak Italian, but pinot grigio means 'slut fuel', right?

Rob Delaney, Twitter

The Italians have a saying, 'Keep your friends close and your enemies closer.' And, although they've never won a war or mass-produced a decent car, in this case they're right.

Jack Donaghy (Alec Baldwin), *30 Rock*

Why can't you people learn to speak my language? I learned to eat your food.

Homer Simpson (Dan Castellaneta), *The Simpsons*

There's an old Italian saying: 'You fuck up once, you lose two teeth.'

Tony Soprano Sr (James Gandolfini), *The Sopranos*

I'm half-Italian and half-Polish, so I'm always putting a hit out on myself.

Judy Tenuta

Japan

The best way to learn Japanese is to be born as a Japanese baby, in Japan, raised by a Japanese family.

Dave Barry

When it comes to Japanese civilisation, it's mostly eyewash. Kabuki theatre is only just preferable to root-canal work. The three-stringed guitar is a sad waste of cat.

A.A. Gill

In Japan, you have no idea what they are saying, and they can't help you either. Nothing makes any sense. They're very polite, but you feel like a joke is being played on you the entire time you're there.

Bill Murray

Jazz

Without the beat in the background, jazz basically sounds like an armadillo was let loose on the keyboard.

Bill Bailey

Sebastian Wilder (Ryan Gosling): What do you mean, you don't like jazz?
Mia Dolan (Emma Stone): It just means that when I listen to it, I don't like it.

La La Land

Louis Balfour (John Thomson): What are you going to play for us today, Jackson?
Jackson Jeffrey Jackson (Colin McFarlane): Trumpet.
Louis Balfour: No, er, what tune?
Jackson Jeffrey Jackson: Tune?! This is jazz!

The Fast Show

This will put fear into your heart; she's a devoted experimental jazz musician. She can do extraordinary things with her voice – not pleasant things, but extraordinary.

Graham Norton, introducing Rona Nishliu, Albania's
2012 Eurovision Song Contest entry

Jazz, isn't that just a series of mistakes disguised as musical composition?
David St Hubbins (Michael McKean), *This Is Spinal Tap*

Jesus

I can't help thinking that Last Supper must have been a bit tense, with Jesus relating the bread to his broken skin and the wine to his own blood. I bet no one touched the meatballs.

Danny Bhoy

Can you imagine Jesus turning up at a nightclub? 'I don't care who your dad is, pal – you're not getting in with sandals on.'

Kevin Bridges

If Jesus can walk on water, can he swim on land?

Bo Burnham

If we're all God's children, what's so special about Jesus?

Jimmy Carr

If Jesus was a Jew, how come he has a Mexican first name?

Billy Connolly

So what if Jesus turned water into wine? I once turned a whole student loan into vodka.

Sean Lock

I think the reason Jesus is so popular, just on a celebrity level, is that he died at the peak of his career.

Marc Maron

Honk if you love Jesus. Text while driving if you want to meet him.

Rev. Bob Marshall

Jesus fed five thousand people with two fishes and a loaf of bread. That's not a miracle. That's tapas.

Mark Nelson

You can spot immediately that Jesus isn't English, because he's very often wearing sandals, but never with socks. I think that would be an English messiah's look – socks, sandals, khaki shorts skimming the knee, little Fair Isle slipover in case it turns, because it's deceptive, the desert . . .

Linda Smith

When Jesus went to heaven, was that not essentially 'moving back in with your parents'?

Iain Stirling

And some people say Jesus wasn't Jewish. Of course he was Jewish! Thirty years old, single, lives with his parents, come on! He works in his father's business, his mom thought he was God's gift, he's Jewish! Give it up!

Robin Williams

Jewellery

Women like jewellery. They're like raccoons: show them some shiny stuff and they'll follow you home.

Alonzo Bodden

I wear a necklace 'cause I wanna know when I'm upside down.

Mitch Hedberg

That's the second fiancée to chuck that ring away. You'd be better off buying a boomerang!

Blanche Hunt (Maggie Jones), *Coronation Street*

Jews

I'm either mentally ill or Jewish. I can't sometimes tell the difference.

Roseanne Barr

Everyone thinks I'm Jewish. I'm not. Last year I got a call: 'Happy Hanukkah.' I said, 'Ma, I'm not Jewish!'

Joy Behar

Yiddish is a combination of German and phlegm. This is a language of coughing and spitting; until I was eleven, I wore a raincoat.

Billy Crystal, *700 Sundays*

If you look at a group of people that had faith, it's got to be the Jews. They followed Moses through the desert for forty years with no map. There had to be one guy in the back, saying, 'I don't think he knows where he's going.'

Adam Ferrara

Look at the insane things the Jews believe. The Jews believe that Barbra Streisand is worth one thousand dollars a ticket.

Greg Giraldo

Jews can't serve on juries because they insist they're guilty.

Cathy Ladman

You take ten Jews at random and put 'em on a basketball court, you get a real estate seminar.

Gregg Rogell

Summer camp: the second worst camp for Jews.

Sarah Silverman, *The Bedwetter: Stories of Courage, Redemption and Pee*

My friend was brought up Orthodox Jewish. He thought the New Testament was the paperback version of the Old Testament.

Lizz Winstead

Boris Johnson

Unlikely school report cards . . . 'Dear Mr and Mrs Johnson, Boris is a very popular and intelligent boy who should go far, just so long as he's not put in charge of anything complex.'

Chris Addison, *Mock the Week*

In the post-referendum fallout, at one point Boris Johnson wanted to punch Michael Gove, and the only reason he didn't is he hates queuing.

Jo Brand, *Have I Got News for You*

Boris Johnson is the most dangerous politician in Britain precisely because of his charm . . . Funny and likeable, even when he errs it's cute, like a shaved Winnie the Pooh eating all the honey.

Russell Brand

He has catwalk hair, *Vogue* cover hair.

Russell Brand

THE CLOWN PRINCE OF BRITISH POLITICS

Daily Mail headline, 2014

Boris Johnson has left the Conservative leadership race to return to the pages of the *Beano*, he has confirmed. The long-running comic character began a trial run in reality back in 1999, when he proved such a success on *Have I Got News for You* that he was given his own spin-off of increasingly ludicrous adventures.

Thedailymash.co.uk

There might have been a moment when Boris Johnson was dangling on his zip-wire when Theresa May thought, There's the man to communicate Britain's vision to the world in a disciplined and structured way . . . But I somehow doubt it.

Dan Hodges

My chances of being Prime Minister are about as good as the chances of finding Elvis on Mars or my being reincarnated as an olive.

Boris Johnson, more than a decade before almost but not quite announcing his intention to stand for the office

Voting Tory will cause your wife to have bigger breasts and increase your chances of owning a BMW M3.

Boris Johnson

I can hardly condemn UKIP as a bunch of boss-eyed, foam-flecked Euro hysterics, when I have been sometimes not far short of boss-eyed, foam-flecked hysteria myself.

Boris Johnson

The dreadful truth is that when people come to see their MP they have run out of better ideas.

Boris Johnson

My speaking style was criticised by no less an authority than Arnold Schwarzenegger. It was a low moment to have my rhetorical skills denounced by a monosyllabic Austrian cyborg.

Boris Johnson

As I have discovered myself, there are no disasters, only opportunities. And indeed, opportunities for fresh disasters.

Boris Johnson

My policy on cake is pro having it and pro eating it.

Boris Johnson

Regardless of party politics, how do you think this bloke isn't an absolute pantomime nincompoop?

Stuart Maconie

The National Health Service would be about as safe in the hands of Boris Johnson and Iain Duncan Smith as a pet hamster would be with a hungry python.

John Major

Boris is the life and soul of the party, but he isn't the man you want driving you home at the end of the evening.

Amber Rudd

An enigma wrapped inside a whoopee cushion.

Will Self

Clearly British humour has no borders.

Belgian MEP Guy Verhofstadt, after Boris Johnson
was appointed Foreign Secretary

The Kardashians

————

It's being reported that the Kardashians were frustrated when they were in Cuba, because most Cubans have not seen their show, so they don't know why they're famous. As opposed to most Americans who have seen their show, and still don't know why they're famous.

Jimmy Fallon

Kim Kardashian said she suffers from anxiety. That has to be hard, not knowing when her fifteen minutes will be over.

Lee Mays, Twitter

If Kim wants us to see a part of her we've never seen, she's gonna have to swallow the camera.

Bette Midler

Kissing

————

Daniel Cleaver (Hugh Grant): First, have some more wine, and then tell me the story about practising French kissing with the art girls at school, because it's a very good story.
Bridget Jones (Renée Zellweger): It wasn't French kissing.
Daniel Cleaver: Don't care, make it up.

Bridget Jones's Diary

You've only kissed three girls. Your type is 'Anyone who'll let you'.
Simon Cooper (Joe Thomas), *The Inbetweeners*

It's a big mouth. I was aware of a faint echo when I was kissing her.
Hugh Grant, on Julia Roberts, his co-star in *Notting Hill*

Sam Malone (Ted Danson): Do these lips remind you of anything?
Rebecca Howe (Kirstie Alley): Yeah. I think the liver in my freezer's gone bad.

Cheers

I'm a sappy romantic, I really like to take it slow. I don't kiss until the fortieth date.

Kate Hudson

Ben Stiller (himself): I've kissed Cameron Diaz, Drew Barrymore! I slapped Jennifer Aniston's butt!
Maggie Jacobs (Ashley Jensen): In films.
Stiller: It still counts! It still counts! It still counts . . . I did it . . .

Extras

The shame of pulling out of a double-cheek kiss too early, then attempting to re-enter it after the moment's passed.

Rob Temple, *Very British Problems*

Lawyers and the Law

If you want to kill an idea without being identified as the assassin, suggest that the legal department take a look at it.

Scott Adams, *Dilbert Gives You the Business*

Michael Bluth (Jason Bateman): I'm not a one-night-stand kinda guy. I don't like lying to women.
George Oscar 'GOB' Bluth II (Will Arnett): These are lawyers. That's Latin for liar.

Arrested Development

C'mon, we hate all our clients. It's good to hate: allows us to overcharge and still sleep at night.

Denny Crane (William Shatner), *Boston Legal*

It takes a long time to become a lawyer because you need three things – a bachelor's degree, a law degree, and a desire to worship Satan.

Craig Ferguson

Let me tell you something. I didn't become a lawyer because I like the law; the law sucks. It's boring, but it can also be used as a weapon. You want to bankrupt somebody? Cost him everything he's worked for? Make his wife leave him, even make his kids cry? Yeah, we can do that.

Richard Fish (Greg Germann), *Ally McBeal*

Recently in court, I was found guilty of being egotistical. I am appealing.

Stewart Francis

We've all broken the rules at some point in our lives. I once sold multi-pack cans of Coke individually at a church fete.

Ivo Graham

Daddy's a litigator. Those are the scariest kind of lawyer. Even Lucy, our maid, is terrified of him. And Daddy's so good he gets five hundred dollars an hour to fight with people. But he fights with me for free because I'm his daughter.

Cher Horowitz (Alicia Silverstone), *Clueless*

Let's make a law that gay people can have birthdays, but straight people get more cake – you know, to send the right message to kids.

Bill Maher

To me, a lawyer is basically the person that knows the rules of the country. We're all throwing the dice, playing the game, moving our pieces around the board, but if there is a problem the lawyer is the only person who has read the inside of the top of the box.

Jerry Seinfeld

Laziness

My husband asked me if we have any cheese puffs. Like he can't go and lift that couch cushion up himself.

Roseanne Barr

You know you're lazy when you run out of toilet paper and use the cardboard roll to wipe with.

Dane Cook

Some people like to keep their grass cut really short so they can see any intruders coming. I say let the grass grow tall so they don't know there's a house behind it. Some call it lazy, I say it's thinking.

Jeff Foxworthy

Michael Bluth (Jason Bateman): You've got to be the laziest person in the world.
Lindsay Fünke (Portia de Rossi): If you weren't all the way on the other side of the room, I'd slap your face.

Arrested Development

Sometimes the only reason I leave my house is so when someone asks about my day I don't have to say, 'Netflix and avoiding responsibilities'.

Anna Kendrick, Twitter

How many of you have ever started dating because you were too lazy to commit suicide?

Judy Tenuta

Liars and Lying

That's how it always starts. You think lies are going to make things easier, so you tell the policeman you don't know what speed you were doing, you keep the 10p you found on the pavement, you tell the poppy day lady you've already given. Next thing you know, you're fiddling your tax and taking paperclips home from work!

Gordon Brittas (Chris Barrie), *The Brittas Empire*

I broke up with a girl once because she lied about her weight. I say that, she died in a bungee-jumping accident.

Jimmy Carr

Just remember, it's not a lie if you believe it.

> George Costanza (Jason Alexander), *Seinfeld*

It wasn't a lie, it was ineptitude with insufficient cover.

> Don Draper (Jon Hamm), *Mad Men*

Pam Byrnes (Teri Polo): What's the matter, sweetie? Can't sleep?
Greg Focker (Ben Stiller): No, no. I was just going over my answers to the polygraph test your dad just gave me.

> *Meet the Parents*

DI Sam Tyler (John Simm): I think she's telling the truth.
DCI Gene Hunt (Philip Glenister): I think she's as fake as a tranny's fanny.

> *Life on Mars*

Unforeseen legacy of the Brexit campaign: 'Written down the side of the bus' now apparently British political shorthand for 'blatant lie'.

> Robert Hutton, Twitter

It's a basic truth of the human condition that everybody lies. The only variable is about what.

> Hugh Laurie

(Jeffrey) Archer has issued a strenuous denial – as good as a signed confession, really.

> Des Lynam, *Have I Got News for You*

There are two things that you have to lie to get through. One is politics and the other is marriage.

> Bill Maher

I know lying is wrong, but if the Elephant Man came in now in a blouse with some make-up on, and said, 'How do I look?', would you say, bearing in mind he's depressed and has got respiratory problems, would you say, 'Go and take that blusher off, you misshapen-headed elephant tranny'? No. You'd say, 'You look nice, John.'

> Alan Partridge (Steve Coogan), *I'm Alan Partridge*

Stan Zbornak (Herbert Edelman): Sophia, you're looking younger and more beautiful than ever.

Sophia Petrillo (Estelle Getty): And may I say that's a beautiful toupee you're wearing. There, now we're both lying!

The Golden Girls

You calling me a liar? You better watch out because the last person's called me a liar was Bethany Ray, and she ended up getting stabbed in the arm with a pencil, but I never done it 'cause I would soooo never do that! And anyone who says I did, I'd stab them in the arm with a pencil.

Vicky Pollard (Matt Lucas), *Little Britain*

Sometimes lying is OK, like when you know what's good for people more than they do.

Rob Reiner, *South Park*

You can always tell when someone's lying to you, because they're male.

Caroline Rhea

Life

Life is half-delicious-yoghurt half-crap, and your job is to keep the plastic spoon in the yoghurt.

Scott Adams

The world isn't fair, but as long as it's tilting in my direction I find that there's a natural cap to my righteous indignation.

Scott Adams

I don't think we're as amazing as our parents are. I'm not going to have any struggles to tell my kids about. What's my story going to be like? 'Ah, son, once, when I was flying from New York to LA, my iPad died!'

Aziz Ansari

To expect life to treat you good is as foolish as hoping a bull won't hit you because you are a vegetarian.

Roseanne Barr

The path of my life is strewn with cowpats from the devil's own satanic herd!

> Edmund Blackadder (Rowan Atkinson), *Blackadder II*

My motto in life is always give one hundred per cent. Which makes blood donation quite tricky.

> Tony Cowards, Twitter

You know, life's a lot like a river: fast, furious, unpredictable. You just have to take it as it comes. Every now and then, though, I wish I was one of those people who had a boat.

> Caroline Duffy (Lea Thompson), *Caroline in the City*

It is a truth universally acknowledged that when one part of your life starts going OK, another falls spectacularly to pieces.

> Helen Fielding, *Bridget Jones's Diary*

Life without risks is like a burrito without Tabasco. Bland, but you'll still fart.

> Martyn V. Halm, *Reprobate: A Katla Novel*

Why don't they just accept that life is sad and cheer up? It's not forever.

> Jeremy Hardy, *The News Quiz*

It's important to live your life by a motto. I chose to live my life by the motto, 'My enemy's enemy is my friend.' Unfortunately, as it turns out, my enemy is his own worst enemy. So I have to invite him to barbecues.

> Richard Herring

I remember watching Mel Gibson on some show once and he was being asked about his belief in the afterlife. Gibson said, 'Well, I can't believe this is all there is.' And I thought: Wait a minute. You're Mel Gibson. You have millions of dollars. You're a great-looking chap with every conceivable blessing that could be bestowed upon a man. And that's not good enough?

> Hugh Laurie, 2009

Life is like a box of chocolates. It doesn't last long if you're fat.

> Joe Lycett

If you're a battery, you're either working or you're dead. It's a shit life.

Demetri Martin

It's one of several neglected areas in my life. I've got no sex life, no frying pan and I'm halfway through a tube of toothpaste I absolutely cannot stand!

Stan Meadowcroft (Duncan Preston), *dinnerladies*

Life goes much more smoothly when everyone's saying 'Sorry'. It's the second most important social lubricant and, unlike the first, it doesn't damage your liver.

David Mitchell, *Thinking About It Only Makes It Worse*

Life is like a musical by Andrew Lloyd Webber – very popular and not as bad as some would have you believe.

Simon Munnery

When you get right down tae it, there's only birth, copulation and death. Everything else is pure bloody guesswork.

Rab C. Nesbitt (Gregor Fisher), *Rab C. Nesbitt*

Out of everything I've lost, I miss my mind the most.

Ozzy Osbourne

Next to Sammy's life, my life has always appeared dull. Then again, next to a barnacle's life, my life has always appeared dull.

Norm Peterson (George Wendt), *Cheers*

There are times in life when people must know when not to let go. Balloons are designed to teach small children this.

Sir Terry Pratchett

Life is basically trying to meet better people than the ones you currently know.

Julius Sharpe, Twitter

Son, if you really want something in this life, you have to work for it. Now, quiet! They're about to announce the lottery numbers.

Homer Simpson (Dan Castellaneta), *The Simpsons*

Life is like animal porn, it's not for everyone.

Doug Stanhope

God put me on Earth to accomplish certain things. Right now, I'm so far behind, I'll never die.

Bill Watterson, *Calvin and Hobbes*

Life's not fair, is it? Some of us drink champagne in the fast lane, and some of us eat our sandwiches by the loose chippings on the A597.

Victoria Wood

Literature

We had one book in our house: the phone book. I've read it, it wasn't a great read, lots of characters, and at the end loads of Polish people turn up.

Stephen K Amos

My girlfriend got me this book on feng shui, but I didn't know where in my home to put it.

Irwin Barker

A classic is a book that everybody is assumed to have read and often think they have.

Alan Bennett

Once I start a book, I finish it. That was the way one was brought up. Books, bread and butter, mashed potato – one finishes what's on one's plate.

Alan Bennett

When I read a book, I always underline the bits I don't understand. That way, if I ever lend it to someone, they'll think I'm really clever.

Adam Bloom

There's a new book about a couple who have sex in unusual places. It's on the shelves Monday, hanging from a chandelier Tuesday . . .

Rob Brydon

When you write books for a living, you come to realise that while not all people who write to authors are strange, all people who are strange write to authors.

Bill Bryson, *The Road to Little Dribbling: More Notes from a Small Island*

Some say that [Rachel] Cusk has no sense of humour, but expecting giggles from this writer would be akin to expecting sonnets from Benny Hill.

Julie Burchill

When I buy a new book, I read the last page first. That way, in case I die before I finish, I know how it ends.

Harry Burns (Billy Crystal), *When Harry Met Sally* . . .

I went to the book shop today because it was a third off all titles. I bought *The Lion, The Witch*.

Jimmy Carr

I wrote a book about poltergeists. I'm pleased to say it's literally flying off the shelves.

Jimmy Carr

I love *Rupert the Bear* stories, especially the one where Bill Badger was gassed.

Jeremy Clarkson

Never trust anybody with only one book.

Billy Connolly

The cover ordered you to '*Mount!* Jilly Cooper' but I'm too old to accommodate you all, so instead I want you to form an orderly line and shake my hand.

Jilly Cooper, at the launch of her 2016 novel *Mount!*

I've just spilled glue on my autobiography. Well, that's my story and I'm sticking to it.

Tony Cowards, Twitter

If you had to pick what Shakespeare did best, most people would pick tragedy – one of the few things he has in common with Steps.

Philomena Cunk (Diane Morgan), *Cunk on Shakespeare*

A library is a place where you can lose your innocence without losing your virginity.

Germaine Greer

So, not even the moths have shown interest in it!

Blanche Hunt (Maggie Jones) to son-in-law Ken Barlow
after he finds an intact copy of his novel manuscript
fifty years later in the loft, *Coronation Street*

What happened to great literature? I mean, there's nothing like getting to the end of a good book and thinking to yourself, 'Ah, *there's* Wally!'

Milton Jones

Hopefully I've got a book coming out soon. Shouldn't have eaten it really.

Milton Jones

A book hasn't caused me this much trouble since *Where's Waldo?* went to that barber pole factory.

Tracy Jordan (Tracy Morgan), *30 Rock*

I'm writing my book in the fifth person, so every sentence starts out with: 'I heard from this guy who told somebody . . .'

Demetri Martin

I like reading in a pub rather than a library or study, as it's generally much easier to get a drink.

Pete McCarthy, *McCarthy's Bar*

A good book is called a page-turner. Surely that is the minimum you expect from any book.

Michael McIntyre

If you only read one book in your life, I highly recommend . . . you keep your mouth shut.

Simon Munnery

I did actually sit down with a blank sheet of paper once. I think the phone rang and that was the end of my literary career.

Bill Nighy

The author of *Fifty Shades of Grey* has been named the world's best-paid author. When J. K. Rowling heard the news, she announced the release of her latest book – *Harry Potter and the Chamber of Gentle Ass Play*.

Conan O'Brien

What two books would I take to a desert island? The first book I'd bring with me would be a big, plastic inflatable book, and the second one would be *How to Make Oars Out of Sand*.

Ardal O'Hanlon

Alan Partridge (Steve Coogan): What's that you're reading?
Dave Clifton (Phil Cornwell): Actually, it's incredible. This is the biography of an East End gangster. It's called *Bad Slags*. It's amazing stuff. It's incredible.
Alan: I think there's another word for it really. I think it's sad that people find it entertaining to read about men who call themselves things like 'Stan the Stabber', who chop people's heads off, in half, set fire to their eyebrows and knock people's teeth out with a toffee hammer just because they couldn't repay a loan at a very uncompetitive rate of interest.

I'm Alan Partridge

What you don't know about post-mortem analysis could fill a book, Mr Castle. In fact, it has. Numerous times.
Dr Sidney Perlmutter (Arye Gross) to crime novelist Richard Castle, *Castle*

Can anyone recommend a few thousand books on hoarding?

Tim Siedell, Twitter

When a writer dies, you get a higher standard of obituary.

Arthur Smith

Should not the Society of Indexers be known as Indexers, Society of, The?

Keith Waterhouse

Loneliness

I suppose doing things you hate is just the price you pay to avoid loneliness.

Mark Corrigan (David Mitchell), *Peep Show*

Love-life . . . may be a rather grandiose term for staring at women on the bus.

Mark Corrigan (David Mitchell), *Peep Show*

I went to a therapy group to help me cope with loneliness, but no one else turned up.

Stewart Francis

Do any of you have a completely unremarkable friend or maybe a house-plant I could go to dinner with on Saturday night?

Miranda Hobbes (Cynthia Nixon), *Sex and the City*

I never feel more alone than when I'm trying to put sunscreen on my back.

Jimmy Kimmel

Even when I was a kid, my imaginary friend would play with the kid across the street.

Daniel Tosh

Single men: convince people you have a girlfriend by standing outside Topshop with bags of shopping, looking at your watch and occasionally glancing inside.

Top Tips, *Viz*

Love

A guy knows when he's in love when he loses interest in his car for a couple of days.

Tim Allen

Love is like a fart. If you have to force it, it's probably shit.

Stephen K Amos

Love is just a system for getting someone to call you 'darling' after sex.

Julian Barnes, *Talking it Over*

Valentine's Day: the holiday that reminds you that if you don't have a special someone, you're alone.

Lewis Black

If love were a product, the queue at the faulty goods desk would stretch right round the universe and back.

Charlie Brooker

Peggy Bundy (Katey Sagal): Tell me you love me, Al.
Al Bundy (Ed O'Neill): I love football, I love beer, let's not cheapen the meaning of the word.

Married . . . with Children

It's a fact of life: people we love leave us. Unless you chain them to a radiator, which for some reason is illegal.

Richard Castle (Nathan Fillion), *Castle*

If grass can grow through cement, love can find you at every time in your life.

Cher

Oh, Ron, there are literally thousands of other men that I should be with instead, but I am seventy-two per cent sure that I love you.

Veronica Corningstone (Christina Applegate),
Anchorman: The Legend of Ron Burgundy

Saying 'I love you' is like firing first in a duel: if you miss, you're fucked.

Mark Corrigan (David Mitchell), *Peep Show*

So what if I don't really love her? Charles didn't really love Diana and they were all right. Sort of.

Mark Corrigan (David Mitchell), *Peep Show*

The language of love may be universal, but it's not one of the options on an ATM machine.

Dov Davidoff

There's nothing better than the love of a good woman, apart from maybe two bad women.

Gary Delaney, Twitter

It's probably not love if you don't press your face to the toilet seat after they've used it to feel their warmth.

Rob Delaney

You don't need to stay with a man you don't love just because he saved your life. It's not like he bought you a car or something.

Donna (Sharon Horgan), *Pulling*

Everything was going great until I said, 'I love you, Ben', and then he got this look on his face like he'd taken a wrong turn in a really bad neighbourhood.

Roz Doyle (Peri Gilpin), *Frasier*

By love, you mean big lightning bolts to the heart, where you can't eat and you can't work, and you just run off and get married and make babies. The reason you haven't felt it is because it doesn't exist. What you call love was invented by guys like me to sell nylons.

Don Draper (Jon Hamm), *Mad Men*

I thought I was in love once. And then, later, I thought it was just an inner ear imbalance.

Constable Benton Fraser (Paul Gross), *Due South*

Rachel Green (Jennifer Aniston): No, you're not an idiot, Ross. You're a guy very much in love.

Ross Geller (David Schwimmer): Same difference.

Friends

Valentine's Day has got blown way out of proportion. Valentine's Day just used to be for your girlfriend or your wife but now everyone's like, 'Oh, happy Valentine's Day!' I even got a Valentine's Day card from my grandmother. How ridiculous is that? We stopped having sex years ago.

Greg Giraldo

There is not a thin line between love and hate. There is, in fact, a Great Wall of China with armed sentries posted every twenty feet between love and hate.

Dr Gregory House (Hugh Laurie), *House*

You can't put a price tag on love. But if you could, I'd wait for it to go on sale.

Jarod Kintz, *This Book is Not for Sale*

Love is telling someone their hair extensions are showing.

Natasha Leggero

Valentine's Day is the day you should be with the person you love the most. I understand Simon Cowell spent the day alone.

Jay Leno

Love without evidence is stalking.

Tim Minchin

Don't talk to me about Valentine's Day. At my age, an affair of the heart is a bypass.

Joan Rivers

Real love amounts to withholding the truth, even when you're offered the perfect opportunity to hurt someone's feelings.

David Sedaris, *Dress Your Family in Corduroy and Denim*

Alfie Moon (Shane Richie): You know what they say, darlin', the course of true love never runs smooth.

Kat Slater (Jessie Wallace): I don't want smooth, just something that's less like roller-blading down the Himalayas with a rocket up me backside.

EastEnders

Manners

Why do people have to spit? That ruined *Titanic* for me, the spitting. The iceberg couldn't come fast enough after I saw that.

Dolly Bellfield (Thelma Barlow), *dinnerladies*

I saw someone peeing in Jermyn Street the other day. I thought, is this the end of civilisation as we know it? Or is it simply someone peeing in Jermyn Street?

Alan Bennett, *The Old Country*

How long is it polite to continue to be interested in what someone says after they reveal they've got a boyfriend?

Russell Brand

(to her sons): Now remember, no throwing ice, no flicking butter at the ceiling, no sticking gum under the table, and no eating gum already stuck under the table.

Lois (Jane Kaczmarek), *Malcolm in the Middle*

The absolute limit that was! You wouldn't believe that anyone could pick their nose all the way through *Dances With Wolves*, would you? Three and a half hours I had to sit next to that! And always the right nostril; he never touched the left one. Always the one at *my* side! You'd think he was digging the Channel tunnel.

Victor Meldrew (Richard Wilson), *One Foot in the Grave*

There's nothing more boring than respect in the bedroom. Why are you being so polite? This is sex, not tea in the duchess's walled garden.

Victoria Coren Mitchell

Alotta Fagina (Fabiana Udenio): How dare you break wind before me!
Austin Powers (Mike Myers): I'm sorry, I didn't realise it was your turn.

Austin Powers: International Man of Mystery

I'm a gentleman, and I was always taught it's rude to talk about a woman's age or weight unless you are breaking up with her.

David Spade

Marriage

My husband and I didn't sign a pre-nuptial agreement. We signed a mutual suicide pact.

Roseanne Barr

Good-looking people marry good-looking people and the others take what's left.

Alan Bennett, *Smut*

I can't get married. I can't fake sleep for thirty years.

Elayne Boosler

Love and marriage go together like angel cake and anthrax.

Julie Burchill

I know a couple who get on like a house on fire. They both feel trapped and are slowly suffocating to death.

Jimmy Carr

I don't think I'll ever meet the perfect woman. I might have to get one of those mail order women. You send away to the Philippines, and they send you a wife. The only thing is, once you're on their mailing list, they keep sending you a relative a month whether you want it or not.

Adam Ferrara

According to a new study, women in satisfying marriages are less likely to develop cardiovascular diseases than unmarried women. So don't worry, lonely women, you'll be dead soon.

Tina Fey

Love means never having to say you're sorry. Marriage means apologising when you know you're right.

Dana Gould

Perhaps Noel isn't the most dynamic man in the world. And perhaps he is quite inhibited sexually. And perhaps our married life won't be a thrilling, torrid sequence of 'I love you', 'I hate you', 'I need you', 'I can't bear you'. And perhaps while I wanted a Heathcliff to my Cathy, I've found a Ken Barlow to my Deirdre.

Janet (Selina Griffiths), *The Smoking Room*

Valentine's Day is a test. It's a test of your commitment, your prepared-ness, of whether you love someone enough to waste one hundred dollars on flowers that on any other day of the year would cost you thirty dollars.

Jimmy Kimmel

Marriage is very difficult. Marriage is like a five-thousand-piece jigsaw puzzle, all sky.

Cathy Ladman

Love prepares you for marriage the way needlepoint prepares you for round-the-world solo yachting.

Kathy Lette, *Courting Trouble*

Many marriages break up for religious reasons. He thinks he's a god and she doesn't.

Kathy Lette, *Men: A User's Guide*

When I was a kid, I asked my mum what a couple was, and she said, 'Oh, two or three.' And she wonders why her marriage didn't work out!

Josie Long

Next year we are celebrating two years of happy marriage. We've been married for twelve.

Lee Mack

(to audience member): How long have you been married? Three-and-a-half years? Aw, you're nearly done.

Sarah Millican

I'm in a same-sex marriage. The sex is always the same.

Alfie Moore

I'm a great supporter of sex before marriage. Otherwise I wouldn't have had sex at all.

Owen Newitt (Roger Lloyd Pack), *The Vicar of Dibley*

Marriage is when two people are joined together to become one desperately boring person.

Ardal O'Hanlon

With marriage, you've just got to stick it out. You can't jump off the boat at the first bump in the waves.

Ozzy Osbourne

Marriage is like a tense, unfunny version of *Everybody Loves Raymond*, only it doesn't last twenty-two minutes. It lasts forever.

Pete (Paul Rudd), *Knocked Up*

A marriage is always made up of two people who are prepared to swear that only the other one snores.

Sir Terry Pratchett, *The Fifth Elephant*

Our date-night rule is no talking about the kids. That lasts about to the end of the driveway.

Paul Reiser

In US and A, if you want to marry a girl, you cannot just go to her father's house and swap her for fifteen gallons of insecticide.

Borat Sagdiyev (Sacha Baron Cohen), *Borat: Cultural Learnings of America for Make Benefit Glorious Nation of Kazakhstan*

My dad said, 'Marry a girl with the same beliefs as the family.' I thought: Why should I marry a girl who thinks I'm a schmuck?

Adam Sandler

All my friends are getting married. I guess I'm just at that age where people give up.

Amy Schumer

Marge Simpson (Julie Kavner): You're my rock, Homey.
Homer Simpson (Dan Castellaneta): And I promise this rock is going to weigh you down for the rest of your life.

The Simpsons

Kids, marriage is like a car. Along the way it has bumps and dings. And this country can't make one that lasts more than five years.

Homer Simpson (Dan Castellaneta), *The Simpsons*

Francine Smith (Wendy Schaal): This man's given me something you haven't for a long time.
Stan Smith (Seth MacFarlane): We've talked about this. My neck gets tired.
Francine: I'm talking about respect, Stan.

American Dad!

The secret to a successful marriage is low expectations.

Jeff Stilson

Jim Trott (Trevor Peacock): Well, I've been married thirty-seven years, and the secret of a successful marriage, Hugo, is sex and plenty of it.
Hugo Horton (James Fleet): Well, hooray.
Jim: With as many different women as possible.

The Vicar of Dibley

If the present Mrs Wogan has a fault – and I must tread carefully here – this gem in the diadem of womanhood is a hoarder. She never throws anything out. Which may explain the longevity of our marriage.

Sir Terry Wogan

I was told a sex therapist could teach me new techniques and put the spice back into my marriage. I don't think I could learn any now. It's taken me twenty years to remember when we are making love not to say, 'Did you do the bins?'

Victoria Wood

Masturbation

There's a fine line between masturbating while you look out of a window and masturbating while you're looking in a window.

Dave Attell

I'm very romantic when I masturbate. I light some candles. Then I try to shoot them out when I'm done. Never invite me to a birthday party.

Dave Attell

(seeing an old school crush): I should speak to her, but what the hell can I say? Anything that doesn't mention I masturbate over her memory is probably good. I think that's a compliment, but women just don't seem to want to hear it.

Mark Corrigan (David Mitchell), *Peep Show*

Maybe if you spent a little less time cavorting with Madam Palm and her five daughters, you'd be a little more alert.

Harvey Denton (Steve Pemberton), *The League of Gentlemen*

I masturbated in the car once. I wouldn't do it again, though, 'cause the cab driver got really pissed off. I was, like, 'I'm sorry, sir, all I saw was the no smoking sign.'

Mitch Fatel

My wife said, 'We are having sex on a Tuesday.' Well, I thought that's great because now I know I can leave myself alone. Because you can get caught out, she comes in a bit frisky, and you have to look at her and go, 'That ship has sailed, darling.'

Micky Flanagan

I'm not an expert on masturbation, but I hold my own.

Stewart Francis

When I masturbate, I fantasise about having my own apartment. I used to think about Cindy Crawford, now I think about leaving a dish in the sink overnight.

Greg Giraldo

Did you know that if a man masturbates four times a week, it reduces the risk of him getting prostate cancer? I've tallied up my weekly counts and I'm immortal.

Sean Lock

Grace Adler (Debra Messing): Karen, are you all right? You haven't touched your muffin.
Karen Walker (Megan Mullally): Honey, please, since Stan left I've done nothing but touch my muffin!

Will & Grace

Mathematics

Rejected exam question . . . Amy is sixteen. Or at least she said she was. How much trouble are you in?

Hugh Dennis, *Mock the Week*

Cher Horowitz (Alicia Silverstone): If it's a concussion, you have to keep her conscious, OK? Ask her questions.
Elton Tiscia (Jeremy Sisto): What's seven times seven?
Cher: Stuff she knows!

Clueless

Here is another area of study for which I have little patience. The killer for me has always been that two negatives make a positive. I don't have two sheep, you don't give me two sheep, suddenly I have four sheep causing havoc in the paddock.

Sandi Toksvig, *The Chain of Curiosity*

Did you know that five out of three people have trouble with fractions?

Calvin Trillin

Maths was always my bad subject. I couldn't convince my teachers that many of my answers were meant ironically.

Calvin Trillin

Men

To get a man's attention, just stand in front of the TV and don't move.

Tim Allen

Men don't like to cuddle. We only like it if it leads to . . . you know . . . lower cuddling.

Ray Barone (Ray Romano), *Everybody Loves Raymond*

I know what men want. Men want to be really, really close to someone who will leave them alone.

Elayne Boosler

Like many men, I am highly skilled in the art of losing things but prefer to outsource the recovery process.

Craig Brown

Guys are like dogs: they never notice if you've changed your hair, but they can sense when there's another guy sniffing around their territory.

Candace Bushnell, *The Carrie Diaries*

Men think about sex every seven seconds, which I think makes talking to your dad very creepy.

Jimmy Carr

Men aren't necessities, they're luxuries.

Cher

Do you know how many middle-aged men go out for a pint of milk and never come home? Not enough.

Jenny Eclair

Dogs are man's best friend because guys want buddies that are dumber than they are. So do women, but they've already got men.

Bill Engvall

Sex is important to guys. We need stories to tell our friends.

Adam Ferrara

Men. Can't live with 'em; can't live . . . nope, that's it.

> Sam Fuller (Regina King), *Miss Congeniality 2: Armed and Fabulous*

At the end of the day, we want someone who is going to do the bloody dishes.

> E. L. James, on what women really look for in a man

Guys love it when you can show them you're better than they are at something they love.

> Leslie Knope (Amy Poehler), *Parks and Recreation*

Men think monogamy is something you making dining tables out of.

> Kathy Lette

If he wants breakfast in bed, tell him to sleep in the kitchen.

> Kathy Lette

If vibrators could light the barbie and kill spiders in the bathtub, would we need men at all?

> Kathy Lette

I think men talk to women so they can sleep with them and women sleep with men so they can talk to them.

> Jay McInerney

Men simply love explaining things . . . They offer their nuggets of wisdom as gifts, like a cat offers a half-eaten bird.

> Victoria Coren Mitchell

God gave men brains larger than dogs' so they wouldn't hump women's legs at cocktail parties.

> Kate Libby (Angelina Jolie), *Hackers*

Although no man is an island, you can make quite an effective raft out of six.

> Simon Munnery

Ladies, if a man says he will fix it, he will. There's no need to remind him every six months about it.

> Bill Murray

Behind every great man is a woman rolling her eyes.

Bruce Nolan (Jim Carrey), *Bruce Almighty*

OK, sex is fine. Sex is good. Sex is great! OK, OK, we need men for sex . . .
Do we need so many?

Maggie O'Connell (Janine Turner), *Northern Exposure*

It's hard for a man to turn down sex. If they chase us, we can't run that
fast.

Chris Rock

I hate when women compare men to dogs. Men are not dogs. Dogs are
loyal. I've never found any strange panties in my dog's house!

Wanda Sykes

Tim Taylor (Tim Allen): You just don't understand the intricacies of the
male mind.
Jill Taylor (Patricia Richardson): Explain it to me, I've got a minute.

Home Improvement

It's not genetically possible for men to have opinions about fabric.

Steve Taylor (Jack Davenport), *Coupling*

What do men want? Men want a mattress that cooks.

Judy Tenuta

Men are simple things. They can survive a whole weekend with only three
things – beer, boxer shorts and batteries for the remote control.

Daniel Tosh

Mental Health

I used to subscribe to *Mental Health Monthly*. I still have a lot of issues.

Tony Cowards, Twitter

My dad was a schizophrenic but he was good people. I remember when I
was five and he was Mussolini.

Stewart Francis

Constable Benton Fraser (Paul Gross): Is there any insanity in our family?
Sgt. Bob Fraser (Gordon Pinsent): No, not that I'm aware of.
Constable Fraser: Good.
Sgt. Fraser: Well, there was your uncle Tiberius who died wrapped in cabbage leaves, but we assumed that was a freak accident.

Due South

My sister was diagnosed with multiple personalities. She phoned me the other day and my caller ID exploded.

Zach Galifianakis

Is it still OK to make fun of schizophrenics? There's a little voice in my head that says, 'No.'

Dana Gould

I lived with a guy who had OCD and I used to put Rice Krispies in his slippers before I went out. He went mental, but not before he counted them all.

Russell Howard

I am not a lunatic. I have the psychiatric report to prove it. A slender majority of the panel decided in my favour.

Owen Newitt (Roger Lloyd Pack), *The Vicar of Dibley*

Tourette's is like predictive talking that people can't turn off.

Lee Mack

Stu Preissler (Steve Martin): Am I nuts, Edith?
Edith Preissler (JoBeth Williams): Are you asking me as a therapist or as a wife?
Stu: Which one is cheaper?

The Big Year

We need a twelve-step group for compulsive talkers. They could call it Anon Anon.

Paula Poundstone

The OCD probably kicked in when I was in my teens and I was pretty much single for my entire twenties. I got a lot done though. It was a productive period – all my old bank statements were in order.

Jon Richardson

I find, as a general rule of thumb, if you see someone wearing more than two badges, they're a nutter.

Frank Skinner, *Frank Skinner*

There's no such thing as addiction; there's only things that you enjoy doing more than life.

Doug Stanhope

Screw normal. You know why? 'Cause if you're normal, the crowd will accept you. But if you're deranged, the crowd will make you their leader.

Christopher Titus

Middle East

Remember when we dug Saddam up out of that hole? He looked like a Father Christmas who had been sacked from Debenhams for being drunk at work.

Russell Brand

The only reason the Arabs and Jews have managed to keep their nasty little war going for fifty years is because it never bloody rains there. If the post-war powers had put Israel in Manchester, there'd have been no bloodshed.

Jeremy Clarkson

I believe that the government that governs best is a government that governs least, and by these standards we have set up a fabulous government in Iraq.

Stephen Colbert

Most people only associate the Middle East with oil and phlegm and halitosis. I'm joking, I'm joking, we're running out of oil.

Omid Djalili

It's no fun being a broody Iranian woman. Every time I said to people, 'My body clock is ticking,' they would hit the ground.

Shappi Khorsandi

What Iran needs now is a more modern leader – a mullah-lite.

Shappi Khorsandi

For exiled Iranian writers, the closest we have to a literary award is a fatwah.

Shappi Khorsandi

On his book tour, President Bush is being very candid. He says he used to do stupid things when he was drunk. But think about it, who among us hasn't had a couple of drinks and invaded Iraq?

David Letterman

Let's see what's going on over in Iraq. A Burger King has opened up and prostitutes are back on the streets of Baghdad after more than twenty years. Fast food and hookers – they are truly living the American dream.

David Letterman

I think Iran and Iraq had a war simply because their names are so similar. They keep getting each other's post.

Paul Merton

Egypt is in the second day of angry street protests. Secretary of State Hillary Clinton is calling for calm. Because nothing calms an enraged Arab country like a powerful woman ordering it around.

Conan O'Brien

Military

Nearly a quarter of American men were in the Armed Forces (in 1968).
The rest were in school, in prison or were George W. Bush.

Bill Bryson, *The Life and Times of the Thunderbolt Kid*

My father was a soldier and when we were young we moved around a
lot . . . because he used us for target practice.

Milton Jones

Mistakes

(answering the phone): The Bouquet residence, the lady of the house
speaking . . . No, I do not have a special offer on spicy prawn balls. This is
not the Chinese takeaway. And will you please get off my white slimline
telephone with last number redial.

Hyacinth Bucket (Patricia Routledge), *Keeping Up Appearances*

I can't go back and keep making the same mistakes, when I can make new ones.

Bridget Jones (Renée Zellweger), *Bridget Jones's Baby*

I was on the street. This guy waved to me and he came up to me and said:
'I'm sorry, I thought you were someone else.' I said, 'I am.'

Demetri Martin

Father Ted Crilly (Dermot Morgan): Anyway Dougal, you were saying . . .
about the school reunion.
Father Dougal Maguire (Ardal O'Hanlon): Ah, yeah, I didn't recognise
anyone. And you know something? They all became firemen. I was the
only one there that wasn't a fireman.
Father Ted: Dougal, you didn't go to a fire station by mistake, did you?
Father Dougal: Ah!

Father Ted

I can't write about my greatest mistakes because I've slept with most of them.

Arabella Weir

Money

Money: the only thing that keeps us in touch with our children.

Gyles Brandreth

Those who pay their bills on time are soon forgotten. It is only by not paying one's bills that one can hope to live in the memory of the commercial classes.

Gyles Brandreth, *Oscar Wilde and a Death of No Importance*

I'm half Scottish and half Jewish, so don't ask me for money.

David Duchovny

You walk into a strip club with a wad of cash: they all flock around you. Strippers are just pigeons with tits: they go where the bread is.

Chris Hardwick

A dollar here, a dollar there. Over time, it adds up to two dollars.

Jarod Kintz, *The* Titanic *would never have sunk if it were made out of a sink*

The only good thing I've ever noticed about money, the only positive aspect of an otherwise pretty vulgar commodity, is that you can use it to buy things.

Hugh Laurie

It's money. I remember it from when I was single.

Jack Lawrence (Billy Crystal), *Fathers' Day*

Money can't buy you love, but it can get you some really good chocolate ginger biscuits.

Dylan Moran

People say that money is not the key to happiness, but I always figured if you have enough money, you can have a key made.

Joan Rivers

Most men would rather show off their bald patch than admit what they earn.

Anne Robinson

From tomorrow the new Bank of England five-pound note comes into circulation. The notes, which feature the head of Iggy Pop, can only be used once.

Collaterlie Sisters (Doon Mackichan), *The Day Today*

Sister Mary Bernard (Melinda Page Hamilton): Money can't buy happiness.
Gabrielle Solis (Eva Longoria): Sure it can. That's just a lie we tell poor people to keep them from rioting.

Desperate Housewives

Morality

There's a gigantic grey area between good moral behaviour and outright felonious activities. I call that the Weasel Zone and it's where most of life happens.

Scott Adams, *Dilbert and the Way of the Weasel*

Doris Block (Caroline Aaron): You have no values. With you it's all nihilism, cynicism, sarcasm, and orgasm.
Harry Block (Woody Allen): Hey, in France I could run for office with that slogan, and win!

Deconstructing Harry

I have no sense of decency – that way my other senses are enhanced.

Bob 'Bulldog' Briscoe (Dan Butler), *Frasier*

I have never taken the high road. But I tell other people to, 'cause then there's more room for me on the low road.

> Tom Haverford (Aziz Ansari), *Parks and Recreation*

Now is not the time to have a one-night stand with your conscience.

> DCI Gene Hunt (Philip Glenister), *Life on Mars*

Mike McLintock (Matt Walsh): Which way are you gonna vote?
Selina Meyer (Julia Louis-Dreyfus): The way that my principles and conscience tell me to go.
Amy Brookheimer (Anna Chlumsky): OK.
Selina: Which way do you think that should be?

> *Veep*

You're an inveterate scum-sucker whose moral dipstick is about two drops short of bone-dry.

> Fox Mulder (David Duchovny), *The X-Files*

That man's so twisted he could hide behind a spiral staircase.

> Rita Sullivan (Barbara Knox), *Coronation Street*

He's got so many politicians in his pocket he walks with a limp.

> Det. Ray Vecchio (David Marciano), *Due South*

Mothers

As a housewife I figure if the kids are still alive when my husband gets home from work, then I've done my job.

> Roseanne Barr

Denise Best (Caroline Aherne): She's a dreadful mother.
Barbara Royle (Sue Johnston): Where are *your* kids, Denise?
Denise: Ooh, Dave, we forgot to pick them up from school!
Dave Best (Craig Cash): They'll be at the headmaster's house again.

> *The Royle Family*

Lucille Bluth (Jessica Walter): I don't have the milk of mother's kindness in me anymore.
Michael Bluth (Jason Bateman): Yeah. That udder's been dry for a while though, hasn't it?

Arrested Development

My mother is no spring chicken, although she has got as many chemicals in her as one.

Dame Edna Everage (Barry Humphries)

I'm sorry I haven't been a very good mother. You can't be good at everything, and I was A1 with a hula hoop.

Petula Gordino (Julie Walters), *dinnerladies*

I hated my mom for not letting me play football as a kid. So when I have kids someday, I guarantee . . . they'll never meet their grandmother.

Anthony Jeselnik

My mother made us eat all sorts of vitamins and supplements until one day I nearly choked on part of the *Sunday Times*.

Milton Jones

I was adopted at birth and have never met my mum. That makes it very difficult to enjoy any lapdance.

Bobby Mair

When I was eleven, I broke the patio window and my mother sued me. She's always been a very aggressive litigator.

Maurice Moss (Richard Ayoade), *The IT Crowd*

If my mum was on her last legs, she'd steal somebody else's!

Fiz Stape (Jennie McAlpine), *Coronation Street*

I've been like a mother to that girl. I've locked her in her room, told her she was fat and once I even left her in a store.

Karen Walker (Megan Mullally), *Will & Grace*

I felt my mother about the place. I don't think she haunts me, but I wouldn't put it past her.

Julie Walters

Motor Sport

I didn't understand NASCAR until I met some NASCAR fans. You talk to a couple of NASCAR fans and you'll see where a shiny car driving in a circle would fascinate them all day. I can make fun of NASCAR fans because if they chase me, I just turn right.

Alonzo Bodden

Looking at the way [Narain] Karthikeyan's car was handling, I imagine his pit stop was for fresh underwear.

Martin Brundle

Racing drivers have balls. Unfortunately, none of them are crystal.

David Coulthard

You win some, lose some and wreck some.

Dale Earnhardt

You can always spot a motorcycle racer in a restaurant. He's the one gripping his fork with the first two fingers of his left hand.

Kenny Roberts

Jenson [Button] is now officially the fastest button in sport, apart from the one on Tiger Woods' trousers.

Jonathan Ross

Movies

My favourite film is the Eddie Redmayne classic, *The Theory of Everything*. Loved it. Should have been called *Look Who's Hawking*, that's my only criticism.

James Acaster

My attention span for films is eighty minutes. As far as I'm concerned, the *Titanic* is still sailing.

Alex Brooker, *The Last Leg*

Until this week the one thing I knew about the *Twilight Saga* was that it had vampires in it, which was enough to put me off. I didn't realise it was a romantic fantasy aimed at teenage girls. Turns out it's possible to be put off something twice before you've actually seen it.

Charlie Brooker

I have never seen *Jaws 4*, but by all accounts it is terrible. However, I have seen the house that it built and it is terrific.

Sir Michael Caine

I'm a huge film star, but you have to hurry to the movies, because I usually die in the first fifteen minutes. I'm the only guy I know who died in a *Muppet* movie.

Billy Connolly

Unlikely things to hear in a horror film . . . 'Uh, no, sorry, Freddy. Your satnav must be on the blink. This is Elm Crescent.'

Hugh Dennis, *Mock the Week*

Why do I have to watch a French movie? I didn't do anything wrong!

Phil Dunphy (Ty Burrell), *Modern Family*

Martin Scorsese's new movie *The Wolf of Wall Street* broke a record by using the F-word five hundred and six times. It beats the previous record, which was set by my dad trying to put together a desk from IKEA.

Jimmy Fallon

The 3D effects in the new *Star Wars* movie are so realistic, you can actually see George Lucas reaching from the screen and taking the money from your wallet.

Craig Ferguson

North Korea referred to *The Interview* as absolutely intolerable and a wanton act of terror. Even more amazing? Not the worst review the movie got.

Tina Fey

In *Titanic*, James Cameron had to invent a Romeo-and-Juliet-style fictional couple to heat up what was a real-life catastrophe. This seems a tiny bit like giving Anne Frank a wacky best friend to perk up the attic.

Libby Gelman-Waxner (Paul Rudnick)

Richard Curtis calls me about Comic Relief every year without fail, and says, 'Want to go to Africa? It's riddled with AIDS, poverty and war.' I say, 'No, it sounds awful.' He also asked me to be in *Love Actually*. I said, 'So, tell me about that Africa trip again.'

Ricky Gervais

(on 3D films): It seems like everything this year was three-dimensional, except the characters in *The Tourist*.

Ricky Gervais, hosting the 2011 Golden Globes

Just got back from *Fight Club*. It was really fun! Got there late so missed the rules being read out but I'm sure it was nothing important.

Phil Gibson via Twitter

Not everyone who wants to make a film is crazy, but almost everyone who is crazy wants to make a film.

Clive James, *May Week Was In June*

Did you ever see the French movie *And*? I think it was released in this country as *ET*.

Milton Jones

Where did people go to eat popcorn before films were invented?

Miles Kington

Think of it as a carefully constructed entertainment for the benefit of people who really, really like beer commercials.

Anthony Lane, on *Lock, Stock and Two Smoking Barrels*

The Catholic Church is still very angry about *The Da Vinci Code*. They don't like anything that makes more money in a weekend than they do.

Jay Leno

Pearl Harbor the movie, arguably, was worse than the invasion itself.

Marc Maron

The best thing about buying illegal DVDs is that you don't have to sit through the warning not to buy illegal DVDs at the start. It just goes straight into the film.

Dara O'Briain

The producers of the *X-Men* movies say their next movie will take place in the 1990s. In it, the X-Men use their superpowers to try and stop the Backstreet Boys.

Conan O'Brien

Unlikely lines from a thriller . . . 'Ah, Pussy Galore, Bond here. I've been told by my doctor that I need to contact all previous partners . . .'

Andy Parsons, *Mock the Week*

They should make a sequel to *Groundhog Day,* but it's the exact same movie.

Will Phillips, Twitter

I saw *Wedding Crashers* accidentally. I bought a ticket for *Grizzly Man* and went into the wrong theatre. After an hour, I figured I was in the wrong theatre, but I kept waiting. 'Cause that's the thing about bear attacks – they come when you least expect it.

Dwight Schrute (Rainn Wilson), *The Office* (US)

A movie that only an eight-year-old Christian environmentalist could love.

Dana Stevens, on *Evan Almighty*

(of *Trainspotting*): Mother walked out – not a locomotive in sight.

Mary Taylor (Patti Clare), *Coronation Street*

Oh God, did you rent *Pretty Woman* again? Face it, Grace, the only things you and Julia Roberts have in common are horse teeth and bad taste in men.

Karen Walker (Megan Mullally), *Will & Grace*

I saw a poster for *Mission Impossible III* the other day. I thought, 'It's not impossible if he's already done it twice.'

Mark Watson

The Hobbit is so unrealistic. How are that many guys with beards not in a band?

Bridger Winegar, Twitter

I can almost always tell if a movie doesn't use real dinosaurs.

Bridger Winegar, Twitter

Andy Millman (Ricky Gervais): I think you doing this is so commendable – you know, using your profile to keep the message alive about the Holocaust.
Kate Winslet (herself): My God, I'm not doing it for that. And I don't think we really need another film about the Holocaust, do we? It's like, how many have there been? You know, we get it; it was grim, move on. No, I'm doing it because I've noticed that if you do a film about the Holocaust – guaranteed Oscar!

Extras

Last time I went to the movies, I was thrown out for bringing my own food. My argument was that the concession stand prices are outrageous. Besides, I haven't had a barbecue in a long time.

Steven Wright

Music

American rock has a sort of self-pitying whine to it.

Bill Bailey

I chose the tuba based on this theory: if you're not cool enough to be a cheerleader, make sure you're carrying something big enough to knock one on her ass.

Amy Barnes

This country singer before every song would go, 'This is a beautiful little song and it goes a little something like this.' I felt like saying, 'Mate, just play it exactly how it goes. How long have you been playing it for? You haven't nailed it yet?'

Carl Barron

MTV is to music as KFC is to chicken.

Lewis Black

The British love of queuing and discomfort and being bossed around seems to have found a new outlet in the pop festival.

Craig Brown

Punk was over in two years. That was the only good thing about it.

Julie Burchill

Piracy doesn't kill music, boy bands do.

Ricky Gervais, Twitter

I went to a record store. They said they specialised in hard-to-find records. Nothing was alphabetised.

Mitch Hedberg

Penny (Kaley Cuoco): Leonard, I didn't know you played the cello.
Leonard Hofstadter (Johnny Galecki): Yeah, my parents felt that naming me Leonard and putting me in advanced placement classes wasn't getting me beaten up enough.

The Big Bang Theory

There's an easy way to make someone sound less powerful; just put DJ in front of their name . . . like DJ Abraham Lincoln.

Demetri Martin

The electric guitar – like making love – is much improved by a little feedback, but completely ruined by too much.

Simon Munnery

You wouldn't catch me at one of those festivals. Three days in a tent, shitting in a bucket like the victim of a natural disaster.

Robin (Robert Webb), *The Smoking Room*

I fell asleep watching the country music channel and woke up racist.

Daniel Tosh

Marty DiBergi (Rob Reiner): It's very pretty.
Nigel Tufnel (Christopher Guest): You know, just simple lines intertwining, very much like . . . I'm really influenced by Bach and Mozart and it's sort of in between those really.
Marty: What do you call this?
Nigel: Well, this piece is called 'Lick My Love Pump'.

– *This Is Spinal Tap*

Men: when listening to your favourite CD, simply turn up the sound to the volume you desire, then turn it down three notches. This saves your wife having to do it.

Top Tips, *Viz*

Musicians

Phil Collins is losing his hearing, making him the luckiest man at a Phil Collins concert.

Simon Amstell, *Never Mind the Buzzcocks*

My sister's going to be in the Sugababes for her gap year.

Simon Amstell, *Never Mind the Buzzcocks*

I found a Justin Bieber concert ticket nailed to a tree, so I took it. You never know when you might need a nail.

Anon

The death of Rick Parfitt merely emphasised that 2016 was a bad year for the status quo.

Anon

Deep down, it really is just a meaningless lyric. 'I got soul, but I'm not a soldier'. You may as well be saying, 'I got ham, but I'm not a hamster'.

Bill Bailey, on the lyrics for The Killers' 'All These Things That I've Done'

If you thought 2016 was bad, I'm releasing an album in 2017.

James Blunt

will.i.am has been romantically linked to Cheryl Cole. When asked if he was going to enter into a long-term relationship with her, he changed his name to will.i.fuck.

Frankie Boyle, *Never Mind the Buzzcocks*

[Kasabian] have an important role to play: they are there to remind us how true *Spinal Tap* was.

Billy Bragg

To attack Dylan for impoliteness is a bit like attacking Humpty Dumpty for being egg-shaped or an octopus for being all hands. Impoliteness is the whole point of Bob Dylan.

Craig Brown

WARNING: if you see posts offering a free clip of the new Nickelback album DO NOT CLICK. It links to a free clip of the new Nickelback album.

Sean Cranbury, Twitter

Which Mumford is the dad?

Rob Delaney, on Mumford & Sons, Twitter

Most of One Direction are so bland and nothingy that you wonder if they could get an automatic door to open for 'em. I've seen holograms with more presence.

Danny Dyer

Lady Gaga is like a carnival ride. From a distance she looks fun, but up close, you don't want to climb on that.

Bill Engvall

Michael Bolton has had nine hits this year . . . on his website.

Dame Edna Everage (Barry Humphries)

I used to be in a band called Missing Cat. You probably saw our posters.

Stewart Francis

(of brother Liam): He's rude, arrogant, intimidating and lazy. He's the angriest man you'll ever meet. He's like a man with a fork in a world of soup.

Noel Gallagher

My musical knowledge is so poor I thought Kanye West was a railway station and Lana Del Rey a holiday destination.

Miranda Hart

With Michael Jackson, what I thought was really interesting was people saying, 'He looked really well in that final video.' No, he didn't. He looked like someone had melted goat's cheese over a sex doll.

Russell Howard

Beyoncé and pathos are strangers. Amy Winehouse and pathos are flat-mates, and you should see the kitchen.

Clive James

Never should it be said that [Rod] Stewart hasn't done his bit for female emancipation. He's seen more sex than a policeman's torch.

Dylan Jones

Barry Manilow famously wrote the words, 'I can't smile, I can't sing, I'm finding it hard to do anything'. Not only the lyrics to one of his biggest hits but also Geri Halliwell's CV.

Mark Lamarr, *Never Mind the Buzzcocks*

When Carlos Santana first met his future wife Deborah, he said, 'She smelled like something I wanted to wake up next to for the rest of my life.' It's beautiful, isn't it? Finding a woman who smells like a bacon sandwich.

Mark Lamarr, *Never Mind the Buzzcocks*

The Rolling Stones say their current US tour is a lot harder than their first, when we had only thirteen states.

Jay Leno

Do you think Beethoven had any inkling in even the darkest recesses of his unconscious, when he was deaf and sweating over his fifth symphony, that one day it would emit from some idiot's pocket and the response would be, 'Hey, it's my mom!'

Marc Maron

The White Stripes are teaming up with The Black Keys to form A Piano.

Ally Maynard, Twitter

Today the stock market plunged six hundred points and One Direction announced they're breaking up. Yes, both of these things happened. It was good timing for me because when people asked why I was sobbing uncontrollably, I was able to blame it on the stock market.

Conan O'Brien

Sometimes I'm scared of being Ozzy Osbourne, but it could have been worse. I could have been Sting.

Ozzy Osbourne

Have you seen U2's live show? It's boring as hell. It's like watching CNN.

Sharon Osbourne

That was 'Big Yellow Taxi' by Joni Mitchell, a song in which Joni complains, 'They paved paradise to put up a parking lot', a measure which actually would have alleviated traffic congestion on the outskirts of paradise, something which Joni singularly fails to point out, perhaps because it doesn't quite fit in with her blinkered view of the world. Nevertheless, nice song.

Alan Partridge (Steve Coogan), *I'm Alan Partridge*

'Sunday Bloody Sunday'. What a great song. It really encapsulates the frustration of a Sunday, doesn't it? You wake up in the morning, you've got to read all the Sunday papers, the kids are running around, you've got to mow the lawn, wash the car, and you just think, 'Sunday, bloody Sunday!'

Alan Partridge (Steve Coogan), *I'm Alan Partridge*

Wings? They're only the band the Beatles could have been.

Alan Partridge (Steve Coogan), *I'm Alan Partridge*

There's nothing more depressing than seeing a band come off stage at a festival, go back stage and just flip their laptop open at online shopping . . . and have some chicken and broccoli.

Kasabian's Serge Pizzorno

I do think certain kinds of music can make you violent. Like, when I listen to Nickelback, it makes me want to kill Nickelback.

Brian Posehn

In America, some people are still upset about Michael Jackson, a singer and dancer who, across a forty-year career, became famous, changed colour and died.

Steve Punt, *The Now Show*

I was very unfortunate in that I was born to very loving and rich parents and I never wanted for anything. I think that's held me back.

Pat Quid (Paul Whitehouse), *The Life of Rock with Brian Pern*

True or false? Jim Kerr from Simple Minds was born in Spain and orginially christened Juan.

Vic Reeves, *Shooting Stars*

We're very lucky in the band that we have two visionaries, David and Nigel, they're like poets, y'know, like Shelley and Byron. They're two distinct types of visionaries – it's like fire and ice, basically. I feel my role in the band is to be somewhere in the middle of that, kind of like lukewarm water.

Derek Smalls (Harry Shearer), *This Is Spinal Tap*

Kiss is like a smell in a paper bag: they just never go away.

Twisted Sister's Dee Snider

I don't care how cute those children are. If I hear one song from that classic rock outfit Journey, I will start pulling catheters.

Sue Sylvester (Jane Lynch), *Glee*

We believed that anything that was worth doing was worth overdoing.

Aerosmith's Steven Tyler

Rod Stewart is a man of principle. He absolutely will not go out with a woman with brown hair.

David Walliams

What's the difference between God and Bono? God doesn't wander down Grafton Street [Dublin] thinking he's Bono.

Louis Walsh

Keith Richards is the only man who can make the Osbournes look Amish.

Robin Williams

We may all be dead and gone, but Keith Richards will still be there with five cockroaches. He'll be going, 'I smoked your uncle, did you know that?'

Robin Williams

I wonder what would happen if Franz Ferdinand were assassinated.

Glenn Wool

Names

How would you like to go through life with the name Cooper Banks-McKenzie? The kid's gonna sound like a law firm.

Matty Banks (Kieran Culkin), Father of the Bride Part II

If you'd spent your life being called Gyles Brandreth, you would crawl across broken glass to achieve the bliss, the simplicity, the purity, the joy of simply being called Bob.

Gyles Brandreth

Greg Focker (Ben Stiller): Gaylord is my legal name. Nobody's called me by it since third grade.
Denny Byrnes (Jon Abrahams): Wait a minute, so your name is Gay Focker?

Meet the Parents

People always give their kids famous names now. I was in Boots the other day and the girl serving me was called Mmmm . . . Danone.

Alan Carr

I've got a friend whose nickname is 'Shagger'. You might think that's pretty cool. She doesn't like it.

Jimmy Carr

We grew up laughing at Frank Zappa for calling his daughter Moon Unit, but today we're naming our kids after remote Himalayan villages and exotic cheeses.

Jeremy Clarkson, *And Another Thing . . .*

We had a Jimmy Glasscock at school. You could always see when he was coming.

Alan Davies, *QI*

When my daughter was born, she had jaundice. She was all round and yellow. We called her Melanie.

Milton Jones

I was in Hawaii, on the Big Island. The 'Big Island', that name cracks me up. First of all, it's not that big, so I'm pretty sure a guy came up with that name.

Carol Leifer

(of Angus Deayton): His name is Angus. The 'G' is silent.

Paul Merton

Louise: beautiful British name. Means born on a council estate.

Al Murray, The Pub Landlord

There was a period where our child's birth was getting really close, and we still had nothing. We were dangerously close to calling him Untitled Baby Project.

Paul Reiser

Marty DiBergi (Rob Reiner): David St Hubbins . . . I must admit I've never heard anybody with that name.

David St Hubbins (Michael McKean): It's an unusual name. He's not a very well-known saint. He was the patron saint of quality footwear.

This Is Spinal Tap

I knew a girl at school called Pandora. Never got to see her box, though.

Spike (Rhys Ifans), *Notting Hill*

You know what was hard for me, coming up with names for our children. I panic when I have to name a new document on my computer. I got so desperate toward the end of my wife's third pregnancy I found myself reading the credits at the end of movies, looking for names – which means at some point I'll have to explain to my little boy that he was named after the key grip on *Dude, Where's My Car?*

Jeff Stilson

Neighbours

My bloody neighbour banged on my front door at two-thirty this morning. Thank God I was still up, playing the drums.

Jo Brand

I love my neighbourhood. It's so quiet there. Especially since the gangs started using silencers.

Woody Boyd (Woody Harrelson), *Cheers*

The tone of this neighbourhood has always been my business! It is not without enormous effort on my part that this district has one of the most sought-after postal codes.

Hyacinth Bucket (Patricia Routledge), *Keeping Up Appearances*

My neighbour is in *Guinness World Records* for having forty-three concussions. He lives very close – just a stone's throw away.

Stewart Francis

Dorien Green (Lesley Joseph): Good afternoon, neighbours.

Sharon Theodopolopoudos (Pauline Quirke): It was, up until now.

Dorien: Now, now, Sharon. Fat people are supposed to be jolly; it's a tradition.

Birds of a Feather

Run along home now, Gail. The curtains won't twitch themselves, you know.

Eileen Grimshaw (Sue Cleaver), *Coronation Street*

My neighbour complains every time my girlfriend and I have sex. We're not that loud, but he used to date my girlfriend.

Anthony Jeselnik

I ordered a book on the internet, *How To Have Absolutely Nothing To Do With Your Neighbours*. Unfortunately, I was out when it was delivered.

Milton Jones

Netherlands

My experience in Amsterdam is that cyclists ride where the hell they like and aim, in a state of rage, at all pedestrians while ringing their bell loudly, the concept of avoiding people being foreign to them. My dream holiday would be a) a ticket to Amsterdam b) immunity from prosecution and c) a baseball bat.

Sir Terry Pratchett

Newspapers and Magazines

Open government, Prime Minister. Freedom of information. We should always tell the press freely and frankly anything that they could easily find out some other way.

Sir Humphrey Appleby (Nigel Hawthorne), *Yes, Prime Minister*

There are moments when we in the British press can show extraordinary sensitivity; these moments usually coincide with the death of a proprietor or a proprietor's wife.

Craig Brown

Journalism could be described as turning one's enemies into money.

Craig Brown

The problem is that if you say to a journalist, 'Can you avoid that topic?', that's when they really go for it. It's like saying to the school bully, 'I'll wet myself if you tickle me.'

Terri Coverly (Joanna Scanlan), *The Thick of It*

How can one not be fond of something that the *Daily Mail* despises?

Stephen Fry

Never worry about bad press. All that matters is that they spell your name right.

Kate Hudson

I've read more about Oprah Winfrey's ass than I have about the rise of China as an economic superpower. I fear this is no exaggeration. Perhaps China is rising as an economic superpower because its women aren't spending all their time reading about Oprah Winfrey's ass.

Caitlin Moran, *How To Be a Woman*

On the plus side, Katie Hopkins said she would leave the UK to live in America. Need help packing?

@Not_A_Doormat, Twitter, on Donald Trump winning the 2016 US presidential election

People who read the tabloids deserve to be lied to.

Jerry Seinfeld

What are we going to do? You're unemployed. I've got no money coming in. How am I going to afford aspirational magazines?

Daisy Steiner (Jessica Stevenson), *Spaced*

Edina Monsoon (Jennifer Saunders): Patsy's got that [magazine] job for life.

Saffron Monsoon (Julia Sawalha): You don't mean to say she's actually good at something?

Edina: No, darling, she slept with the publisher.

Patsy Stone (Joanna Lumley): And I'm bloody good at it!

Absolutely Fabulous

North Korea

Kim Jong-un reportedly threw a huge outdoor dance party to celebrate the successful test of North Korea's ballistic missile. Residents described the party as fun, exciting and mandatory.

Jimmy Fallon

Experts say one of the biggest threats facing Donald Trump's presidency could be North Korea. Evidently, Kim Jong-un is so incompetent and unstable, they're worried Trump will give him a Cabinet post.

Conan O'Brien

Nostalgia

My grandfather always said that, in the old days, people could leave their back doors open. Which is probably why his submarine sank.

Milton Jones

Nostalgia is heroin for old people.

Dara O'Briain

Uncle Albert Trotter (Buster Merryfield): You know, once upon a time, ships from all over the world used to sail in here. The water used to be covered with a film of oil and when the sun shone on it, it sparkled, all different colours. When I was a kid, I used to think rainbows lived in the water.

Del Trotter (David Jason): So you was a bit of a divvy in them days an' all, were you?

Only Fools and Horses

Under my derationalisation programme. Yorkshire would get back its Ridings, the red telephone box would be a preserved species, there would be Pullman cars called Edna, a teashop in every High Street and a proper card index in the public library.

Keith Waterhouse

Nudity

Celia (Celia Imrie): I've never been naked in front of anyone in my life.

Chris Harper (Helen Mirren): Not even Frank?

Celia: Frank's a major. We approach nudity on a strictly need-to-know basis.

Calendar Girls

Nudists are like people who do amateur dramatics: those who are most enthusiastic are those who should do it least.

Jeremy Hardy

The last time I was this naked in public I was coming out of a uterus.

Gracie Hart (Sandra Bullock), *Miss Congeniality*

I went to a nude beach for the first time. I thought it would be all sexy and hot, but what a flubber fest! It didn't make me want to take off my clothes, it made me want to take out my contacts.

Carol Leifer

I was driving along the highway and I saw a sign that said, 'Live Nude Girls'. And I was thinking, You probably don't need the 'live'. I wasn't even thinking about the girls' mortality until you brought it up.

Demetri Martin

(to Demi Moore): Would you ever consider keeping your clothes on if the script demanded it?

Dennis Pennis (Paul Kaye)

Obesity

My husband is almost as heavy as I am. We were married in adjoining churches.

Roseanne Barr

You know you're getting fat when you step on the dog's tail and it dies.

Elayne Boosler

You know you are fat when you hug a child and it gets lost.

Marcus Brigstocke

When I was a kid, I used to hate getting picked for team sports. It would be the fit and sporty guys over there, and me and the fat kids over here. Those kids were fat! One girl had to be cut out of a hula hoop!

Alan Carr

My friend was told by her doctor that she was morbidly obese . . . as if she doesn't have enough on her plate.

Jimmy Carr

There's a lot of discrimination against obese people in the NHS. I knew one doctor who would write 'DTS' in the notes, which means 'Danger to Shipping'.

Dr Phil Hammond

Anti-wrinkle cream there may be, but anti-fat bastard cream there is none.

Dave Horsefall (Mark Addy), *The Full Monty*

There is an obesity epidemic. One out of every three Americans weighs as much as the other two.

Richard Jeni

I decided to lose weight as I have learned obesity is the leading cause of heart disease, stroke, and your flirting at work being construed as harassment.

Pete Johansson

When you have a fat friend, there are no see-saws, only catapults.

Demetri Martin

There's a song called 'Big Girls Don't Cry'. Yeah, they do, 'cause they're fat, 'cause they can't get a boyfriend and 'cause there's no trifle left.

Sarah Millican

You know what African mothers tell their children every day? 'Be grateful for what you have. Because there are fat children starving in Mississippi.'

Trevor Noah

Due to the recent heatwave, doctors are warning obese people to stay indoors – not for their health, but because no one wants to see them in short pants.

Conan O'Brien

I stay fat because it just wouldn't be fair to all the thin people if I were this good-looking, intelligent, funny and thin. It's a public service really.

Rebel Wilson

Occupations and Professions

Give a man a fish, and you'll feed him for a day. Teach a man to fish, and he'll buy a funny hat. Talk to a hungry man about fish, and you're a consultant.

Scott Adams

The only options for girls then were mother, secretary or teacher. At least, that's what we all thought and were preparing ourselves for. Now, I must say how lucky we are, as women, to live in an age where 'dental hygienist' has been added to the list.

Roseanne Barr

He works in pizza delivery, which just answers all your prayers, doesn't it? Man, motorbike, has own food!

Jane Christie (Gina Bellman), *Coupling*

Richard Finch (Neil Pearson): Why do you want to work in television?
Bridget Jones (Renée Zellweger): I've got to leave my job because I shagged my boss.
Richard: Fair enough. Start on Monday.

Bridget Jones's Diary

I quit my job at the helium gas factory. I refused to be spoken to in that tone.

Stewart Francis

I remember the shouts of 'Scab!' as my father went to work during the great dermatologists' strike.

Harry Hill

I used to work in a shoe recycling shop. It was sole-destroying.

Alex Horne

'Early in the morning when the day is dawning'?! Your real Postman Pat rolls up around noon wearing a pair of shorts and his breakfast. And if he's not chucking elastic bands around like confetti he'll be rifling through your birthday cards for cash or leaving your valuables on the step.

Blanche Hunt (Maggie Jones), *Coronation Street*

The worst job I ever had was as a forensic scientist. Once I thought I'd come across the mass grave of a thousand snowmen, but it turns out it was just a field of carrots.

Milton Jones

My wife travels a lot with her job. She's a drug mule. They're always on the go.

Brian Kiley

A guy gave me a job at an information booth, no questions asked.

Jay London

If you enjoy shaming people, I suggest denistry as a profession.

Bonnie McFarlane

In Hawaii, I was the chief chunker in a pineapple canning factory. I used to come home smelling like a compote.

Bette Midler

Receptionists are just secretaries who can't type.

Al Murray, The Pub Landlord

Noël Coward said work is more fun than fun, but then he didn't work in the Bird's Eye factory packing frozen fish fingers nine hours a day, did he?

Paul O'Grady

I got a job as a litter removal man. I didn't have any training – I just thought I'd pick it up as I go along.

Tim Vine

Old Age

———

I'm getting old but at least I can multi-task now. I piss when I sneeze.

Roseanne Barr

At eighty, things do not occur; they recur.

Alan Bennett, *The Uncommon Reader*

Surely getting old is just depressing. Being married in your sixties is like being a member of the National Trust – you've got free entry to an old ruin but nobody wants to use it.

Frankie Boyle, *Mock the Week*

Old people shouldn't be allowed to have sex because there is a certain age when the body's fluids stop running. I don't want to be too graphic, but if you've ever tried eating muesli without any milk . . .

Marcus Brigstocke, *Argumental*

Old? I stopped ageing at thirty-eight. I still am thirty-eight . . . except when they say, 'Run up those stairs.'

Sir Michael Caine

I think it would be interesting if old people got anti-Alzheimer's disease where they slowly began to recover other people's lost memories.

George Carlin

My nan used to say, 'Run up the stairs, your legs are younger than mine.' I'd say, 'No, they're not. You've had two hip replacements and a plastic knee; from the waist down you're a toddler.'

Alan Carr

You cannot correct an old person every time they say something offensive. You would never make it through Thanksgiving dinner.

Stephen Colbert

I won't say that all senior citizens who can't master technology should be publicly flogged, but if we made an example of one or two, it might give the others the incentive to try harder.

Sheldon Cooper (Jim Parsons), *The Big Bang Theory*

Older people are still people. They're just people who think when they open a new window on the computer that the previous window has disappeared for good.

Mark Corrigan (David Mitchell), *Peep Show*

A sure sign that you're getting old is when a bag for life is something you have fitted.

Jack Dee

Come on, everybody, party's over, let's be having ya. And you, Tommy, come on, you better hurry up or your mates'll lock the gates back at the cemetery.

Pub landlord Ken Dixon (John Henshaw), *Early Doors*

Pomposity and indignation grow in old age, like nostril hairs and earlobes.

Stephen Fry, *The Fry Chronicles*

Senior citizens' chat-up line . . . I could take you to a hip joint.

Graeme Garden, *I'm Sorry I Haven't a Clue*

You know you're getting old when you start to like your mum and dad again. 'Yes, I'd love to come caravanning to Tenby with you. No, I'll bring a packed lunch. I'm not paying café prices.'

Jeff Green

Kids, your grandfather's ears are not gross and they're certainly not an enchanted forest.

Lois Griffin (Alex Borstein), *Family Guy*

Everyone over fifty should be issued every week with a wet fish in a plastic bag by the Post Office so that, whenever you see someone young and happy, you can hit them as hard as you can across the face.

Richard Griffiths

Chloe (Emma Pike): Those old people are swingers.
Susan Harper (Zoë Wanamaker): Swingers? As in Glenn Miller or as in Glenn Miller, his wife and the rest of his band?

My Family

You're going to have to learn to take pleasure in the misfortunes of others, Ken, or you're going to have a very miserable old age.

Blanche Hunt (Maggie Jones), *Coronation Street*

Old ladies in wheelchairs with blankets over their legs? I don't think so. Retired mermaids.

Milton Jones

If you mention the idea of home birth to someone of an older generation, they're always instantly mistrustful. But that's just a generational thing, like racism and never indicating.

Miles Jupp

Betty White is so old that on her first game show ever, the grand prize was fire.

Lisa Lampanelli

Why is it old people say, 'There's no place like home', yet when you put them in one . . . ?

Stuart Mitchell

The great thing about the elderly is that there's always a conversational trump card: health. It's a topic that distracts them like chocolate buttons distract a labrador (or me).

Victoria Coren Mitchell

As you grow old, you lose interest in sex, your friends drift away and your children often ignore you. There are other advantages, of course, but these are the outstanding ones.

Sir Richard Needham

It's not so nice when you are seventy-one and looking for some action. Happily, when it comes to girls hitting on me, I'm not undernourished.

Jack Nicholson, 2008

The human male is physically capable of enjoying sex up to and even beyond the age of eighty. Not as a participant, of course . . .

Denis Norden

Sex is better when you're older, because we don't have to change our sheets. The nurses do it for us.

Joan Rivers

You know you're getting old when you get that one candle on the cake. It's like, 'See if you can blow this out.'

Jerry Seinfeld

I did a gig at an old people's home. Tough crowd. They wouldn't respond to my knock-knock jokes until I showed ID.

Frank Skinner

Dorothy Zbornak (Bea Arthur): Ma, I cannot believe that all these years you've been hoarding away all this money.
Sophia Petrillo (Estelle Getty): Dorothy, please. That money is for my old age.
Dorothy: Old age?! Ma, you don't leave fingerprints anymore!

The Golden Girls

Olympic Games

The synchronised swimmers would've kept their stories straight.

Nelson Bighetti, Twitter, after 'Lochtegate' at the 2016 Rio Olympics

It's good they're holding the Olympics in the East End of London. It means the athletes will have to use extra skills to work out which gunshot is the starting pistol.

Frankie Boyle, on the 2012 Olympics

Would you like the oldest, most historically significant athletic competition the world has ever known, attracting athletes from every known nation on the face of the planet, to come here and perform at the peak of their abilities, in the very city where you live? Most Londoners go, 'Where will we park?'

Marcus Brigstocke, on the 2012 Olympics

Just let everyone do drugs or make peeing in a cup into an Olympic sport.

James Corden

Where are the Olympics for people with minor afflictions? Dressage for haemorrhoid sufferers? The 4 x 100 relay for multiple personality disorders?

Hal Cruttenden

[Ryan] Lochte won five medals in London and only two of them are damaged when he tried to find out if there was chocolate inside.

Jon Hamm

Performance-enhancing drugs are banned in the Olympics. OK, we can swing with that. But performance-debilitating drugs should not be banned. Smoke a joint and win the 100 metres, fair play to you. That's pretty damn good. Unless someone's dangling a Mars Bar off in the distance.

Eddie Izzard

As I write these words there are semi-naked women playing beach volley-ball in the middle of the Horse Guards Parade . . . They are glistening like wet otters.

Boris Johnson at the 2012 Olympics

Every Olympic event should include one average person competing, for reference.

Bill Murray

The Olympic torch arrived in Rio in preparation for the opening ceremony. And the cool thing about Rio is, if the torch runs out of fuel, you can just dip it in the ocean and it'll reignite.

Seth Meyers

I retain no knowledge from one Olympics to the next. Every time, 'What's a repechage? What's the peloton? Is judo fought to the death?'

Olly Richards via Twitter

The Olympics is really my favourite sporting event. Although I have a problem with the silver medal. Because when you think about it, when you win the gold, you feel good. You win the bronze, you think, At least I got something. But when you win the silver, it's like, 'Congratulations, you almost won. Of all the losers you came in first of that group. You're the number one loser. No one lost ahead of you.'

Jerry Seinfeld

The Olympics is a giant competition to determine whose ruined childhoods were worth it.

Julius Sharpe, Twitter

When sychronised swimming first appeared on TV, we laughed very heartily and I, for one, applauded the decision to introduce humour into the Olympics.

Arthur Smith

Aristotle compiled the first known comprehensive list of all winners of the Olympic Games. Which means that quite probably he was sat in a bar with Plato, muttering, 'Go on then, give me any year you like and I'll tell you who won the four-man bobsleigh.'

Mark Steel

There are too many weird Olympic events now, like that one where the gymnasts prance around the mat swirling a piece of ribbon. It's called rhythmic gymnastics – unless you're five, then it's called playing.

Jeff Stilson

The Olympics are for everyone, not just someone who happens to own a dancing horse.

Glenn Wool, on dressage

Opera

His productions are brilliant! He staged a Philip Glass opera last year and no one left.

Niles Crane (David Hyde Pierce), *Frasier*

The only thing worse than opera is someone who hums along with opera.

Josh Lanyon, *A Dangerous Thing*

Oral Sex

(on his friend Will's dilemma): She's offering to put your penis in her mouth, not paying you to lie in parliament.

Simon Cooper (Joe Thomas), *The Inbetweeners*

Who do I have to blow to never have to blow anyone, ever again?

Whitney Cummings

Receiving oral sex from an ugly person is like rock climbing; you should never look down.

Stewart Francis

I will not be judged by you or society. I will wear whatever and blow whomever I want as long as I can breathe – and kneel.

Samantha Jones (Kim Cattrall), *Sex and the City*

My mother told me: 'You don't have to put anything in your mouth you don't want to.' Then she made me eat broccoli, which felt like double standards.

Sarah Millican

I was licking jelly off my boyfriend's penis and all of a sudden I'm thinking, 'Oh my God, I'm turning into my mother!'

Sarah Silverman

Orgasm

I give women two types of orgasm: fake and none.

Adam Carolla

I'm thirty-three years old; I haven't outgrown the problems of puberty; I'm already facing the problems of old age. I completely skipped healthy adulthood. I went from having orgasms immediately to taking forever. You could do your taxes in the time it takes me to have an orgasm.

George Costanza (Jason Alexander), *Seinfeld*

Yes, Martin, I have learned my lesson: if you're going to shag a pie-eating mummy's boy, then at least choose one who knows the difference between a sneeze and an orgasm.

Karen (Tanya Franks), *Pulling*

Having an orgasm for women is something you need to practise for yourself, over time, like Etch A Sketch or the Fosbury Flop.

Rachel Parris

To a man, sex is like a car accident, and trying to determine a female orgasm is like asking, 'What did you see after the car went out of control?' 'Well, there were a lot of screeching noises, I was facing the wrong way at one point and, in the end, my body was thrown clear.'

Jerry Seinfeld

Guys always wonder, why do we fake it? To get you the hell off us!

Wanda Sykes

Paranoia

Paranoia is a bad personality trait for a comedian . . . What are you laughing at?

Danny Bhoy

No, I don't think you're paranoid. I think you're the opposite of paranoid. I think you walk around with the insane delusion that people like you.

Harry Block (Woody Allen), Deconstructing Harry

Being slightly paranoid is like being slightly pregnant – it tends to get worse.

Molly Ivins

Parties

I'm somewhat socially inept. Slide me between two strangers at any light-hearted jamboree and I'll either rock awkwardly and silently on my heels or I'll come out with a stone-cold conversation-killer like, 'This room's quite rectangular, isn't it?' I glide through the social whirl with all the elegance of a dog in high heels.

Charlie Brooker

Somewhere in the back of their minds, hosts and guests alike know that the dinner party is a source of untold irritation and that even the dullest evening spent watching television is preferable.

Craig Brown

When I'm in social situations, I always hold on to my glass. It makes me feel comfortable and secure, and I don't have to shake hands.

Larry David (himself), Curb Your Enthusiasm

Lines that would change the atmosphere at a dinner party . . . 'Help yourself to Nibbles – he was our favourite hamster.'

Hugh Dennis, Mock the Week

Hosting your children's party is like an exercise in riot control. You find yourself spotting the ringleaders, appealing to the more moderate children to try and keep order, abandoning the living room to the mob and trying to consolidate your power base in the kitchen.

Jeremy Hardy

My wife and I want to try swapping. We want to go to one of those key parties where you put your keys in a bowl. But we just want to upgrade our car.

Andy Kindler

Margaret Meldrew (Annette Crosbie): You haven't forgotten we're going to Ronnie and Mildred's tonight?
Victor Meldrew (Richard Wilson): I try to forget we're going to Ronnie and Mildred's tonight, like you try to forget you're going to die, but it doesn't work.

One Foot in the Grave

The last time I went back to a girl's house for an impromptu house party, I spent most of the night straightening out rugs, putting down coasters and alphabetising DVDs while all around me, people got off with whoever was closest and gradually headed off to various rooms – to make more mess, no doubt.

Jon Richardson

Susan Mayer (Teri Hatcher): How could we have all forgotten about this?
Lynette Scavo (Felicity Huffman): We didn't exactly forget; it's just usually when the hostess dies, the party is off.

Desperate Housewives

I went to a party dressed as sodium chloride. Someone threw hydrochloric acid over me. I didn't know how to react.

Tim Vine

I once went to one of those parties where everyone throws their car keys into the middle of the room. I don't know who got my moped, but I drove that Peugeot for years.

Victoria Wood

Patriotism

Sometimes I wonder if I'm patriotic enough. Yes, I want to kill people, but on both sides.

Jack Handey

Nationalism does nothing but teach you how to hate people that you never met.

Doug Stanhope

Peace

How come the dove gets to be the peace symbol? How about the pillow? It has more feathers than the dove and it doesn't have that dangerous beak.

Jack Handey

Everyone wants peace, and they will fight the most terrible war to get it.

Miles Kington

How are we going to achieve global peace if the world can't decide on one universal plug socket?

Chris Martin

People

I consider myself to be a pretty good judge of people – that's why I don't like any of them.

Roseanne Barr

The majority of people perform well in a crisis and when the spotlight is on them; it's on the Sunday afternoons of this life, when nobody is looking, that the spirit falters.

Alan Bennett, *Writing Home*

Creepy people do the things that decent people want to do, but have decided are not a great idea.

Mike Birbiglia

There are two types of people in the world: one who opens a packet of biscuits, has one and puts the rest back in the cupboard, and one who eats the whole packet in one go.

Jo Brand

In life there are two types of people: those who catch the waiter's eye and those who don't.

Gyles Brandreth, *Oscar Wilde and a Death of No Importance*

I can't abide other people, with their stink and their noise and their irritating ringtones. Bill Hicks called the human race 'a virus with shoes', and if you ask me he was being unduly hard on viruses. I'd consider a career in serial killing if the pay wasn't so bad.

Charlie Brooker, *Screen Burn*

I have no time for people like that. This one time, someone rang me, saying, 'If you come down to the corner, I'll let you see my willy.' The dirty bastard! He never showed up!

Agnes Brown (Brendan O'Carroll), *Mrs Brown's Boys*

People are like music; some speak the truth and others are just noise.

Bill Murray

There are two types of people in this world: there are those who have lots of casual sex with strangers, and jealous people.

– Ardal O'Hanlon

I haven't the slightest idea how to change people, but still I keep a long list of prospective candidates just in case I should ever figure it out.

David Sedaris, *Naked*

There is no such thing as an impartial jury because there are no impartial people. There are people that argue online for hours about who their favourite character in *Friends* is.

Jon Stewart

You have to remember one thing about the will of the people: it wasn't that long ago that we were swept away by the Macarena.

Jon Stewart

Periods

Gary doesn't understand periods. He thinks they're something to do with the moon.

Dorothy Bishop (Caroline Quentin), *Men Behaving Badly*

I have no problem with buying tampons. I am a fairly modern man. But apparently they're not a 'proper' present.

Jimmy Carr

A woman cut in front of me at the store with a box of tampons, ice cream and wine in her basket. I wasn't about to mess with that situation.

Abby Heugel, Twitter

She's so cold, sweetie, I'll just bet she has her period in cubes.

Edina Monsoon (Jennifer Saunders), *Absolutely Fabulous*

Periods are like a friend who comes bearing good news but then stays for a week, eats all your food and borrows and ruins your clothes.

Mara Wilson, Twitter

Perseverance

From watching my dad, I learned a lesson that still applies to life today. No matter how difficult a task may seem, if you're not afraid to try it – and if you really put your mind to it – you can do it. And when you're done, it will leak.

Dave Barry

My father was a quitter, my grandfather was a quitter, I was raised to give up. It's one of the few things I do well.

George Costanza (Jason Alexander), *Seinfeld*

Look, I'm a Simpson. And a Simpson never gives up until he tries at least one easy thing.

Bart Simpson (Nancy Cartwright), *The Simpsons*

In school they told me: 'Practice makes perfect'. And then they told me, 'Nobody's perfect', so then I stopped practising.

Steven Wright

Personality

You know, sometimes when I think you're the shallowest man I've ever met, you somehow manage to drain a little more out of the pool.

Elaine Benes (Julia Louis-Dreyfus), *Seinfeld*

I am in the pigeon-hole marked 'No threat' and did I stab Judi Dench with a pitchfork I should still be a teddy bear.

Alan Bennett, *Keeping On Keeping On*

The girl is wetter than a haddock's bathing costume.

Edmund Blackadder (Rowan Atkinson), *Blackadder the Third*

If you truly believe you need to pick a mobile phone that 'says something' about your personality, don't bother. You don't have a personality. A mental illness, maybe – but not a personality.

Charlie Brooker

Cher Horowitz (Alicia Silverstone): Would you call me selfish?
Dionne Davenport (Stacey Dash): No, not to your face.

Clueless

I'm not a competitive person. I'll be the first to admit it.

Stewart Francis

I keep my own personality in a cupboard under the stairs at home so that no one else can see it or nick it.

Dawn French

If you think a weakness can be turned into a strength, I hate to tell you this, but that's another weakness.

Jack Handey

Susan Harper (Zoë Wanamaker): You don't think I'm a control freak, do you?
Ben Harper (Robert Lindsay): No, no, course not. You're more of a control . . . enthusiast.

My Family

I'm superstitious, but not like 'wear the same underwear for two weeks' superstitious.

Kate Hudson

DCI Gene Hunt (Philip Glenister): I think you have forgotten who you are talking to.
DI Sam Tyler (John Simm): An overweight, over-the-hill, nicotine-stained, borderline-alcoholic homophobe with a superiority complex and an unhealthy obsession with male bonding.
DCI Hunt: You make that sound like a bad thing.

Life on Mars

I'm a man of my word, and that word is 'unreliable'.

Demetri Martin

Remember, when you're with me, it's the only time you're not the strangest person in the room.

Ally McBeal (Calista Flockhart), Ally McBeal

I'm compulsive, but I'm also very indecisive. I don't know what I want, but I know that I want it now.

Dylan Moran

I can tell people are judgemental just by looking at them.

Daniel Plainview, Twitter

I'm not superstitious, but I am a little stitious.

Michael Scott (Steve Carell), The Office (US)

All of us take pride and pleasure in the fact that we are unique, but I'm afraid that when all is said and done the police are right: it all comes down to fingerprints.

David Sedaris, Holidays on Ice

Whenever I hear girls say, 'I'm not religious, but I'm spiritual,' I like to reply with, 'I'm not honest, but you're interesting.'

Daniel Tosh

I am not a malicious woman, and I will strike down the first person who says I am.

Jill Tyrell (Julia Davis), Nighty Night

Pessimism

Kids do have to learn that life is a humiliating charade of endless disappointment and tragedy ultimately culminating in pain, decay and death. My parents used to sing me to sleep with that one.

Samantha Bee

I try to look on the bright side, but it really hurts my eyes.

Dana Gould

My mum's so pessimistic that if there was an Olympics for pessimism . . .
she wouldn't fancy her chances.

Nish Kumar

One thing you can be sure about in life: just when you think that things
are never ever going to get better, they suddenly get worse.

Victor Meldrew (Richard Wilson), One Foot in the Grave

I'm one of the more pessimistic cats on the planet. I make Van Gogh look
like a rodeo clown.

Dennis Miller

I've always been a pessimist. I like the thought of being some kind of
depressive drunk, smoking opium like some old poet. That's very
appealing.

Michael Parkinson

I'm a total pessimist. It's not the glass is half empty; someone stole the
glass.

Joan Rivers

Pets

I'm at the vet's. A man opposite me weeps with an empty cage in his arms.
I'd be crying too if I were that forgetful.

Anon

I had a parrot. The parrot talked, but it did not say, 'I'm hungry', so it died.

Mitch Hedberg

Pets are always a help in times of stress. And in times of starvation, too, of
course.

Sir Terry Pratchett, Small Gods

It reminds me of when my dad made me choose which of my pet calves to slaughter with my own hands for my sixth birthday. I couldn't choose, so I slaughtered both of them. And they were delicious.

Ron Swanson (Nick Offerman), *Parks and Recreation*

Philosophy

My philosophy is that every phone conversation has a loser.

Scott Adams

'If you want the rainbow, you've gotta put up with the rain.' Do you know which 'philosopher' said that? Dolly Parton. And people say she's just a big pair of tits.

David Brent (Ricky Gervais), *The Office*

As the wise man once said, 'So?'

Ron Burgundy (Will Ferrell), *Anchorman 2: The Legend Continues*

Sorry, two's company and three's an adult movie.

Roland T. Flakfizer (John Turturro), *Brain Donors*

I'm a firm believer that there's no such thing as the worst bits of anything. What we call worst bits are, in fact, just best bits with the wrong clothes on.

Ian Fletcher (Hugh Bonneville), *W1A*

You can't lick the system, but you can give it a damn good fondling.

Stephen Fry

Normal is nothing more than a cycle on a washing machine.

Whoopi Goldberg

Sometimes when you make an omelette you've got to break a few eggs. What's the alternative? No omelettes at all? Who wants to live in that kind of world? Maybe birds. Then all their babies would live.

Leslie Knope (Amy Poehler), *Parks and Recreation*

We do not go in for philosophy in this country. We have our own system. It's called wondering.

> Al Murray, The Pub Landlord

You know, another layer of icing on a shit cake doesn't make it taste good.

> Nicky Nichols (Natasha Lyonne), *Orange is the New Black*

I got an A in philosophy because I proved my professor didn't exist.

> Judy Tenuta

Police

Deputy Wendell (Garret Dillahunt): It's a mess, ain't it, Sheriff?
Sheriff Ed Tom Bell (Tommy Lee Jones): If it ain't, it'll do till the mess gets here.

> *No Country for Old Men*

I'll tell you what separates the men from the boys: Operation Yewtree.

> Maff Brown

Insp. Frank Butterman (Jim Broadbent): Your predecessor assumed rural policing was easy. Ended up having a nervous breakdown and Sergeant Powell was an exceptional officer. Truly exceptional. And he had one thing you haven't got.
Sgt. Nicholas Angel (Simon Pegg): What's that, sir?
Insp. Butterman: A great, big, bushy beard!

> *Hot Fuzz*

There was a time when the police in this country were friends of the church; speeding tickets torn up, drunk-driving charges quashed, even a blind eye turned to the odd murder!

> Father Ted Crilly (Dermot Morgan), *Father Ted*

Ed Hocken (George Kennedy): You haven't shot anybody in six months.
Lt. Frank Drebin (Leslie Nielsen): That's true. Funny how you miss the little things.

> *Naked Gun* $33\frac{1}{3}$*: The Final Insult*

State trooper (Harland Williams): Pull over!

Harry Dunne (Jeff Daniels): No, it's a cardigan, but thanks for noticing.

Dumb and Dumber

I don't like this. Gene Hunt smashes doors down, he does not pick girly locks.

DCI Gene Hunt (Philip Glenister), *Life on Mars*

A quick word about police brutality . . . plenty of it!

DCI Gene Hunt (Philip Glenister) about to
raid a suspect's house, *Ashes to Ashes*

Policemen know nothing about computers. I don't know if you've been down to PC World . . .

Milton Jones

There are only two places to get robbed: TV and the real world. On television you get your stuff back. In the real world, if you're lucky, the policeman who responds to your call will wonder what kind of computer it was. Don't let this get your hopes up. Chances are he's asking only because he has a software question.

David Sedaris, *Let's Explore Diabetes with Owls*

This policeman came up to me with a pencil and a piece of very thin paper. He said, 'I want you to trace someone for me.'

Tim Vine

In England, the police don't have a gun and you don't have a gun. If you commit a crime, the police will say, 'Stop or I'll say "Stop" again!'

Robin Williams

Political Correctness

A joke is either funny or it's not funny. If I hear a funny joke, you know what I do? I laugh, that's what I do. I don't start a focus group to see who got hurt by the joke.

Alonzo Bodden

Political correctness is the language of cowardice.

Billy Connolly

Pat Healy (Matt Dillon): I work with retards.
Mary Jensen (Cameron Diaz): Isn't that a little politically incorrect?
Pat: Yeah, maybe, but hell, no one's gonna tell me who I can and can't work with.

There's Something About Mary

Do you prefer 'fashion victim' or 'ensembly challenged'?

Cher Horowitz (Alicia Silverstone), *Clueless*

Political correctness seems to me to be about an institutionalised politeness at its worst.

Stewart Lee

Justin [Bieber]'s fans are called Beliebers because it's politically incorrect to use the word 'retards'.

Natasha Leggero

Maybe I should understand yobbos or not even call them yobbos. Call them 'young men with issues around stabbing'.

Peter Mannion (Roger Allam), *The Thick of It*

You're not allowed to call them dinosaurs anymore. It's speciesist. You have to call them pre-petroleum persons.

Sir Terry Pratchett, *Johnny and the Bomb*

Politicians

If he can't ignore facts, he's got no business being a politician.

Sir Humphrey Appleby (Nigel Hawthorne), *Yes, Prime Minister*

Sir Humphrey Appleby Nigel Hawthorne: We write him a speech that makes him nail his trousers to the mast.

Bernard Woolley (Derek Fowlds): Oh, you mean nail his colours to the mast.

Sir Humphrey: No, nail his trousers to the mast. Then he can't climb down.

Yes, Minister

It's what we've known for many years outside of Australia – you can't have a world leader called Kevin.

Bill Bailey, on Australian prime minister Kevin Rudd's ousting in 2010

I don't really want to hang out with politicians. I'd rather go straight to hell and not collect two hundred dollars.

Roseanne Barr

I dislike Ted Cruz as much as the next person. But that's no reason to be rude to Ted's loving wife and possible hostage.

Samantha Bee

You think the President of the United States wants to fuck every woman he meets . . . ? Well, bad example.

Harry Block (Woody Allen), *Deconstructing Harry*

Andrea Leadsom: a sort of defrosted Theresa May.

Frankie Boyle

He looks terrible, doesn't he, [Gordon] Brown? He looks like a sad face that someone has drawn onto their scrotum.

Frankie Boyle

Do you think George W. Bush actually knows who Gordon Brown is? He probably just thinks Tony Blair's put on weight and had a mild stroke.

Frankie Boyle

Three million [pounds] for the funeral of Margaret Thatcher? For three million, you could give everyone in Scotland a shovel and we could dig a hole so deep we could hand her over to Satan in person.

Frankie Boyle

Barack Obama didn't just appeal to black voters who think he'll change society. He also appealed to white voters who think he's Tiger Woods.

Frankie Boyle

I've got a soft spot for Nick Clegg – face down on Hackney Marshes.

Jo Brand

(of Nigel Farage): A pound-shop Enoch Powell.

Russell Brand

John Major, he dresses so well. And so quickly.

Gyles Brandreth

Silvio Berlusconi's entry into a room is less likely to be greeted with the Italian national anthem than by the Benny Hill theme tune.

Rory Bremner

Describing Tony Blair as a Middle East peace envoy is like asking a mosquito to find a cure for malaria.

Rory Bremner

I can't look at John Prescott without thinking of Les Dawson.

Rory Bremner

David Cameron plays by far the most convincing [Tony] Blair. The rest of us just do the voice and the mannerisms, but Cameron does the whole career.

Rory Bremner

Future generations will use [Tony] Blair's name as a swearword so offensive it currently has no equivalent in the English language.

Charlie Brooker

George Osborne . . . is so posh he probably weeps champagne.

Charlie Brooker, *I Can Make You Hate*

A lot of people think right-wingers aren't capable of being amusing at all. Not true. Mussolini looked hilarious swinging from that lamppost.

Charlie Brooker

We just don't see enough of Nigel Farage. Sometimes you can eat an entire Twix without seeing a photograph of him raising a pint and guffawing or hearing his voice on the radio.

Charlie Brooker, January 2015

John Howard is by far the dullest man in Australia. Imagine a very committed funeral home director – someone whose burning ambition from the age of eleven was to be a funeral home director, whose proudest achievement in adulthood was to be elected president of the Queanbeyan and District Funeral Home Directors' Association – then halve his personality and halve it again and you have pretty well got John Howard.

Bill Bryson, *Down Under: Travels in a Sunburned Country*

The House has noticed the prime minister's remarkable transformation in the last few weeks from Stalin to Mr Bean, creating chaos out of order rather than order out of chaos.

Vince Cable, on Gordon Brown

We Americans only voted for George W. Bush to prove to the British that Americans understand irony.

Scott Capurro

These days, many politicians are demanding change. Just like homeless people.

George Carlin

(Jeb Bush running in the 2016 US presidential election): Of course, America is hungry for another leader from that talented family!

Stephen Colbert

For the Blairs' official Christmas card, Cherie decided not to smile, in case they couldn't fit the card into the envelope.

Ronnie Corbett, *Have I Got News For You*

On being told he was going to be the new Home Secretary, Charles Clarke couldn't believe his ears. Well, quite frankly, none of us can believe his ears!

Ronnie Corbett, *Have I Got News for You*, December 2004

Expectations of Ed Miliband are so low that when he comes on stage and doesn't soil himself . . . he will out-perform expectations.

> Professor Philip Cowley on 2015 UK general election TV debate

Michael Gove is to stand as Tory leader on the basis that he will betray absolutely anyone without a second's hesitation. Taking the stage to the O'Jays classic 'Back Stabbers', he said: 'Knifing Boris [Johnson] is nothing. It's like letting the air out of one of those giant parade inflatables, everyone's tempted . . . I am the only candidate endorsed by Judas.'

> Satirical website thedailymash.co.uk

David Cameron will be remembered as the only man who could get a removal van in two days.

> Hugh Dennis, *Mock the Week*, after Cameron's hasty exit from 10 Downing Street following the EU referendum of June 2016

Jeremy Corbyn moves forward with all the dynamism and energy of a canal boat.

> Hugh Dennis, *Mock the Week*

Do you think kids might confuse Jeremy Corbyn with Father Christmas? He's got a beard, he's promised people lots of presents and adults laugh at you for believing in him.

> Hugh Dennis, *Mock the Week*

Al Gore campaigned for Hillary Clinton at a Florida rally attended by sixteen hundred people. Unfortunately for Gore, a recount showed that it was only thirteen hundred people.

> Jimmy Fallon

Sarah Palin's book just came out. It has just over three hundred pages and just under nine hundred made-up words.

> Jimmy Fallon

[George W.] Bush doesn't know the names of countries, he doesn't know the names of foreign leaders, he can't even find the Earth on a globe.

> Doug Ferrari

Gaddafi. What an idiot! A dictator and he only made himself colonel. A guy who put chicken in a bucket made it to colonel!

Rich Hall

The Tory conference are not an attractive lot, are they? If all those people were born in the same village, you'd blame pollution, wouldn't you?

Jeremy Hardy

He's charming and northern; he's the man tasked with crushing the poor in their own accent, isn't he really?

Jeremy Hardy, on Vince Cable, 2010

[Nicholas] Soames was magnificent, a vast, florid spectacle, a massive inflatable frontbench spokesman. You could tow him out to a village fete and charge children 50p to bounce on him. They could have floated him over London to bring down the German bombers.

Simon Hoggart

Seeing John Major govern the country is like watching Edward Scissorhands try to make balloon animals.

Simon Hoggart

In Gordon Brown's Britain there is always a review. If he had been stopped by Dick Turpin demanding, 'Your money or your life', he would have announced a review to consider the options.

Simon Hoggart

Peter Mandelson is the only man I know who can skulk in broad daylight.

Simon Hoggart

I'm often amazed at the way politicians, who spend hours poring over opinion poll results in a desperate attempt to discover what the public thinks, are certain they know precisely what God's views are on everything.

Simon Hoggart

Every sentence he manages to utter scatters its component parts like pond water from a verb chasing its own tail.

Clive James, on George W. Bush

What's the difference between IDS and IBS? One is an irritable arse, the other is a gastric complaint.

Alan Johnson, on Iain Duncan Smith

[Tony Blair] is a mixture of Harry Houdini and a greased piglet. He is barely human in his elusiveness. Nailing Blair is like trying to pin jelly to a wall.

Boris Johnson

(of Gordon Brown): He is like some sherry-crazed old dowager who has lost the family silver at roulette, and who now decides to double up by betting the house as well.

Boris Johnson, 2008

Jack Whitehall: UKIP politicians are rather like clowns because they're funny, wear silly clothes . . . and frankly are terrifying.
Lloyd Langford: . . . And they all have white faces.

QI

How did Ed Miliband manage to make the Labour Party less popular than under Blair? That's like catching a baby that's been thrown out of an airplane and then tripping up and dropping it in a gutter.

Stewart Lee

We pick politicians by how they look on TV and Miss America on where she stands on the issues. Isn't that a little backwards?

Jay Leno

Republicans are always criticising President Obama for using the tele-prompter. Is that a big deal? After eight years of George W. Bush, I'm glad we have a president that can read.

Jay Leno

Hillary Clinton is going to try and unite the Democrat party. But Bill Clinton says, according to his experience, the party is usually over whenever Hillary shows up.

Jay Leno

Hillary Clinton said that her childhood dream was to be an Olympic athlete. But she was not athletic enough. She said she wanted to be an astronaut, but at the time they didn't take women. She said she wanted to go into medicine, but hospitals made her woozy. Should she be telling people this story? I mean, she's basically saying she wants to be president because she can't do anything else.

Jay Leno

Sarah Palin has admitted she tried marijuana several years ago, but she did not like it. She said it distorted her perceptions, impaired her thinking, and she's hoping that the effects will eventually wear off.

Jay Leno

Sarah Palin looks like the flight attendant who won't give you a second can of Pepsi . . . She looks like the nurse who weighs you and then makes you sit alone in your underwear for twenty minutes . . . She looks like the real-estate agent whose picture you see on the bus stop bench . . . She looks like the hygienist who makes you feel guilty about not flossing . . . She looks like the relieved mom in a Tide commercial.

David Letterman

President Obama is going to take two weeks to unwind, as opposed to President Bush, who never wound.

David Letterman

I really fancy Ed Miliband, mainly because he looks like David Miliband reflected in a spoon.

Gráinne Maguire

Rudy Giuliani's first wife was his cousin. Did you know this? I think that's a very cheap way to go after the southern vote.

Bill Maher

This week Sarah Palin's memoir became a bestseller. It's not even out yet. It's being translated into English.

Bill Maher

I do miss George W. Bush. Compared to these teabaggers and the people who are pandering to them, he looks like a professor.

Bill Maher

George W. Bush has that weird mixture of born-again Christian and stupid that some people mistake for courage and focus.

Marc Maron

Never a frown with Gordon Brown.

Paul Merton, *Have I Got News for You*

Jacob Rees-Mogg looks like he was cultivated in a greenhouse.

Paul Merton, *Have I Got News for You*

[Michael] Gove's slide down the greasy pole could hardly have been less dignified if he'd been wearing nipple tassels.

David Mitchell

(of Michael Gove): There's something magnetic about his loathsomeness. He's like the Bond villain who's about to get dissolved in acid. A four-eyed, reptilian tosspot.

David Mitchell, *Have I Got News for You*

Silvio Berlusconi has had so many facelifts, his face has moved to the top of his head. You have to get on a stepladder to watch him lie.

Dylan Moran

Berlusconi is so crooked, he sleeps on a spiral staircase.

Dylan Moran

We've gotten so close that in some places in Indiana they won't serve us pizza anymore.

Barack Obama, on vice president Joe Biden

California governor Arnold Schwarzenegger's approval rating is down to thirty per cent. After hearing this, Arnold said, 'I'm not going to act all hurt and upset, because I don't have that kind of range.'

Conan O'Brien

According to a new poll, Hillary Clinton is more unpopular than ever, but still not as unpopular as Donald Trump. So this election is kind of like asking people if they'd rather have chlamydia or gonorrhoea.

Conan O'Brien, on the US presidential election of 2016

Politicians are interested in people. Not that it is always a virtue. Fleas are interested in dogs.

P. J. O'Rourke, *Parliament of Whores: A Lone Humorist Attempts to Explain the Entire US Government*

Prime Minister Tony Blair was re-elected for a record-setting third term as George W. Bush's bitch.

Amy Poehler

I saw George W. Bush at a benefit concert actually waving at Stevie Wonder. Someone had to tell him: 'He can't see you.'

Anne Robinson

The only reason I'm not running for president this year, I swear to God, is I am afraid no woman would come forward to say she had sex with me.

Larry Sanders (Garry Shandling), *The Larry Sanders Show*

(of John Prescott): I suspect language isn't his first language.

Linda Smith

Ann Widdecombe's confused us all by going blonde. I was watching *Question Time*, thinking, 'Blimey, Sue Barker's slapped on a bit of weight!'

Linda Smith

George W. Bush and Donald Rumsfeld are like an old couple with some holiday brochures. 'Where shall we invade next? Cuba looks nice.'

Mark Steel, *Have I Got News for You*

Donald Rumsfeld. Love him or hate him, you've got to admit: a lot of people hate him.

Jon Stewart

Andy Burnham looks like someone who'd get to the sixth week of *The Apprentice* because you hadn't noticed him.

Josh Widdicombe

When the results came in, Nigel Farage said it was his dream come true. I thought, I'd quite like my dream to come true because I once dreamed I'd run him over with a plough.

Joe Wilkinson

Having George W. Bush giving a lecture on business ethics is like having a leper give you a facial.

Robin Williams

(on the end of George W. Bush's presidency): It's the end of the reign of George the Second. The reign of error is over. America is officially out of rehab.

Robin Williams

Where did they get Sarah Palin? Did Ronald Reagan have a kid with Posh Spice?

Robin Williams

Hillary Clinton aimed to show that any woman can become president, as long as your husband did it first.

Michelle Wolf

I'd say to Hillary Clinton, 'Why are your jackets always so big? What are you hiding under there? Is that where your emails are?'

Michelle Wolf

She said, 'What do you think of Marx?' I said, 'I think their pants have dropped off, but you can't fault their broccoli.'

Victoria Wood

Politics

Glenn Cullen (James Smith): So, Hugh, this new word 'citizenship', did the PM tell you what it meant?

Hugh Abbot (Chris Langham): Honestly, I think he was making up the reshuffle as he went along. I think we're lucky that 'citizenship' was the first thing that came to mind. Otherwise we could have been the Department for Social Affairs and Woodland Folk.

The Thick of It

An article on playwrights in the *Daily Mail* was listed according to hard left, soft left, hard right, soft right and centre. I am not listed. I should probably come under soft centre.

Alan Bennett

I think it should be made clear that the Conservatives and the Liberal Democrats have not got into bed together, they are merely sharing a room.

Gyles Brandreth, on the 2010 UK coalition government, *The News Quiz*

We have a presidential election coming up, and I think the big problem, of course, is that someone will win.

Barry Crimmins

If you've half a mind to vote UKIP, don't worry, it's all you need.

Andy de la Tour

The difference between Democrats and Republicans? Democrats remind us that life is unfair, and Republicans make sure it is.

David Feldman

There shouldn't have been a [EU membership] referendum. Why did they ask the general public what they think? The average person is an idiot. On bottles of bleach we've got 'Do not drink'. I say take that off for two years and *then* have a referendum.

Ricky Gervais, *The Last Leg*

If there's one thing we've learned in 2016, it's to ignore the polls and go only on the terrible foreboding in the pit of your stomach.

Jemima Goldsmith

If Abe Lincoln took part in the Republican debates, he would look out of place with his intelligence, compassion and gaping head wound.

Dana Gould

Honesty always gives you the advantage of surprise in the House of Commons.

Jim Hacker (Paul Eddington), *Yes, Prime Minister*

All socialists have bad backs because we slouch – except when we're watching the news when we sit on the edge of our seats, shout and wave our arms. Generally, we sit hunched, arms crossed in a judgemental way, the whole of our bodies pulled into a frown.

Jeremy Hardy

The only way you can ever accuse a Conservative of hypocrisy is if they walk past a homeless person without kicking him in the face.

Jeremy Hardy

The Tea Party is a sort of UKIP with guns.

Ian Hislop, *Have I Got News for You*

The formal Washington dinner party has all the spontaneity of a Japanese imperial funeral.

Simon Hoggart

It's true. I no longer have highly trained, professional campaign managers. So what? Are most murders committed by highly trained, professional assassins? No, they're committed by friends and co-workers.

Leslie Knope (Amy Poehler), *Parks and Recreation*

Brexit will be like getting an egg out of an omelette.

Pascal Lamy, French politician

A protest vote for UKIP is like shitting your hotel bed as a protest against bad service, then realising you now have to sleep in a shitted bed.

Stewart Lee

A new poll shows only three per cent strongly approve of the job Congress is doing, with a margin error of four per cent, so it's possible that less than no one thinks they're doing a good job.

Jay Leno

America really has no left party. We have a centre-right party – which I would call what the Democrats are now – and then we have the Republicans, a party that drove the Crazy Bus straight into Nut Town.

Bill Maher

Republicans have called for a National African-American Museum. The plan is being held up by finding a location that isn't in their neighbourhood.

Conan O'Brien

Lest we forget, when Europe goes far right, they go far right through Belgium.

John Oliver

If you're looking for morals in politics, you're looking for bananas in the cheese department.

Harry Shearer

(on the 2016 EU membership referendum): I wanted to stay in Europe, so I voted Leave – to leave things as they are.

Barry Shitpeas (Al Campbell), *Charlie Brooker's Year Wipe*

The Senate seems like the place where smart people go to die.

Jon Stewart

(At the next election) I'm voting UKIP, just to see where they send me back to.

British-Malaysian Phil Wang

A consultation process is what some authority sets in motion preparatory to doing what it intended all along.

Keith Waterhouse

In a way I'm quite pleased by Brexit. I wish I'd been here before Britain joined the Common Market because, from what I hear, it must have been an absolute paradise. You got to work three days a week. Let's hope we can all live through that again in the very near future.

Henning Wehn

Pope

I think it'd be great if you had a kid that ended up being pope. That would be the ultimate bragging rights. 'Oh, your son's a doctor? Yeah, ours is pope. Oh, they have a house? He has his own city.'

Jim Gaffigan

As you know, we have a new pope. He is Pope Francis of Argentina. He is a seventy-six-year-old man with only one lung. This could be just the burst of youth and vitality the Catholic church needs.

Jay Leno

When the pope's plane lands in the United States, President Obama is going to be there to greet him. President Obama is going to be the guy at arrivals holding a sign that says 'Pope'.

Conan O'Brien, on the 2015 papal visit to the US

The moment the pope dies, they take him through St Peter's Basilica and fifty thousand cellphones are clicking away. And I'm sure that was his last wish: 'When I die, I want to be a screensaver.'

Robin Williams

Popularity

When people say to me, 'Would you rather be thought of as a funny man or a great boss?', my answer's always the same. To me, they're not mutually exclusive.

David Brent (Ricky Gervais), The Office

Fire officer (Chris Walker): Now then, you've no idea who these pranksters are that keep ringing us up?
Victor Meldrew (Richard Wilson): No. Presumably somebody I've annoyed in the past who's trying to get their own back.
Margaret Meldrew (Annette Crosbie): We've drawn up a short list of five thousand names.

One Foot in the Grave

I'm telling you, I have a real problem. Twenty people could say they liked me, Artie, and I am telling you I'd still be thinking: seventeen of them are lying, two of them probably have severe emotional problems and one of them is probably confusing me with Larry King.

Larry Sanders (Garry Shandling), The Larry Sanders Show

(To Lisa): Honey, you could be popular. You've just got to be yourself. In a whole new way.

Marge Simpson (Julie Kavner), The Simpsons

Pornography

One time my father caught me watching a porno movie. The one thing you never want to hear in that situation is, 'Son, move over.'

Dave Attell

I watched the director's cut of a porn film. At the end he actually fixes the washing machine.

Gary Delaney

That was hardly porn. It was a topless woman on a tractor. You know what they call that in Europe? A cereal commercial.

> Phil Dunphy (Ty Burrell), *Modern Family*

If you watch porn while listening to banjo music, everyone on screen seems related.

> Dana Gould

I reckon porn gives kids an unrealistic idea of what it's like to be a plumber.

> Lee Nelson (Simon Brodkin)

Pornography is often frowned upon, but that's only because I'm concentrating.

> George Ryegold

You know the funny thing about child pornography: the lack of credits at the end. No ego on *that* side of Hollywood. Not even a nom de plume. Some people are in it just for the art.

> Doug Stanhope

I was just out of college, I was broke; it's the oldest story in the world. Boy meets girl, boy wants girl to do dominatrix film. Girl says, 'Naked?', boy says, 'Yeah', girl says, 'Forget it'. Boy says, 'OK then, just wear this rubber maid's uniform and beat the old man with a scrub brush', girl says, 'How hard?'

> Karen Walker (Megan Mullally), *Will & Grace*

Pregnancy

Everything's twice the size it was nine months ago and I'm growing another head inside me.

> Dorothy Bishop (Caroline Quentin), *Men Behaving Badly*

Adam Williams (James Nesbitt): You're sure it's safe for the baby if we have sex while you're pregnant?
Rachel Bradley (Helen Baxendale): No offence, but I don't think you're going to reach.

Cold Feet

My girlfriend recently had a phantom pregnancy. And now we have a little baby ghost.

Jimmy Carr

Stop teenage pregnancy – bring back fingering.

Micky Flanagan

Roz Focker (Barbra Streisand): Many unplanned pregnancies happen because the man is such a sexual dynamo, and the woman craves his sperm on an unconscious but very powerful level.
Greg Focker (Ben Stiller): Mom, I'm truly not comfortable having this conversation with you. I've been telling you that since I was eleven!

Meet the Fockers

When she was pregnant, she would get these cravings in the middle of the night . . . for other men.

Brian Kiley

At first I didn't even realise my girlfriend was pregnant. I'd kinda gotten used to her throwing up every time we had sex.

Larry the Cable Guy (Daniel Whitney)

Amy Brookheimer (Anna Chlumsky): Selina might be pregnant. What do we want to do?
Mike McLintock (Matt Walsh): Is this for real? 'Cause if it is, the best thing for her legacy is if she's assassinated before she starts showing.

Veep

It's never a good idea to ask a woman if she's pregnant. If she's not, you're in huge trouble. I don't care if she's in the delivery room and the baby is halfway out. I would still play it safe and say, 'Excuse me, you've got a little something on your leg there.'

Kevin Nealon, *Yes, You're Pregnant, But What About Me?*

Is it OK to ask a very pregnant librarian if she's overdue?

Conan O'Brien

So when Lena Dunham says she wishes she had an abortion everyone has a go at her, but when my mum says it my birthday party was ruined.

Sara Pascoe, Twitter

If men could get pregnant, abortion clinics would be like Starbucks. There would be two on every block and four in every airport and the morning-after pill would come in different flavours like sea salt and cool ranch.

Nasim Pedrad

Peanut butter and lamb chops were not foods that had ever been a significant part of our life before pregnancy. In fact, my wife almost never ate either. So where did these cravings come from? I concluded it's the baby, ordering in.

Paul Reiser

One of my friends is pregnant. And I'm really excited. Not for the baby, but because she's one of my skinniest friends.

Michelle Wolf, Twitter

I thought you could get pregnant if you swam the backstroke in the same lane as a boy who'd just swum the butterfly.

Victoria Wood

I looked up the symptoms of pregnancy – moody, irritable, big bosoms. I've obviously been pregnant for thirty-six years.

Victoria Wood

Prison

Common sense dictates the term 'hot fudge sundae' has a totally different meaning in prison.

Dana Gould

Listen, you're not the one who's going to have to knit himself a new arse after twenty-five years of aggressive male affection in prison showers.

DCI Gene Hunt (Philip Glenister), *Life on Mars*

I've been working like a Japanese prisoner of war. But a happy one.

Alan Partridge (Steve Coogan), *I'm Alan Partridge*

Wait, are you guys laughing extra loud because somebody's trying to build a tunnel right now?

Comedian Jeff Ross, performing at a Texas prison

Carlos Solis (Ricardo Antonio Chavira): You don't know what it was like in prison. Twenty hours a day, eight-by-ten cell, just you and your mind.
Gabrielle Solis (Eva Longoria): So, pretty much just you.

Desperate Housewives

I found out one of my old partners, Larry, is in jail now. Larry got twenty-five years for something he didn't do. He didn't run fast enough.

Damon Wayans

Problems

As you know, the best way to solve a problem is to identify the core belief that causes the problem; then mock that belief until the people who hold it insist that you heard them wrong.

Scott Adams

Problems are like toilet paper: you pull on one and ten more come.

Woody Allen

If you have some problem in your life and you need to deal with it, then use religion, it's fine. I use Google.

Simon Amstell

There are a lot of problems in the world, but it's OK because wristbands are sorting them all out.

Ed Byrne

A problem shared is attention gained.

Pippa Evans

I'm a firm believer that problems are just solutions waiting to happen.

Ian Fletcher (Hugh Bonneville), *Twenty Twelve*

Even if I did get past all my problems, I'm just gonna go out and get new ones.

Ally McBeal (Calista Flockhart), *Ally McBeal*

I always say a problem shared is . . . gossip.

Graham Norton

Procrastination

My life is a monument to procrastination, to the art of putting things off until later or much later or possibly never.

Craig Brown

Procrastinate now, don't put it off.

Ellen DeGeneres

A wrong decision is better than indecision.

Tony Soprano Sr (James Gandolfini), *The Sopranos*

My mother always told me I wouldn't amount to anything because I procrastinate. I said, 'Just wait.'

Judy Tenuta

Promiscuity

People want sex education out of the schools. They believe sex education causes promiscuity. Hey, I took algebra, but I never do maths.

Elayne Boosler

I thought I was promiscuous, but it turns out I was just thorough.

Russell Brand

Sleeping around is a great way to meet people.

Chelsea Handler

I have a rule and that is never to look at somebody's face while we're having sex; because, number one, what if I know the guy?

Laura Kightlinger

I went out with a promiscuous impressionist. She did everybody.

Jay London

Dorothy Zbornak (Bea Arthur): Blanche, how long did you wait to have sex after George died?
Sophia Petrillo (Estelle Getty): Till the paramedics came.

The Golden Girls

Promises

I promise you, we're gonna find you a kidney. I would swear on my father's grave, but whenever I go there I end up dancing on it.

Dr Perry Cox (John C. McGinley), *Scrubs*

Promises are like children. Fun making them. Regret keeping them.

Ed Goodson (William Shatner), *$#*! My Dad Says*

Property

I got on the property ladder this year. It's murder getting that deposit together. You start having dark thoughts, looking at your mum and dad, thinking: 'If only they had an accident . . .'

Alan Carr

They said it was split-level and open plan but, then again, so is an NCP car park.

Alan Carr, on house hunting

My mum gave me some advice when buying an apartment: 'Don't get one with a balcony, because, what with living on your own, there'll be a high suicide risk.' Thanks, Mum.

Sarah Millican

Prostitution

Paddy O'Shea (Paddy McGuinness): Prostitutes are rough in Amsterdam. First one I went with made me wash me old man in the sink.
Max Bygraves (Peter Kay): You took your dad?

Peter Kay's Phoenix Nights

Sleeping with prostitutes is like making your cat dance with you on its hind legs. You know it's wrong, but you try to convince yourself that they're enjoying it as well.

Scott Capurro

Politics and prostitution have to be the only jobs where inexperience is considered a virtue.

Tina Fey

Mary Jo Shively (Annie Potts): We think that your friend Monette might be practising the oldest profession.
Charlene Frazier Stillfield (Jean Smart): You think that Monette is a carpenter?

Designing Women

Psychics

Karen Smith (Amanda Seyfried): I'm kinda psychic. I have a fifth sense.

Cady Heron (Lindsay Lohan): What do you mean?

Karen: It's like I have ESPN or something. My breasts can always tell when it's going to rain.

Cady: Really? That's amazing.

Karen: Well . . . they can tell when it's raining.

Mean Girls

Punctuation

So far as good writing goes, the use of the exclamation mark is a sign of failure. It is the literary equivalent of a man holding up a card reading 'LAUGHTER' to a studio audience.

Miles Kington

I'm still of an age – and a bent – where I can't help finding the bowdlerisation of texting quite insufferable. I'd rather fiddle with my phone for precious seconds than neglect an apostrophe; I'd rather insert a word laboriously keyed out than resort to predictive texting for a – acceptable to some – synonym.

Will Self, 2008

There are people who embrace the Oxford comma and those who don't, and I'll just say this: never get between these people when drink has been taken.

Lynne Truss, *Eats, Shoots & Leaves*

Why did the Apostrophe Protection Society not have a militant wing? Could I start one? Where do you get balaclavas?

Lynne Truss, *Eats, Shoots & Leaves*

Radio

We have a caller on the line who fears he might be gay. He's married, so we'll only refer to him by his Christian name. This is Domingo from Little Oakley . . .

Alan Partridge (Steve Coogan), *I'm Alan Partridge*

Later we'll be taking dedications for anyone wrongly turned down for planning permission. Also, I'll be asking: 'Which is the worst monger? Fish . . . iron . . . rumour . . . or war?'

Alan Partridge (Steve Coogan), *Alan Partridge: Alpha Papa*

Rev. Geraldine Granger (Dawn French): You're on in fifteen seconds, Frank, and I need to hear a little bit for level, so tell us what you had for breakfast.
Frank Pickle (John Bluthal): Toast.
Rev. Granger: Yeah . . . I need a little bit more than that, so just make something up: you know, let your imagination run wild.
Frank: Wild! Great. Two pieces of toast.

The Vicar of Dibley

Television contracts the imagination and radio expands it.

Sir Terry Wogan

I am being paid to come on and be Cheerful Charlie. You don't go to the doctor for him to tell you he is not well.

Sir Terry Wogan

Gratuitously hurtful folk declare that I am very popular in hospitals because the listeners abed there are too weak to reach out and switch me off.

Sir Terry Wogan

Rejection

Dan Conner (John Goodman): What happened to Jimmy? I liked Jimmy.
Darlene Conner (Sara Gilbert): So did Becky, until he dumped her.
Becky Conner (Lecy Goranson): He didn't dump me!
Darlene: Get real, you hit the ground like a safe.

Roseanne

Her lips were saying, 'No', but her eyes were saying . . . 'Read my lips'.
Niles Crane (David Hyde Pierce), *Frasier*

Just because you dump someone on the day before your wedding doesn't mean you stop caring about them.
Donna (Sharon Horgan), *Pulling*

I told the ambulance driver the wrong blood type for my ex, so he knows what rejection feels like.

Pippa Evans

Plenty of guys have broken up with me. You just beat them up and move on.
Sam Fuller (Regina King), *Miss Congeniality 2: Armed and Fabulous*

He doesn't even know me. The least he could do is get to know me before he rejects me.
Miranda Hobbes (Cynthia Nixon), *Sex and the City*

Things don't get better when you become well known or go on TV. I'm just being rejected by a better class of woman.

Stephen Merchant

Every dumped woman cuts off all her hair – it's the law.

Sarah Millican

Oh, Wayne, I'm the only married woman on the estate – it's not fair on our kids, they get teased at school. 'You've got a daddy, you've got a daddy!' they all shout. I wanna be a single mum, Wayne, and I want a brown baby. All the other mums have got at least one brown baby and I want one. And for that I need a big black man, and that ain't you. You'd best leave, lover.

Waynetta Slob (Kathy Burke), *Harry Enfield and Chums*

I didn't know how to feel. I'd been rebuffed. I hadn't even been trying to buff.

Danny Wallace, *Who is Tom Ditto?*

Relationships

When I leave a relationship I always like to burn down the house so there's no discussion about it later.

Ron Bennington

I just broke up with my girlfriend. The reason we broke up is because I caught her lying . . . under another man.

Doug Benson

Peter Bretter (Jason Segel): How are things going with the lady?
Darald Braden (Jack McBrayer): Not awesome. She's complicated, like the *Da Vinci Code*, except harder to crack.

Forgetting Sarah Marshall

If you're a guy, you have absolutely no idea what's going on at any time in the relationship, ever. Here's what you know: you know when you're getting laid and you know when it's all over. Those are the only two things you're aware of.

Adam Carolla

My girlfriend sat me down the other day for a chat. I say 'chat', it was her talking at me for six hours. I didn't realise that when men say they're 'spoken for', that's actually what they mean.

Jimmy Carr

Yin needs yang, not another yin. Yin-yang is harmony, Yin-Yin is . . . a name for a panda.

Richard Castle (Nathan Fillion), *Castle*

Karen (Tanya Franks): You do know you're supposed to enjoy being with your boyfriend?
Donna (Sharon Horgan): I do. I love being with him. It's just spending time with him I find stressful.

Pulling

Frasier Crane (Kelsey Grammer): What do you do when the romance goes out of a relationship?
Roz Doyle (Peri Gilpin): I get dressed and go home.

Frasier

I've been with the same bloke for over thirty years. He always says it's a one-night stand that went horribly wrong.

Jenny Eclair

Singletons should not have to explain themselves all the time but should have an accepted status – like geisha girls do.

Helen Fielding, *Bridget Jones's Diary*

Isn't it strange? When you're single, all you see are couples and, when you're part of a couple, all you see are hookers.

Jim Gaffigan

Joey Tribbiani (Matt LeBlanc): It's never taken me a week to get over a relationship.
Monica Geller (Courteney Cox): It's never taken you more than a *shower* to get over a relationship.

Friends

Almost all of us will, at some point in our lives, choose to live romantically with someone else – if only to say, 'I did it once, now leave me alone with my cats.'

Jeff Green, *The A–Z of Living Together*

My girlfriend is named Lynn. She spells her name 'Lynn'. My old girlfriend's name is Lyn, too, but she spells it 'Lyn'. Every now and then I screw up, I call my new girlfriend by my old girlfriend's name, and she can tell because I don't say 'n' as long.

Mitch Hedberg

The only way a relationship can exist successfully is if, on some fundamental level, the man is scared shitless of his wife.

Dustin Hoffman

I just ended a long-term relationship. Don't worry, it wasn't mine.

Jim Jefferies

In any relationship there are certain doors that should never be opened. The bathroom door, for example.

Richard Jeni

Failed relationships can be described as so much wasted make-up.

Marian Keyes, *Watermelon*

I'm in a relationship at the moment . . . sorry, girls . . . it's going to have to be your place.

Lee Mack

Relationships should go in twos. Or at least in even numbers.

Ally McBeal (Calista Flockhart), considering a threesome, *Ally McBeal*

You let me put my penis in your mouth, but you won't let me put my T-shirts in your drawer?

Rob Norris (Rob Delaney), on moving in with his girlfriend, *Catastrophe*

For me, being single is a choice. It's my second choice . . .

Graham Norton

Sarah Platt (Tina O'Brien): Me and him are so over.

Gail Platt (Helen Worth): Again? You and him have been on and off more times than the light in Eileen Grimshaw's fridge!

Coronation Street

If you come home, and he's using your diaphragm for an ashtray, it's over.

Carol Siskind

I still see my ex-girlfriend every year at the restraining order renewal breakfast.

Christopher Titus

I always just hoped that I'd meet some nice friendly girl, like the look of her, hope the look of me didn't make her physically sick, then pop the question and settle down and be happy. It worked for my parents. Well, apart from the divorce and all that.

Tom (James Fleet), *Four Weddings and a Funeral*

Well, you know what it's like at the start, when they're all fiery-eyed and eager, and they haven't seen you naked yet. And it's like he's smashing at your door with his mighty battering ram. And he's promising to ravish you forever. So you brace yourself for man overload, and throw open the doors, and what do you find standing there? An oversized toddler who wants his dinner. And before you can say, 'There's been a terrible mistake,' he's snoring on your sofa, the fridge is full of empty bottles and the whole place smells of feet.

Susan Walker (Sarah Alexander), *Coupling*

Relaxation

I don't do yoga for several reasons. First off, you can't win at it. There are no medals or trophies awarded for yoga. So what's the point if you can't be champion?

Nick Cody

I'm the least spiritual person in the world. I can't even abide a smelly candle. I know it's meant to make me relax and that immediately makes my hackles rise.

Jenny Eclair

From now on I'm going to employ relaxation techniques to turn off stress river and mosey gently down contentment creek.

Gus Hedges (Robert Duncan), *Drop the Dead Donkey*

If I want to act relaxed, it's going to take all my cunning, skill and concentration.

David Mitchell

Roy Hess (Sam McMurray): How was your weekend?
Earl Sinclair (Stuart Pankin): I had two days of pure enjoyment all mapped out, then I got home on Friday and remembered I had kids.
Roy: Oh, you had to change your plans, huh?
Earl: No, no, I just turned up the volume on the TV so I couldn't hear the little monsters screaming.

Dinosaurs

Dorothy Zbornak (Bea Arthur): Rose, what are you listening to?
Rose Nylund (Betty White): A relaxation tape. The rain is supposed to relax me.
Dorothy: Is it working?
Rose: Not really. I keep worrying that I left my car windows down.

The Golden Girls

Religion

(to audience): I was brought up a very strict Muslim . . . No, don't be scared, there aren't enough of you to make it worthwhile.

Bisha K Ali

The Taliban ethos was never going to work, was it? It was just cobbled together from different beliefs. The anti-intellectualism of the Khmer Rouge, the religious persecution of the Nazis, the enforced beard-wearing from the world of folk music and the subjugation and humiliation of women from the world of golf.

Bill Bailey

The Jews had holidays that turned up out of the blue and the Catholics had children in much the same way.

Alan Bennett, *Smut*

Wouldn't it be great if you could only get AIDS by giving money to television preachers?

Elayne Boosler

The Church of England has brought out prayers for Monday morning. It has a prayer you can say if you're on a train and can't find a seat. When I'm on a train, I pray loudly to Allah and I generally get the whole carriage.

Frankie Boyle

Religion is like a pair of shoes. Find one that fits for you, but don't make me wear your shoes.

George Carlin

Bishops tried to take a step forward by introducing female bishops. It failed. Everyone knows bishops can only move diagonally.

Jimmy Carr

It's fabulous being a priest; think of all that comfort you bring to the sick and dying. They love it, they can't get enough of it!

Father Ted Crilly (Dermot Morgan), *Father Ted*

That's the great thing about Catholicism: it's so vague.

Father Ted Crilly (Dermot Morgan), *Father Ted*

As far as I'm concerned, the scariest thing to come out of the Muslim world is algebra.

Rob Delaney, Twitter

Basically the Catholic religion is: 'If it feels good, stop.'

Adam Ferrara

My favourite Catholic holiday is Easter. That is the day we celebrate Jesus rising from the grave and coming back to Earth as a rabbit that hides coloured eggs.

Adam Ferrara

Force your children to read the Bible. If they are smart and kind, it will put them off religion for life.

Ricky Gervais, Twitter

The Virgin Mary . . . We have a whole religion based on a woman who really stuck to her story.

Greg Giraldo

I was an altar boy in the Roman Catholic Church and no priest ever laid a hand on me. That's me, always the bridesmaid . . .

Dana Gould

Christians are like a thirteen-year-old kid who still believes in Santa.

Jim Jefferies

My faith is a bit like Magic FM in the Chilterns, in that the signal comes and goes.

Boris Johnson

If they make it illegal to wear the veil at work, bee keepers are going to be furious.

Milton Jones

It's difficult, isn't it, when you're in a mosque and everyone's praying . . . and you really enjoy leapfrog.

Milton Jones

I phoned the spiritual leader of Tibet and he sent me a kind of goat with a long neck. It turned out I'd phoned 'Dial-a-Llama'.

Milton Jones

I actually love Catholicism, it's my favourite form of clandestine global evil.

Stewart Lee

People say churches are half empty. They're not; they're too big.

Sean Lock

My mother wears the burka, mainly because she doesn't want to be seen with my dad.

Shazia Mirza

Religion is what people had before television.

Dylan Moran

Religion is basically a formalised panic about death.

Dylan Moran

Catholicism is the most adhesive religion in the world. If you joined the Taliban, you'd merely be regarded as a bad Catholic.

Dara O'Briain

New York City mayor Mike Bloomberg criticised the church of Scientology, saying the religion doesn't make sense. In response, a furious Tom Cruise said, 'Cupcakes, zipper, armadillo.'

Conan O'Brien

I like the Ten Commandments, but I have a problem with the ninth. It should be, 'Thou shalt not covet thy neighbour's ox, except in Scrabble.'

David O'Doherty

Never, never criticise Muslims. Only Christians. And Jews a little bit.

Alan Partridge (Steve Coogan), *Alan Partridge: Alpha Papa*

Last Christmas I bought an advent calendar from the Jehovah's Witnesses. Big mistake. Every time I opened one of the little windows, someone told me to get lost.

Anson Richards

I was raised Catholic. That's why I don't take religion too seriously.

Joe Rogan

I was surprised how British Muslims reacted to the Danish cartoons. How can you get this worked up about a cartoon? But then I remembered how angry I was when they gave Scooby Doo a nephew.

> Paul Sinha, on satirical drawings of the prophet
> Muhammad in Danish newspapers in 2005

Yes, reason has been a part of organised religion ever since two nudists took dietary advice from a talking snake.

> Jon Stewart

Religion: it's given some people hope in a world torn apart by religion.

> Jon Stewart

Restaurants

An American offshoot of a restaurant in Tokyo, Ninja intends to evoke a Japanese mountain village inhabited by ninjas, a special breed of stealthy warriors. In this case they come armed not only with swords and sorcery but also with recipes, which may be their most dangerous weapons of all.

> Frank Bruni, on New York City's Ninja restaurant

Remember the last time we took Dad to a four-star restaurant? He had a miserable time. The restaurant lost a whole star.

> Niles Crane (David Hyde Pierce), *Frasier*

Restaurants always boast about proper homemade cooking. I don't want homemade cooking. That's why I'm here, because I don't like the shit at home.

> Lee Evans

Food and pubs go together like frogs and lawnmowers.

> A. A. Gill, on gastropubs

It gives you the feeling of being in a second-class railways carriage in the Balkans. It's painted a shiny, distressed dung brown. The cramped tables are set with labially pink cloths, which give it a colonic appeal and the awkward sense that you might be a suppository.

A. A. Gill, reviewing a Parisian restaurant

I went to a restaurant with my friend and he said: 'Pass the salt.' I said, 'Screw you! Sit closer to the salt.'

Mitch Hedberg

They had a sign up; the lobsters were flown in. How cruel is that? Think about that, let's say you're a lobster, you've never been on an airplane before – what else can you think but you've won the lobster sweepstakes?

Richard Jeni

Drive-Thru McDonald's was more expensive than I thought . . . once you've hired the car.

Tim Key

Wiener schnitzel, which I assume will be in seasoned crumbs, is coated in batter and lies on the plate like a carpet tile after a flood.

Camilla Long, reviewing a London restaurant

The Subway slogan is 'Where winners eat'. Most of the people in there can't win custody of their own children.

Joe Lycett

Don't eat anything that's served to you out of a window unless you're a seagull.

Bill Maher

The meat inside the shells is small and shrivelled and dry; each shell contains what looks like the retracted scrotum of a hairless cat.

Jay Rayner, reviewing a London restaurant

As to the kale and cauliflower macaroni cheese, I genuinely do not understand how anybody in the food business can taste that and think it's a good idea. It needs to be put in a burlap sack and drowned in the nearest canal.

Jay Rayner

I think that if you're going to eat beef, you want to know it has come from an animal that has moved. This steak slips down like something that has spent its life chained to a radiator in the basement.

Jay Rayner

I like a bit of uric tang as much as the next offal freak, but this was pure essence of NCP car park stairwell.

Jay Rayner

White gazpacho, made with marcona almonds . . . had a texture and astringent flavour that brought paint primer to mind.

Anna Roth, reviewing a San Francisco restaurant

There's a lot of stupid rules connected with eating out, like you should only ever drink white wine with fish. That's stupid – have you ever tried getting pissed with a haddock?

Alexei Sayle

Sometimes I've looked at a plate of food and wondered if it wouldn't look better as a hat.

Janet Street-Porter

I just had lunch at an excellent Christian restaurant called The Lord Giveth. They also do takeaways.

Tim Vine

I called a blind date to set up a meeting at a restaurant. I said, 'I'll be the one in the leather jacket.' She said, 'I'll be the one drinking sake.' Turned out it was one of those biker-sushi places. We never met.

Steven Wright

Royalty

No matter what they say, the royal family aren't like us. We've never accidentally been to a part of our house that we haven't been to before.

Chris Addison

I feel sorry for Prince Harry because with every new royal baby he decreases in value.

Aisling Bea, *8 Out of 10 Cats*

Prince Charles and Camilla went on tour to a really rural area of India. The locals must have thought, 'Diana's let herself go a bit.'

Frankie Boyle

We're always told the royal family are good for business and tourism. Perhaps if we had a country worth visiting we wouldn't have to parade around the product of centuries of incest in order to help sell fridge magnets.

Frankie Boyle, *Have I Got News for You*

Out of respect for the Queen, when I lick a stamp I always do it with my eyes closed.

Russell Brand

Queen Elizabeth I was bald and had wooden teeth and yet somehow managed to remain a virgin.

Jack Dee, *Have I Got News for You*

Prince Charles's vocal cords are plainly trying to strangle him. He may well become the first monarch to lose his head from the inside out.

A. A. Gill

It's the job of the first son to be boring, and Prince William's doing it terrifically well.

Ian Hislop, *Have I Got News for You*

A dead body was discovered this week on the grounds of a country estate owned by Queen Elizabeth. The Queen said today she hopes this serves as a reminder to anybody on her staff that there is a right way and a wrong way to polish sterling silver.

Jay Leno

Whatever Kate Middleton wears sells out in seconds, so it would be great if you put her in a Carlisle away kit.

Sean Lock

For fifty years or more, Elizabeth Windsor has maintained her dignity, her sense of duty and her hairstyle.

Helen Mirren

(on the Queen's Jubilee celebrations): They could have just had a massive pile of burning tyres and more people would have turned up. Especially if they put S Club 7 on the top of it.

Ross Noble

According to a poll of British citizens, eighty-three per cent of people say they forgive Princess Di for her infidelity. Apparently, the other seventeen per cent has never gotten a look at Prince Charles.

Conan O'Brien

I'm nineteenth in line to the Turkish throne. But unofficially. A title without any of the glamour. It's like working in MI6, but in catering.

Naz Osmanoglu (a.k.a.: His Imperial Highness Prince Nazim Ziyaeddin Nazim Osmanoglu)

How could Princess Di not be happy? She was tall, thin, gorgeous and rich with a husband who didn't want to sleep with her.

Joan Rivers

I gave her my all-American smile, where I show wall-to-wall teeth and said, pathetically: 'Hope you like your trip to America.' I was quickly moved on like some old wilted tuna on the conveyor belt at Yo! Sushi.

Ruby Wax, on her meeting with the Queen

I want to see Buckingham Palace on *Homes Under the Hammer*: 'Three hundred and seventy million pounds of repairs, but what would it fetch on the rental market?'

Josh Widdicombe

Rugby

A friend once said to me that he did have a sneaking liking for rugby union in that 'it was always nice to see coppers and barristers getting knocked about a bit on their day off'.

Rugby league fan Stuart Maconie

Rugby, posh man's sport, fifteen men on a team, because posh people can afford to have more friends.

Al Murray, The Pub Landlord

Don't ask me about emotions in the Welsh dressing room. I'm someone who cries when he watches *Little House on the Prairie*.

Bob Norster

Jack Rowell has the acerbic wit of Dorothy Parker and, according to most New Zealanders, a similar knowledge of rugby.

Mark Reason on the former England coach

Rugby is a game for men with no fear of brain injury.

Linda Smith

Russia

The Russian government gave all forty-four of its Olympic medallists a new Mercedes. When asked what happened to the athletes who didn't medal, Vladimir Putin said, 'Do not open trunk.'

Jimmy Fallon

Some Russians are claiming that Putin's election was rigged and that he has no legitimate claim to power. You know what these Russians are called? Missing.

Craig Ferguson

Russian vodka is OK if you need to clean the oven. For drinking, it must henceforth be Polish.

Hugh Laurie

Cher has turned down an invitation to sing at the 2014 Winter Olympics in Russia because of Russia's anti-gay laws. Their anti-gay laws are so strict, men can be arrested just for showing up at a Cher concert.

Jay Leno

In Russia, show the least athletic aptitude and they've got you dangling off the parallel bars with a leotard full of hormones.

Victoria Wood

Salespeople

The first guy who persuaded a blind person they needed sunglasses – he must have been a hell of a salesman.

Jimmy Carr

If that's another man that looks like Buddy Holly trying to sell us Sky television, tell him that we're both blind and deaf. We don't need one of his satellite dishes. I'll weld a bidet to the side of the house and it will be less of an eyesore.

Victor Meldrew (Richard Wilson), *One Foot in the Grave*

They're not a scintillating lot, carpet dealers. They only get excited about bonded underlay.

Eddie Reynoldson (George Costigan), *Calendar Girls*

School

High school is not unlike a Mormon fundamentalist cult where the women are claimed by the older and more powerful.

Mike Birbiglia, *Sleepwalk With Me and Other Painfully True Stories*

Bernard Black (Dylan Moran): But you hated school, you had a terrible time.

Fran Katzenjammer (Tamsin Greig): I've never said that!

Bernard: You don't have to say anything, I just look at your life now and work backwards.

Black Books

When I went to school, sex education was mainly muttered warnings about the janitor.

Frankie Boyle

Technical high school, that's where dreams are narrowed down. We tell our children, 'You can do anything you want.' Their whole lives. 'You can do anything!' But at high school, we take fifteen-year-olds and we tell them, 'You can do eight things. We got it down to eight for you.'

Louis C.K.

When I got out of high school they retired my jersey, but it was for hygiene and sanitary reasons.

George Carlin

I live near a remedial school. There is a sign that says: 'Slow . . . Children.' That can't be good for their self-esteem.

Jimmy Carr

The first school I ever went to was a pretty soft school. At St Pansy's primary, you could have a reign of terror with a balloon on a stick while we were paying protection money to the Brownies.

Ronnie Corbett

In high school, I was the class comedian as opposed to the class clown. The difference is, the class clown is the guy who drops his pants at the football game; the class comedian is the guy who talked him into it.

Billy Crystal

At school the other kids used to push me around and call me lazy. I loved that wheelchair.

Stewart Francis

I was going to join the school debating team, but someone talked me out of it.

Stewart Francis

Dolly Bellfield (Thelma Barlow): Didn't they teach you anything at school?
Twinkle (Maxine Peake): How to put a condom on a cucumber.
Dolly: Honestly, what's the point in that?
Brenda Furlong (Victoria Wood): Be fair, Dolly. There's not many cucumbers that could manage it for themselves.

dinnerladies

Lois Griffin (Alex Borstein): Oh, I haven't been on a college campus for years. Everything seems so different.
Stewie Griffin (Seth MacFarlane): Really? Perhaps if you laid on your back with your ankles behind your ears, that would ring a few bells.

Family Guy

My school had a big problem with drugs. Especially Class A.

Milton Jones

My parents made us take Latin. It comes in handy if someone in the family gets possessed.

Kathleen Madigan

When I was at school, all the boys used to go and snog Julie Miller in the art cupboard. And you know, they don't make teachers like Julie Miller anymore.

Jason Manford

I was thrown out of recorder class for 'not taking it seriously enough'. This seemed preposterously unfair. It was a roomful of nine-year-olds, all obliged to play 'London's Burning' on the recorder. At the same time. Can you imagine what that sounded like? How could *anyone* take it seriously?

Victoria Coren Mitchell

I hated school; they were the worst three days of my life.

Lee Nelson (Simon Brodkin)

I skipped school only once. It turned out to be the day they taught everything.

Rose Nylund (Betty White), *The Golden Girls*

I had to go to Greek school where I learned valuable lessons such as, 'If Nick has one goat and Maria has nine, how soon will they marry?'

Toula Portokalos (Nia Vardalos), *My Big Fat Greek Wedding*

School is not for asking questions. It's a place you go to be out of this house.

Earl Sinclair (Stuart Pankin), *Dinosaurs*

I've got to be in a regular school, one with metal detectors and pregnant cheerleaders.

Tommy Solomon (Joseph Gordon-Levitt), *3rd Rock from the Sun*

I always say that boarding schools are run by therapists to turn out future clients.

Sandi Toksvig

Anyone who has been to an English public school will always feel comparatively at home in prison.

Daniel Tosh

I used to wear my school skirt so high you would have thought it was a serviette.

Shirley Valentine (Pauline Collins), *Shirley Valentine*

Science

It's a scientific fact that your body will not absorb cholesterol if you take it from someone else's plate.

Dave Barry

(of Stephen Hawking): He's not a genius, he's pretentious. Born in Kent and talks with an American accent!

Ricky Gervais

We're all basing this on what Stephen Hawking said and, the fact is, he's subject to interference from minicabs.

Jeremy Hardy, QI

Stephen Hawking operates his voice synthesiser by moving one muscle in his face, so he's already doing better than Roger Moore.

Ian Hislop, on hearing that Hawking wants to be
a Bond villain, Have I Got News for You

Was it my imagination or have they just started building the world's biggest sub-atomic particle accelerator to explain the very origins of the universe as we know it? Strange then that they can't produce a toilet roll where the perforations are on the same place on either side of the paper!

Victor Meldrew (Richard Wilson), One Foot in the Grave

How much *actual* science is involved in being a sports scientist? I mean them no disrespect but they're PE teachers with laptops.

Alan Partridge, Nomad

Someone should tell scientists they don't need to keep finding reasons for us to drink a glass of wine at night.

Michelle Wolf

They say the universe is expanding. That should help ease the traffic.

Steven Wright

Scotland

I'm half-Scottish half-Indian which means, unlike most Scots, I don't get sunburn watching fireworks.

Danny Bhoy

Edinburgh is the only place you can be sunburned and get trench foot on the same day.

John Bishop

We had the Commonwealth Games in Glasgow. A great choice of venue: a place where people think hepatitis B is a vitamin.

Frankie Boyle

The average life expectancy in some parts of Glasgow is fifty-four. If you've ever been there, you'll realise that's maybe a bit long.

Frankie Boyle

The English are worried about the Euro being brought in because of loss of national identity and rising prices. In Scotland, people are just worried in case they have to close Poundstretcher.

Pre-referendum Frankie Boyle

Being a great believer in Scottish tradition, I followed the example of my fellow countrymen and moved to England.

Rory Bremner

In the same week Glasgow was announced as Europe's murder capital but was also voted the UK's friendliest city. You might get the shite kicked out of you but you'll get directions to the hospital.

Kevin Bridges

That is the problem with Scotland, I find. You never know whether the next person you meet is going to offer you his bone marrow or nut you with his forehead.

Bill Bryson, *The Road to Little Dribbling: More Notes from a Small Island*

Scotland had oil, but it's running out thanks to all that deep frying.

Scott Capurro

One in three Scottish girls is obese. As are the other two.

Jimmy Carr

In Scotland, the forbidden fruit is fruit.

Gary Delaney

In a Scottish opera, it ain't over till the fat lady bitch-slaps you.

Craig Ferguson

I grew up in Scotland in the 1970s. There was not much money. The most popular Christmas toy was a potato.

Craig Ferguson

Nobody knows what the original people of Scotland were: cold is probably the best-informed guess, and wet.

A. A. Gill

I think most Scottish cuisine is based on a dare.

Charlie McKenzie (Mike Myers), *So I Married An Axe Murderer*

If you think you're an alcoholic, go to Scotland. People in Scotland drink while they're drinking.

Jay Mohr

Scotland: the country where they invented bacon flavour mouthwash.

Dylan Moran

Sex

Sex can lead to nasty things like herpes, gonorrhea, and something called relationships.

Ali G (Sacha Baron Cohen)

Sex with my first boyfriend was a little bit like learning how to put in a tampon, but only half as enjoyable.

Samantha Bee

In the past few years, I've only had sex in months that end in 'arch'.

Doug Benson

I don't know why people video tape sex because after I have sex, the only thing I can think of is that I'm glad nobody saw that.

Mike Birbiglia

Men put all kinds of expectations on you. They want you to scream,
'You're the best!', while swearing you've never done this with anyone
before.

Elayne Boosler

I've had three lovers in the past four years and they all ran a distant
second to a good book and a warm bath.

Dorothy Boyd (Renée Zellweger), *Jerry Maguire*

Recent surveys show three out of ten men have a problem with premature
ejaculation. The rest just didn't really think it was a problem.

Frankie Boyle

I like threesomes with two women. Not because I'm a cynical sexual pred-
ator – oh, no – but because I'm a romantic. I'm looking for 'the one'. And
I'll find her more quickly if I audition two at a time.

Russell Brand

Premature ejaculation isn't a laughing matter for anyone, except for your
friends when you tell them about it on the phone the next morning.

Julie Burchill

The last woman I had sex with hated me. I could tell by the way she asked
for the money.

Drew Carey

My dad's become obsessed by dogging since he read about it in the *Mail
on Sunday*. He'll be driving along and say, 'Look at that dogging,' and I say,
'No, Dad, it's a car boot sale.'

Alan Carr

Women reach their sexual peak after thirty-five years. Men reach theirs
after about four minutes.

Jimmy Carr

There was one time where I failed to perform sexually. My girlfriend said
to me, 'Oh, don't worry, it happens to a lot of guys.' There are two things
wrong with that. First, who are these other guys, and second, if it's
happening to more than one of us, don't you think it could be *your* fault?

Jimmy Carr

I think that you [Leonard] have as much chance of having a sexual relationship with Penny as the Hubble telescope does of discovering at the centre of every black hole is a little man with a flashlight searching for a circuit breaker.

Sheldon Cooper (Jim Parsons), *The Big Bang Theory*

An orgy sounds great, but you're basically just multiplying the number of people you're not going to be able to look in the eye afterwards.

Mark Corrigan (David Mitchell), *Peep Show*

Frasier Crane (Kelsey Grammer): Would we sleep together?
Lilith Sternin (Bebe Neuwirth): I was thinking we could freeze your sperm.
Frasier Crane: Is that a 'Yes' or 'No'?

Frasier

What is sex addiction? I asked a doctor and the guy goes, 'With sex addiction, people will end up doing something they don't want to do just for sex.' Isn't that called a first date?

Dov Davidoff

The last time I was here, a girl asked me for sex. I had to disappoint her. We had sex.

Gary Delaney

The great thing about going to bed with an older man is that at least he vaguely knows what he's doing, especially since the cataract op. And, afterwards, he can bleed the radiators.

Jenny Eclair

It takes a million sperm to find one egg 'cause they're all males and not one of them is gonna pull over and ask for directions.

Adam Ferrara

Roland T. Flakfizer (John Turturro): Lillian, I could make love to you right here.

Lillian Oglethorpe (Nancy Marchand): Roland, let's keep this professional.

Roland: Fine. I'll charge you fifty bucks a pop.

Brain Donors

Three guys at once? That's a nightmare. That is literally a recurring stress dream that I have. I can only think of jobs for two.

Claire Foster (Tina Fey), *Date Night*

If you can't remember the last time you had sex with a woman, you're either gay or married.

Jeff Foxworthy

Kiss of death . . . Let's do it right here and now, while everyone's concentrating on the sermon.

Graeme Garden, *I'm Sorry I Haven't a Clue*

If you are anxious about your sexual abilities don't worry, you're not alone. We all have the same fears. That is why, after sex, men ask questions like, 'Was I OK?', 'Did you orgasm?' and, 'Do you take Visa?'

Jeff Green, *The A–Z of Being Single*

I believe box-sets are a threat to the nation's sex lives. When it gets to the point where you wake up with popcorn kernels or crumbs from crisps in bed, you really need to re-evaluate your relationship.

Professor Green

If you do talk dirty, make sure that you enunciate because there's nothing more embarrassing than having to repeat yourself.

Chelsea Handler

Sally Harper (Kate Isitt): I hate having sex at home. I've got a listening flatmate.

Jane Christie (Gina Bellman): Oh no, I hate those. Do you have to be really quiet for her?

Sally: No, I have to be really loud. We're very competitive.

Coupling

You can tell I've been married for a while. I went to the doctor's last week, and he said, 'Have you had sex in the last seven days?' And I said, 'No, my birthday's in April.'

Brian Kiley

Sex is not a dirty thing. Sex is not a crime. It's a loving act between two or more consenting adults.

Hank Kingsley (Jeffrey Tambor), *The Larry Sanders Show*

Usually I'm on top to keep the guy from escaping.

Lisa Lampanelli

A survey asked married women when they most want to have sex. Eighty-four per cent of them said right after their husband is finished.

Jay Leno

There are three types of sex. One: brand new, kitchen-table sex. Two: bedroom sex. Then number three: hallway sex, when you pass each other in the hallway and say 'Fuck you!'

Kathy Lette, *To Love, Honour and Betray*

I knew nothing about bondage. I'd always presumed it was just an inventive way of keeping your partner from going home.

Kathy Lette

Relationships are like sharks, Liz; if you're not left with several bite marks after intercourse, then something's wrong.

Jenna Maroney (Jane Krakowski), *30 Rock*

(fearing that he is impotent): Since this thing began my work has suffered. I used to be a power in the office. Now I have to queue for coffee.

David Marsden (Robert Bathurst), *Cold Feet*

Don't have sex. It leads to kissing and pretty soon you have to start talking to them.

Steve Martin

Beware the old truism: 'It's sexy for men to be funny.' This is not the case during sex. So avoid squeezing her breast while making a honking noise. If you genuinely want to do that, you'll be losing your virginity to a gloomy hooker on the eve of your fortieth birthday.

Victoria Coren Mitchell

During foreplay, you must talk about absolutely nothing but sex itself; a joke is no better than saying, 'What do you make of the economic situation in Greece?' Afterwards, of course, a bit of warm giggling is lovely. (With your partner, that is. Not derisively into your phone.)

Victoria Coren Mitchell

I've never had casual sex with a sober person before.

Sharon Morris (Sharon Horgan), *Catastrophe*

Well, Sonja, that was classic intercourse.

Alan Partridge (Steve Coogan), *I'm Alan Partridge*

I'm glad he's single, because I'm going to climb that like a tree.

Megan Price (Melissa McCarthy), *Bridesmaids*

My love life is like a piece of Swiss cheese. Most of it is missing, and what's there stinks.

Joan Rivers

My sex life is so bad, my G-spot has been declared a historical landmark.

Joan Rivers

I have no sex appeal. The only way I can ever hear heavy breathing from my husband's side of the bed is when he's having an asthma attack.

Joan Rivers

My first sexual experience took about a minute-and-a-half, and that included me buying the dress.

Joan Rivers

I was in bed with this woman and she said, 'Hey, not in the ass!' And I said, 'Hey, it's my thumb and my ass. If you don't like it, go in the other room.'

Garry Shandling

As I've got older, I've found that sex from behind has been a godsend. Because with sex from behind, you don't have to look interested.

Frank Skinner

She lay on the bed, her hands nonchalantly behind her head, with the banana between her legs. Only half of it was alfresco. It was as if we'd had sex and then, before heading for the bathroom, I'd bookmarked her vagina so as not to lose my place.

Frank Skinner, *Frank Skinner on the Road*

I'm not against orgies, but I'm not a good multitasker.

Grace Slick

If size doesn't matter, how come my girlfriend's vibrator isn't three inches and crooked?

Doug Stanhope

Anal sex is a lot like spinach: if you're forced to have it as a child, you won't enjoy it as an adult.

Daniel Tosh

Trust me, Bart, it's better to walk in on both your parents than just one of them.

Milhouse Van Houten (Pamela Hayden), *The Simpsons*

Sometimes when I'm having sex, I'm already thinking about what I'm going to write in the thank-you letter.

Holly Walsh

Someone asked me recently – what would I rather give up, food or sex? Neither! I'm not falling for that one again, wife.

Mark Watson

People think I hate sex. I don't. I just don't like things that stop you seeing the television properly.

Victoria Wood

In my day we didn't have sex education, we just picked up what we could off the television. As far as I was concerned, if *Pinky and Perky* didn't do it, I didn't want to know about it.

Victoria Wood

Dorothy Zbornak (Bea Arthur): I really like him, and I think he likes me.
Sophia Petrillo (Estelle Getty): Just don't ruin it and sleep with him.
Dorothy: Of course not, Ma. I only do that with men I plan to scar psychologically.

The Golden Girls

Sexism

Ed Harken (Fred Willard): Sweetheart, you and I have had this discussion a million times. There's never been a woman anchor.
Veronica Corningstone (Christina Applegate): Mr Harken, this city needs its news. And are you going to deprive them of that because I have breasts . . . exquisite breasts?

Anchorman: The Legend of Ron Burgundy

I'm not sexist – I'm not! That's why I let my female workers work longer than the men so they can make the same money.

Guv (Al Murray), *Time Gentlemen Please*

Right! How many birds does it take to screw in a light bulb? Two! One to run around screaming, 'What do I do?' and one to shag the electrician!

DCI Gene Hunt (Philip Glenister), *Ashes to Ashes*

Women in the workplace – we still have big strides to make. A girlfriend of mine just got a new job. First question the new boss asked her was if she could make a good cup of coffee. Yeah, she stormed right out of that Starbucks.

Carol Leifer

The danger is that all this equality might spell the end of the office affair . . . If there's absolutely no chance of bad sex in a cupboard, why would anyone go to work at all?

Victoria Coren Mitchell

The Taliban were bang out of order. If the dishes are done, there's no need for a mask.

Al Murray, The Pub Landlord

I love it when I get whistled at by builders. If they don't, I'll walk past again until they do.

Su Pollard

(after a fire): Yes, I was the first one out. And yes, I've heard 'women and children first'. But we do not employ children. We are not a sweatshop, thankfully. And women are equal in the workplace by law. So if I let them out first, I have a lawsuit on my hands.

Michael Scott (Steve Carell), The Office (US)

Shoes

Roberto Volare (George de la Peña): My dance shoes are in the Louvre in Paris.
Roland T. Flakfizer (John Turturro): Big deal. Last year I left a raincoat in Cleveland.

Brain Donors

If you have a choice of selling shoes to ladies or giving birth to a flaming porcupine, look into that second, less painful career.

Richard Jeni

Give a girl the right shoes and she can conquer the world.

Bette Midler

There's a reason why men experience pain more acutely than women – that's because there's always part of a woman's brain thinking about shoes.

Ardal O'Hanlon

Husbands come and go, but the Chanel slingbacks are for life.

Karen Walker (Megan Mullally), *Will & Grace*

Shopping

My first rule of consumerism is never to buy anything you can't make your children carry.

Bill Bryson

I knocked a whole display over in Poundland – four pounds worth of damage.

Alan Carr

I love going shopping. I have a black belt in it.

Russell Crowe

The great thing about Sainsbury's is it keeps the scum out of Waitrose.

Stephen Fry, *QI*

I staunchly bought one frame during a two-for-one frame sale and barely left the store alive.

Dana Gould

Our grocery store now has self-checkout, for your convenience. It's like getting punched in the throat, for your comfort.

Dana Gould

Ian Hislop: You bought one courgette?
Miranda Hart: I live alone!

Have I Got News for You

I bought a seven-dollar pen because I always lose pens and I got sick of not caring.

Mitch Hedberg

What I don't get are these people who, instead of buying a four-pack or an eight-pack of toilet paper, buy the single individual roll. Are you trying to quit?

Brian Kiley

I went into a clothing store, and a lady came up to me and said: 'If you need anything, I'm Jill.' I've never met anyone with a conditional identity before.

Demetri Martin

I went into a clothing store, and the lady asked me what size I was. I said, 'Actual. I'm not to scale.'

Demetri Martin

I know a guy who called up the Home Shopping Network. They said, 'Can I help you?' and he said, 'No, I'm just looking.'

George Miller

Hear my wife speak of John Lewis and you might picture a stately pleasure dome of ornamental cascades and hanging gardens, staffed by muscular centaurs who know all there is to know about kitchenware and soft furnishings. But really it's just a big hall full of wanky chrome fridges.

Tim Moore, *You Are Awful (But I Like You); Travels Around Unloved Britain*

I saw a shop window displaying 'essential oils'. I didn't have any of them. I'm lucky to be alive!

Ardal O'Hanlon

My mother is the kind of woman you don't want to be in line behind at the supermarket. She has coupons for coupons.

Chris Rock

My girlfriend asked me to go to the shop and get her butternut squash – then got angry when I came back with three different things.

Seann Walsh

Show Business

There are no requests for jugglers – only, 'Don't juggle!'

Simon Amstell

I've become the most successful impresario since the manager of the Roman coliseum thought of putting the Christians and the lions on the same bill.

Capt. Edmund Blackadder (Rowan Atkinson), *Blackadder Goes Forth*

We know that the most important thing in the world is love and friendship and family and if people don't have those things, well, then they usually get into show business.

Ellen DeGeneres

I've seen a topless lady ventriloquist. No one has ever seen her lips move.

Ken Dodd

Sometimes I wonder what my grandfather would think of what I do. He spent his whole life in the kebab business . . . was buried with all his equipment . . . probably turning in his grave.

Milton Jones

Always remember, if you decide to come to the showbiz party, the dress code is 'Thick skin'.

Graham Norton, *The Life and Loves of a He Devil*

This occasion is all about helping those in show business who've fallen on hard times. Just fifty pounds will give Simon Cowell the Botox he desperately needs. He hasn't had any since two o'clock this afternoon. And two hundred pounds would pay for a life-changing operation to remove Piers Morgan's tongue from Donald Trump's bum.

David Walliams, hosting the 2016 Royal Variety Performance

Sincerity

Michael Bluth (Jason Bateman): Are you serious?
Wayne Jarvis (John Michael Higgins): Almost always. I was once voted
the worst audience participant Cirque du Soleil ever had.

Arrested Development

Singing

I don't know what cats being squashed sound like in Lithuania, but I now
have a pretty good idea.

Simon Cowell on Dreamgirls, two sisters from Lithuania, *The X Factor*

You sounded like Dolly Parton on helium.

Simon Cowell, *American Idol*

You take singing lessons? Do you have a lawyer? Get a lawyer and sue
your singing teacher.

Simon Cowell, *American Idol*

Have you ever heard somebody sing some lyrics that you've never sung
before, and you realise you've never sung the right words in that song?
You hear them and all of a sudden you say to yourself, '"Life in the Fast
Lane?" That's what they're saying? Why have I been singing, "Wipe in the
vaseline"?'

Ellen DeGeneres, *My Point . . . And I Do Have One*

My singing voice is somewhere between a drunken apology and a plumb-
ing problem.

Colin Firth

I have to mime at parties when everyone sings 'Happy Birthday' . . . mime
or mumble and rumble and growl and grunt so deep that only moles,
manta rays and mushrooms can hear me.

Stephen Fry, *Moab is my Washpot*

Life would be a lot more exciting if every single person had a theme song they had to sing when you met them.

Julius Sharpe, Twitter

My girlfriend told me to stop singing 'Wonderwall'. I said, 'Maybe' . . .

Kieran Tobin, Twitter

Skiing

Stretch pants – the garment that made skiing a spectator sport.

Anon

Skiing is the only sport where you spend an arm and a leg to break an arm and a leg.

Henry Beard, Skiing

A ski jacket is the larval stage of a blimp.

Henry Beard, Skiing

I never understand why people ski down a slope to a bar and then go on a lift so they can ski down the same slope again. That's like walking to the pub on a Sunday, then going home and walking to the pub again. Madness.

Jeremy Clarkson, And Another Thing . . .

Sleep

The last refuge of the insomniac is a sense of superiority to the sleeping world.

Leonard Cohen

Howard Wolowitz (Simon Helberg): How's the air mattress?
Sheldon Cooper (Jim Parsons): It's OK, if you don't mind sleeping on a bouncy castle.

The Big Bang Theory

Carla Borrego (Julia Sawalha): Have you ever slept in a castle with a moat before?
Jonathan Creek (Alan Davies): I once passed out in front of a blocked urinal.

Jonathan Creek

Most harm is done by people who are awake.

Jeremy Hardy

I haven't slept for ten days, because that would be too long.

Mitch Hedberg

If you can't sleep, count sheep. Don't count endangered animals. You will run out.

Mitch Hedberg

I don't know if you've ever fallen asleep whilst eating a plate of cauliflower and then woken up and thought you were in the clouds . . .

Milton Jones

There is no sunrise so beautiful that it is worth waking me up to see it.
Mindy Kaling, *Is Everyone Hanging Out Without Me?*

I'm not a very good sleeper, but you know what? I'm willing to put in a few extra hours every day to get better. That's just the kind of hard worker I am.

Jarod Kintz, *Whenever You're Gone, I'm Here for You*

A new study says that people who snore have a higher risk of cancer. But the good news is at least they're not losing any sleep over it.

Jay Leno

I wrote my nightmares out this afternoon so I can get a good night's sleep tonight.

Richard Lewis

Dorothy Zbornak (Bea Arthur): Ma, I don't snore!
Sophia Petrillo (Estelle Getty): Please, I had to turn you away from the window so you wouldn't inhale the drapes!

The Golden Girls

Sleep is the best of both worlds: you get to be alive and unconscious.

Rita Rudner

I woke up the other morning and found that everything in my room had been replaced by an exact replica.

Steven Wright

Smoking

I've stopped smoking. I think the cost was a lot of it, and not being able to breathe.

Dave Allen

I quit because I'm so tired of hearing bad news about cigarettes. Even if they discover good news, they don't publicise it – like the fact that smoking seriously reduces the risk of jogging.

Arj Barker

I quit smoking. I feel better. I smell better. And it's safer to drink out of old beer cans lying around the house.

Roseanne Barr

I'm only not smoking in front of baby David until he's old enough to get up and walk out of the room, then it's his choice.

Denise Best (Caroline Aherne), *The Royle Family*

I did think about giving up smoking, but I decided not to because I'm not a quitter. And I know that every cigarette I smoke takes five minutes off my life, but I also know it takes ten minutes to smoke it. That's a clear five-minute net gain, I reckon.

Ed Byrne

Isn't making a smoking section in a restaurant like making a peeing section in a swimming pool?

George Carlin

Scientists have demonstrated that cigarettes can harm your children. Fair enough: use an ashtray.

Jimmy Carr

Cigarettes are very much like weasels – perfectly harmless unless you put one in your mouth and try to set fire to it.

Boothby Graffoe

The only legitimate reason for smoking an electronic cigarette is if you are a robot that has just had sex with another robot.

Lloyd Langford

A tobacco company now advertises that you can get a packet of cigarettes for one dollar. The cost of dying is really going down.

Jay Leno

People always come up to me and say that my smoking is bothering them. Well, it's killing me!

Wendy Liebman

I hate not being able to smoke in pubs. People say to me, 'Think of the money you'll save by not smoking.' But actually I won't save any money at all, because I'll live longer.

Sean Lock

They're talking about banning cigarette smoking now in any place that's used by ten or more people in a week, which, I guess, means that Madonna can't even smoke in bed.

Bill Maher

There are various ways to give up smoking – nicotine patches, nicotine gum. My auntie used to pour a gallon of petrol over herself every morning.

Paul Merton

It should not be an act of social disobedience to light a cigarette. Unless you're actually a doctor working at an incubator.

Dylan Moran

No, I don't smoke. I'm one of the anti-cancer set. We're a dying breed. Well, we're not, you are. I don't mean you've got cancer. Maybe you have. If you haven't, I apologise. If you have, please take the rest of the day off.

Alan Partridge (Steve Coogan), *I'm Alan Partridge*

Snakes

'But don't worry,' she continued. 'Most snakes don't want to hurt you. If you're out in the bush and a snake comes along, just stop dead and let it slide over your shoes.' This, I decided, was the least-likely-to-be-followed advice I have ever been given.

Bill Bryson, *Down Under: Travels in a Sunburned Country*

A giant python was discovered in Florida. Spooky news for a state that derives half its income from a giant mouse.

Dana Gould

Soccer

When I score, I don't celebrate because it's my job. When a postman delivers letters, does he celebrate?

Mario Balotelli

If brains were chocolate, Robbie Savage wouldn't have enough to fill a Smartie.

Alan Birchenall

Being an England supporter is like being the over-optimistic parents of the fat kid on sports day.

John Bishop

British ferries have stopped transporting live animals to the continent. This has made it very difficult for England fans to get to away matches.

Jo Brand

On PlayStation you only get to control one player at a time, while the others all charge about randomly like . . . England.

Pete Brockman (Hugh Dennis), *Outnumbered*

Back in the 1930s, when men with handlebar moustaches played football in long johns and tails and the ball was a spherical clod of bitumen, did fans weep in the stands when their team lost? No. They limited their responses to a muttered, 'Blast', or a muted, 'Hurrah', before going home to smoke a pipe and lean on the mantelpiece.

Charlie Brooker, *I Can Make You Hate*

It's hard being a football loather, a football unfan. I sometimes feel as lonely as the sole survivor in the last reel of a zombie film as, one by one, old friends reveal themselves, with their glassy stares and outstretched arms, to have succumbed to the lure.

Craig Brown

When they asked her to be on the touchline for David's first game [in Los Angeles], Victoria Beckham thought they wanted her to be a cheerleader. In fact, they needed a corner flag.

Jo Caulfield, *Mock the Week*

If all the creatures on Earth were the same size, it's said a lobster would have the smallest brain. But then someone invented Wayne Rooney.

Jeremy Clarkson

Scotland has the only football team in the world that does a lap of disgrace.

Billy Connolly

Nicky Butt's a real Manchester boy. He comes from Gorton where it is said they take the pavements in of a night time.

Sir Alex Ferguson

Eric Cantona couldn't tackle a fish supper.

Sir Alex Ferguson

He has the most savage tongue you can imagine. As I was arguing with him, his eyes started to narrow, almost to wee black beads. It was frightening to watch. And I'm from Glasgow!

Sir Alex Ferguson, on Roy Keane

When I was in prison, I played football for the stalkers. When one of us went for the ball, we'd all go. There was no one looking for space.

Rhod Gilbert

When you look at other sports, like golf, the players earn a lot more money without running around. I wish I had that little cart to take me to the corner kicks.

Thierry Henry

I am a football manager, I can't see into the future. Last year I thought I was going to Cornwall on my holidays but I ended up going to Lyme Regis.

Ian Holloway

I couldn't be more chuffed if I were a badger at the start of the mating season.

Ian Holloway

Right now, everything is going wrong for me. If I fell in a barrel of boobs, I'd come out sucking my thumb.

Ian Holloway

The World Cup in South Africa was amazing. The last time I saw African kids that excited, Madonna was at their school with a net.

Russell Howard

There are some things you just can't do with a modern player – and sheep-herding is one of them.

Manager Eddie Howe, on an unsuccessful
team bonding exercise at Burnley

(of an injury to German defender Mats Hummels): We will wait for him like a good wife waiting for her husband who is in jail.

Jürgen Klopp

(after victory at Bayern Munich in 2011): When Borussia Dortmund last won here, most of my players were still being breastfed.

> Jürgen Klopp

[Henrikh] Mkhitaryan fits us like an arse on a bucket. What he offers is exactly what we need.

> Jürgen Klopp

Even Jesus Christ wasn't liked by everyone. What hope is there for me?

> José Mourinho

(David Luiz) plays football like he's being controlled by a ten-year-old on a PlayStation.

> Gary Neville

I've just seen a video recording of the game, and I'm going to tape *Neighbours* over it.

> Harry Redknapp

I lay in bed the other night thinking about strikers. It's a few years ago now but I can remember there were always much better things to do in bed.

> Harry Redknapp

Congratulations to Wayne Rooney. He scored three times on Tuesday. He hasn't done that since he crashed a pensioners' bingo night.

> Jonathan Ross

It wasn't my choice to become a goalkeeper, but I was probably too violent to play outfield.

> Peter Schmeichel

You look at Sven [Göran Eriksson] and you think he's a pharmacist. He should be saying, 'Here's your pile ointment.'

> Frank Skinner

Wayne Rooney's entitled to let his hair down because, let's face it, it's let him down.

> Frank Skinner, after Rooney was accused of getting drunk following an England game in 2016

Dennis Wise is never involved in anything but he's always there. He's like the old lady who has been driving for fifty years and never been in an accident – but has seen dozens.

Gordon Strachan

You want a quick word? Velocity.

Gordon Strachan, to a TV reporter

Social Media

If you haven't got anything interesting to say, post it on Facebook.

Anon

The past tense of 'tweet' is 'twat'.

Aisling Bea

Getting your news from Twitter is like asking a cat for directions.

Andy Borowitz

It used to be that people could be painfully boring in private. Facebook changed all that.

Andy Borowitz

Facebook's new relationship status option: 'No longer able to interact with actual people.'

Andy Borowitz

When you've got five minutes to fill, Twitter is a great way to fill thirty-five minutes.

Matt Cutts, Twitter

I'm retiring from tweeting to spend more time with my family.

Alan Davies

I tried to follow my dreams but they'd already blocked me.

Gary Delaney, Twitter

'Poking' someone on Facebook is exactly as creepy as showing them your soft penis in an elevator.

Rob Delaney, Twitter

Newton's law of the internet: For every action there is an unequal and opposite overreaction.

Damien Fahey, Twitter

Twitter has become a stalking ground for the sanctimoniously self-righteous.

Stephen Fry

Twitter is where people come to miss the point and then get angry about it.

Ricky Gervais

Twitter is not a good place for people who feel they're being followed.

Dana Gould

Sheldon Cooper (Jim Parsons): Everyone at the university knows I eat breakfast at 8.00 and move my bowels at 8.20.
Leonard Hofstadter (Johnny Galecki): Yes, how did we live before Twitter?

The Big Bang Theory

Have people always been this angry? I've got an idea that before the internet people were just writing 'Fuck you' and attaching it to pigeons.

Russell Howard

My little sister, she got me on Facebook because I was on MySpace. 'No, no, no, you don't want to be on MySpace, you want to be on Facebook!' So I joined both. But I keep muddling them up, so I keep asking people to come on MyFace. Still, eighty thousand friends . . .

Shappi Khorsandi

To find out who views your Facebook profile the most, look in the mirror.

Rob Lathan, Twitter

Yesterday morning Facebook was temporarily offline, leaving millions of workers unable to do anything except their jobs.

Jay Leno

Twitter provides us with a wonderful platform to discuss/confront societal problems. We trend Justin Bieber instead.

Lauren Leto

Twitter is perfect for people who can't shut up, even when they're on their own.

Sean Lock, *8 Out of 10 Cats*

There's something very macho about how many followers you have on Twitter. Jesus had followers but he had something important to say, not, 'Had a bath, watched *Sex and the City*.'

Sean Lock

Can we go back to using Facebook for what it was originally for – looking up exes to see how fat they got?

Bill Maher

I think the only people who should have Twitter accounts are comedians. Because it's all about one-liners. I would love it if Conan O'Brien were to walk into a room, tell me a joke and leave. But you don't want Gore Vidal telling you, 'I'm doing the dishes right now.'

Jack White

When speaking to me, please remember you're addressing someone who's had at least one account password described as 'strong'.

Bridger Winegar via Twitter

Space

Once you get up there, there's nothing really there. It's a bit like Norfolk.

Sean Lock

So today is the last shuttle flight. From this day on, all American-made rockets will be aimed at people.

Steve Punt, *The Now Show*, 2011

Sports

Sport belongs in a news bulletin about as much as a mummified cat's head belongs in a Caesar salad.

Charlie Brooker

For me, snowboarding is basically like being beaten up by a mountain.

Ed Byrne

I'm not very interested in tobogganing, but I would do it if pushed.

Gary Delaney

Wrestling is only gay when you make eye contact.

Felipe Esparza

I haven't seen an Englishman take a blow like that since Hugh Grant!

Sportscaster Frank, *South Park*

I was watching sumo wrestling on the television for two hours before I realised it was darts.

Hattie Hayridge

There's two positions in snowboarding. One is looking cool and the other is dead.

Eddie Izzard

There are only two categories in cliff diving. There's Grand Champion and Stuff on a Rock.

Norm Macdonald

A sports bar is a way to take a bar and fill it with even more annoying people than usual.

Demetri Martin

The guy that designed girls' volleyball uniforms definitely never had daughters.

Jay Mohr

Look at the sea and think of your evolutionary past. Look at the sky and imagine the future. Look at the land and think of the present. And at the most profound place, where land, sea and sky meet, there ye shall play volleyball.

Simon Munnery

I first played with my left hand when I was seventeen. Things weren't going well, I needed to find a way through, and it felt good. My left hand is like a mistress. My wife is my right hand, my mistress is my left. It's been good to me.

Ambidextrous snooker player Ronnie O'Sullivan

I don't know if I'm still The Rocket. Perhaps I'm more like Thomas the Tank Engine these days.

Ronnie O'Sullivan, 2004

(interviewing a martial arts instructor): Now, self-defence is not just about punching someone repeatedly in the face until they're unconscious, is it?

Alan Partridge (Steve Coogan), *The Day Today*

I don't believe for a second that weightlifting is a sport. They pick up a heavy thing and put it down again. To me, that's indecision.

Paula Poundstone

My favourite pub game is, of course, snooker. Any game whose rules basically amount to finding a table covered in mess and slowly and methodically putting it all away out of sight is one with which I can empathise emphatically.

Jon Richardson, on his OCD (obsessive compulsive disorder)

Black people dominate sports in the United States: basketball, baseball, football, golf, tennis, and, as soon as they make a heated hockey rink, we'll take that too.

Chris Rock

By the age of eighteen, the average American has witnessed two hundred thousand acts of violence on television, most of them occurring during the NHL play-off series.

Steve Rushin, on ice hockey

America national sport is called baseballs. It very similar to our sport, shurik, where we take dogs, shoot them in a field, and then have a party.

Borat Sagdiyev (Sacha Baron Cohen), *Borat: Cultural Learnings of America for Make Benefit Glorious Nation of Kazakhstan*

Curling is just housework on ice.

Linda Smith

You think the luge is a sport? It's not a sport; it's a bet.

Jon Stewart

Somebody said to me the other day that there were no characters in snooker any more. I asked him who his favourite player was and he replied, 'Terry Griffiths'. That threw me completely.

John Virgo

If we'd had [darts champion] Phil Taylor at Hastings against the Normans, they'd have gone home.

Sid Waddell

William Tell could take an apple off your head, Phil Taylor could take out a processed pea.

Sid Waddell

Then there's the luge, for which I have only one question: what drunken German gynaecologist invented that sport? What guy said, 'You know what? I want to dress like a sperm, shove an ice skate in my ass and go balls first down an ice chute. *Ja*, that would be fun!'

Robin Williams

Strength

My gym has two-pound weights. If you're using two-pound weights, how did you even open the door to the gym? What's your dream? To pump up and open your mail?

Dave Attell

Niles Crane (David Hyde Pierce) (as Frasier spots a famous author on the other side of the road): We're a stone's throw away from one of the giants of American literature!
Roz Doyle (Peri Gilpin): Not the way you throw!

Frasier

Studies have shown that an ant can carry one hundred times its own weight, but there is no known limit to the lifting power of the average, tiny, eighty-year-old Spanish peasant grandmother.

Sir Terry Pratchett, *Reaper Man*

Boys who spent their weekends making banana-nut muffins did not, as a rule, excel in the art of hand-to-hand combat.

David Sedaris, *Dress Your Family in Corduroy and Denim*

Stress

My ability to turn good news into anxiety is rivalled only by my ability to turn anxiety into chin acne.

Tina Fey

Look at her. She's as nervous as a very small nun at a penguin shoot.
DCI Gene Hunt (Philip Glenister), *Life on Mars*

Permission to panic, sir!

L/Cpl. Jones (Tom Courtenay), *Dad's Army*

There's no panic like the panic you momentarily feel when your hand or head is stuck in something.

Peter Kay

They say that moving is one of the most stressful things in life. Death in the family is the second most stressful, and moving your dead spouse is the third.

Kevin Nealon

Do I look like I suffer from panic attacks? I've had one panic attack – in a car wash. It was a perfect storm of no sleep, no wife and angry brushes whirring towards me. By the time the giant hair dryer came on, I was in the footwell.

Alan Partridge (Steve Coogan), *Alan Partridge: Alpha Papa*

Stress is a designer ailment that many of the so-called afflicted suffer from with pride.

Janet Street-Porter

Stupidity

Everything goes over your head, doesn't it, George? You should go to Jamaica and become a limbo dancer.

Capt. Edmund Blackadder (Rowan Atkinson), *Blackadder Goes Forth*

Your head is as empty as a eunuch's underpants.

Edmund Blackadder (Rowan Atkinson), *Blackadder: The Cavalier Years*

Who the hell is Julius Caesar? You know I don't follow the NBA.

Ron Burgundy (Will Ferrell), *Anchorman 2: The Legend Continues*

Harry Dunne (Jeff Daniels): Woh! Check out the hotties at twelve o'clock.
Lloyd Christmas (Jim Carrey): That's three hours away. Why can't I check 'em out now?

Dumb and Dumber To

Becky Conner (Lecy Goranson): All I have to do is count to ten.

Darlene Conner (Sara Gilbert): Don't wear mittens. It'll slow you down.

Roseanne

I thought PPI was something you got through not wearing goggles at the swimming baths.

Gary Delaney

I don't date these girls because they're well read. I gave one of them a copy of *A Farewell to Arms*. She thought it was a diet book.

Henry Fine (George Segal), *The Mirror Has Two Faces*

Trigger still doesn't know which end of the dart to throw.

Mike Fisher (Kenneth MacDonald), *Only Fools and Horses*

When you are dead, you do not know you are dead. It is only painful and difficult for others. The same applies when you are stupid.

Ricky Gervais, Twitter

Dr Alan Harper (Jon Cryer): She looks up to me. She thinks I'm special. She thinks I'm smart.

Charlie Harper (Charlie Sheen): She thinks gazpacho is Pinocchio's father.

Two and a Half Men

Phil Connors (Bill Murray): Do you ever have déjà vu, Mrs Lancaster?

Mrs Lancaster (Angela Paton): I don't think so, but I could check with the kitchen.

Groundhog Day

Adam Green (Arye Gross): You may as well walk in there wearing an 'I am a sucker' T-shirt.

Ellen Morgan (Ellen DeGeneres): I actually have one of those. I can't believe I paid sixty dollars for it!

Ellen

Percy (Tim McInnerny): Only this morning in the courtyard, I saw a horse with two heads and two bodies!

Prince Edmund (Rowan Atkinson): Two horses standing next to each other?

Percy: Yes, I suppose it could have been.

The Black Adder

Norm Peterson (George Wendt): Woody, are you in pain, buddy?

Woody Boyd (Woody Harrelson): No, no, I was just thinking.

Norm: Well, the first time's always the worst.

Cheers

He's out of his depth on a wet pavement.

Sir Terry Pratchett

You want to get Cindy Crawford confused? Ask her to spell 'mom' backwards.

Joan Rivers

Mirror, mirror, on the wall, who's the dumbest of you all?

Anne Robinson, *The Weakest Link*

How come things that happen to stupid people keep happening to me?

Homer Simpson (Dan Castellaneta), *The Simpsons*

Mike Fisher (Kenneth MacDonald): All the lights are out!

Trigger (Roger Lloyd Pack): I know.

Mike: You've been standing in the dark for an hour?

Trigger: Yeah, I thought we were all gonna jump out and surprise someone.

Mike: But there was no one else in there.

Trigger: But I didn't know that, did I? The lights were out.

Only Fools and Horses

He's useless. He's absolutely useless. He's as useless as a marzipan dildo.

Malcolm Tucker (Peter Capaldi), *The Thick of It*

He's so dense that light bends around him.

Malcolm Tucker (Peter Capaldi), *The Thick of It*

Style

Hyacinth Bucket (Patricia Routledge): Rose! Have you been drinking?
Rose (Mary Millar): I haven't been drinking. I took a pill and it seems to have gone straight to my knees.
Hyacinth: I wish you could say the same about your skirt.

Keeping Up Appearances

I'm a schizophrenic mix of wannabe glamour puss and absolute slob and my style is very much magistrate-meets-barmaid.

Jenny Eclair

I'm like old shoes. I've never been hip. I think the reason I'm still here is that I was never enough in fashion that I had to be replaced by something new.

Harrison Ford

I've never been cool and I don't really care about being cool. It's just an awful lot of time and hair gel wasted.

Chris Martin

I wouldn't say I invented tacky, but I certainly brought it to its present high popularity.

Bette Midler

I am the drinking woman's George Clooney . . . if he had an Irish dentist and an entirely different set of life values.

James Nesbitt

If you ever see me in a social setting wearing any sort of sportswear, then you know I'm in crisis.

Bill Nighy

I find it hard to relax around any man who's got the second button on his shirt undone.

Bill Nighy

I don't think I've got bad taste. I've got no taste.

Graham Norton

I try and keep up with what's cool. I was talking to this black kid the other day and I said, 'Hey, man, what's the word on the street?' And he said, 'No parking.'

Alexei Sayle

Is it mandatory that people that roll their own cigarettes do it while staring at you so you can see how cool they are?

Chrissy Teigen, Twitter

I don't fit in. I'm like the only one in a nudist colony with a duffel coat.

Victoria Wood

Success

In Washington, success is just a training course for failure.

Simon Hoggart

The biggest challenge after success is shutting up about it.

Criss Jami

Success is like toilet paper; it only seems important when you don't have it.

Richard Jeni

In America, one sure sign of success is the presence of an unnecessary waterfall in a person's yard.

Demetri Martin

The worst part of success is trying to find someone who is happy for you.

Bette Midler

If you expect a kick in the balls and you get a slap in the face, then it's a victory.

Ardal O'Hanlon

It is well known that a vital ingredient of success is not knowing that what you're attempting can't be done.

Sir Terry Pratchett

The only time success comes before work is in the dictionary.

> Harvey Specter (Gabriel Macht), *Suits*

Sorry, I can't hear you over the sound of how awesome I am.

> Harvey Specter (Gabriel Macht), *Suits*

When you're a baby, success is not wetting your bed. When you're a teenager, success is going all the way. When you're a young man, success is making money. When you are middle-aged, success is being happy. When you're an old man, success is going all the way. And when you're really old, success is not wetting your bed.

> David Steinberg

As soon as you find the key to success, somebody always changes the lock.

> Tracey Ullman

Suicide

Rose, you will not commit suicide. I forbid it! No one in this family has ever committed suicide and I'm sure we're not going to start on the day I'm having the new vicar for tea and light refreshments.

> Hyacinth Bucket (Patricia Routledge), *Keeping Up Appearances*

I couldn't commit suicide if my life depended on it.

> George Carlin

Suicide bombing: now there's a bright idea. I want to see how the instructor does it. 'Right lads, I'm only going to show you this once . . .'

> Billy Connolly

Jeff Greene (Jeff Garlin): How did she die?

Larry David (himself): Killed herself.

Jeff: Why?

Larry: Why? Nobody knows why. She didn't leave a note. That is so rude, isn't it?

Jeff: That is really rude.

Larry: I let my wife know before I go anywhere.

Curb Your Enthusiasm

Dave Horsefall (Mark Addy): Drowning. Now there's a way to go.

Lomper (Steve Huison): I can't swim.

Gary Schofield (Robert Carlyle): Well, you don't have to fucking swim, you divvy, that's the whole point. God, you're not very keen, are you?

Lomper: Sorry.

The Full Monty

Guns are always the best method for a private suicide. They are more stylish looking than single-edged razor blades and natural gas has got so expensive. Drugs are too chancy. You might miscalculate the dosage and just have a good time.

P. J. O'Rourke

Why did the chicken commit suicide? To get to the other side.

Sara Pascoe

I wrote a suicide note once and it said, 'I'm not mad at anybody, this is just something I wanted to do for myself.'

Garry Shandling

Smithy (James Corden): I've been thinking about ending it all, to be honest. Suicide. Big time. How many Nurofen would I need to finish me off?

Gavin Shipman (Mathew Horne): You? You'd need hundreds.

Smithy: Can't afford that, can I? Not if I'm gonna have a holiday this year.

Gavin & Stacey

Suicide? No. Too many people to get even with, and the best way to do that is outlive them.

Diana Trent (Stephanie Cole), *Waiting for God*

I have a paper cut from writing my suicide note. It's a start . . .

Steven Wright

Superheroes

Crime's the disease, meet the cure. OK, not the cure, but more like a topical ointment to reduce the swelling and itch.

Deadpool (Ryan Reynolds), *Deadpool*

I got no respect for Batman. He is this high-powered millionaire who's got all this technology, and he only uses it on street-level crime. He don't focus on corporate, white-collar crime, he only cares about the purse-snatcher on the street. Batman is a conservative's wet dream!

Reginald D. Hunter, *Have I Got News for You*

Most kids prefer Batman to Superman. He's dressed in black, whereas Superman looks like he's just come straight from a Gay Pride march.

Gary Oldman

Surprises

One surprise you should particularly avoid is that which befalls Anastasia on her first date with Christian Grey: 'Turning to face him, I am shocked to find he has his erection firmly in his grasp.' In real life, I promise, this is a very bad idea.

Victoria Coren Mitchell, on *Fifty Shades of Grey*

I don't really like surprises. Not big ones anyway. Just having a pack of Revels holds enough of a surprise for me.

Karl Pilkington, *An Idiot Abroad: The Travel Diaries of Karl Pilkington*

Sweden

Sweden is where they commit suicide and the king rides a bicycle.

Alan Bennett

Eating in Sweden is really just a series of heartbreaks.

Bill Bryson, *Neither Here Nor There: Travels in Europe*

Swimming

Gordon Brittas (Chris Barrie): It is seven years to the day since the first member of the public came through those hallowed portals.
Gavin (Tim Marriott): And you threw him out, Mr Brittas!
Gordon: He was wearing unauthorised water wings, Gavin.

The Brittas Empire

Swimming is good for you . . . especially if you're drowning.

Jimmy Carr

I always wanted to go swimming with dolphins. But when it came to it they both died in the car on the way to the baths.

Milton Jones

Nobody learns swimming as fast as a spider in a rapidly filling bath.

Miles Kington

I've never been swimming, and that's because it's never more than half an hour since I last ate.

Artie Lange

I think everybody pees in the pool.

Michael Phelps

There is water in every lane, so it's OK.

Australian swimming champion Ian Thorpe,
on drawing lane five in competition

When I go swimming, it's like the *Queen Mary* coming into port.

Sandi Toksvig

Of course he [Lord Nelson] couldn't swim, he only had one bloody arm. He would have gone round in circles, wouldn't he?

Del Trotter (David Jason), *Only Fools and Horses*

Switzerland

Since its national products – snow and chocolate – both melt, the cuckoo clock was invented solely in order to give tourists something solid to remember it by.

Alan Coren

Pity the Swiss. They've got France to the left, Austria to the right, Germany up above, Italy down below. You'd never sell that flat!

Al Murray, The Pub Landlord

How can you trust an army that has a wine opener on its knife?

Robin Williams

Tact

Honey, tact is for people who aren't witty enough to be sarcastic.

Karen Walker (Megan Mullally), *Will & Grace*

Talent

Interviewer: Do you have any other skills?
Nobby Butcher (Sacha Baron Cohen): I can make my balls look like Sir Ian McKellen.

Grimsby

I am a lucky woman because I was born with a priceless gift: the ability to laugh at the misfortunes of others.

Dame Edna Everage (Barry Humphries)

When choosing sexual partners, remember: talent is not sexually transmittable.

Tina Fey, *Bossypants*

Let's move on to the Gala. Any progress there, or is the climax of our show still 'Owen and His Amazing Farting Duck'?

David Horton (Gary Waldhorn), *The Vicar of Dibley*

Some are blessed with musical ability, others with good looks. Myself, I was blessed with modesty.

Sir Roger Moore

I've always thought that parallel parking was my main talent.

Calvin Trillin

I have a photographic memory. I just haven't developed it yet.

Jonathan Winters

Tattoos

I get a new tattoo every two years, because that's how long it takes me to forget what 'forever' means.

Caitlin Bergh

Tattoo on the lower back? Might as well be a bullseye.

Jeremy Grey (Vince Vaughn), *Wedding Crashers*

I want to get the words 'Courage' and 'Bravery' tattooed across my back, so people could associate me with those things as they read them while they chase me.

Jarod Kintz, *I Want*

If Jesus had known that his image would end up on Justin Bieber's calf, he would never have started Christianity.

Natasha Leggero

The tattooist said to me that she didn't believe in anaesthetic. I said, 'I assure you, it does exist.'

Diane Spencer

You get that tattoo of barbed wire when you're eighteen, but by the time you're eighty, it's a picket fence.

Robin Williams

Taxation

One third of a pint of beer is tax. Not until about halfway through your pint do you stop drinking for the government and start drinking for yourself.

Al Murray, The Pub Landlord

Blanche Devereaux (Rue McClanahan): I never had to pay a penny in back taxes. I have a way with auditors. The last time I was audited, I even got money back from the government.
Sophia Petrillo (Estelle Getty): Blanche, it's not a refund when the auditor leaves two twenties on your nightstand.

The Golden Girls

Taxation is just a sophisticated way of demanding money with menaces.

Sir Terry Pratchett

I love paying tax so much, the sight of a gritter lorry gives me an erection.

Jon Richardson

Teaching

I had a geography teacher who fancied me, but she said, 'I'm going to wait until you finish school.' So at half-past-three she fucked me.

Jimmy Carr

Do you think when gym teachers are younger, they're thinking, 'I want to teach, but I don't want to read'?

Jim Gaffigan

Remember that kid who had sex with his high school teacher? I read that he died . . . from high-fiving.

Zach Galifianakis

Teachers don't start each day by swearing allegiance to the education fairies under a portrait of the Queen. It's not so much a calling as a graveyard for the unlucky and the unambitious. Between you and me, the only reason anyone teaches these days is that they've taken a more relaxed stance on police checks in recent years.

Mr Gilbert (Greg Davies), The Inbetweeners

Karen (Tanya Franks): I need the cash. They don't pay teachers very much, Donna, in case you've been living under a rock. We are virtually paupers.
Donna (Sharon Horgan): You take a taxi to the off licence, Karen!

Pulling

I was tucking my son in last night and he told me that he hates his teacher. She's 'an idiot' and she's 'out to get' him, which is the last thing you want to hear when your kid's home-schooled.

Brian Kiley

You know how to tell if the teacher is hungover? Movie day.

Jay Mohr

Unless you sit down and shut up immediately, I will write down on the board the name of a character who dies in *Game of Thrones*, season five.

Alfie Wickers (Jack Whitehall), Bad Education

Technology

Ten years I've been Skypeing my mother and I've never seen more than the top of her head.

Aisling Bea

I check my phone messages and email about forty-five times a day. I don't even know what I'm expecting to get in these messages. Maybe Visa will call and say, 'We just realised that we owe you money', or I'll get an email from a high school classmate that says, 'We've reconsidered and we've decided that you were cool after all.'

Mike Birbiglia, *Sleepwalk With Me and Other Painfully True Stories*

My husband proposed to me on Skype. He got down on one knee and disappeared off the screen.

Brenda Blethyn

If my granny had even seen a laptop, she would have tried to toast a sandwich in it.

Frankie Boyle

To the people who've got iPhones: you just bought one, you didn't invent it!

Marcus Brigstocke

When I tell people I don't own a mobile phone and wouldn't know how to text, they react as though I have just confessed that I can't read.

Craig Brown

My office password's been hacked. That's the third time I've had to rename the cat.

Liz Buckley, Twitter

I finally figured out what email is for. It's for communicating with people you'd rather not talk to.

George Carlin, *When Will Jesus Bring the Pork Chops?*

Elliot Carver (Jonathan Pryce): Mr Jones, are we ready to release our new software?

Philip Jones (Rolf Saxon): Yes, sir. As requested, it's full of bugs, which means people will be forced to upgrade for years.

Elliot: Outstanding.

Tomorrow Never Dies

The most useless app on my smartphone is the phone.

Abbi Crutchfield, Twitter

I really hope cell phones aren't bad for us, but I would like the excuse, 'I can't talk right now. You're giving me cancer.'

Whitney Cummings

The smartphone has become almost cutlery – fork in one hand, phone in the other.

Jenny Eclair

I bought my mum a Kindle because she likes reading so much. She still licks her fingers when she changes the page.

Lee Evans

Why does turning on a TV these days require three remotes with ninety buttons?

Helen Fielding, *Bridget Jones: Mad About the Boy*

At some point, the computer industry decided that if you have an email address, you must have some kind of penis problem.

Greg Fitzsimmons

One technology doesn't replace another, it complements. Books are no more threatened by Kindle than stairs by elevators.

Stephen Fry

It's amazing how email has changed our lives. If you ever get a handwritten letter in the mail, you go, 'What the . . . ? Has someone been kidnapped?'

Jim Gaffigan

If you're selling something on Craigslist, it's never a good idea to end the description with 'May have lice'.

Dana Gould

Because of Bluetooth headsets, it's getting more and more difficult to tell who's schizophrenic and who's on a conference call.

Dana Gould

Old women with mobile phones look wrong.

Peter Kay

There's a new app that tells you if your date is a relative. You just press a button, and Bob's your uncle!

David Mitchell, *Have I Got News for You*

My iPod holds three thousand albums. I own, like, ninety albums. My iPod sits at home sullen, frustrated and underused, like a wife who gave up her career and the kids turned out to be shite.

Dara O'Briain

The Catholic church has approved a new app that lets you make confessions over your iPhone. It also raises the possibility of accidentally butt-dialling God.

Conan O'Brien

A new sports bra recently went on sale that features a special pocket to hold an iPod. In fact, I saw a woman today who looked like she was carrying at least twenty thousand songs.

Conan O'Brien

If my mobile was switched off, it was switched off for a reason. I was at an owl sanctuary. I was worried that the ringing might have sounded like a mating call. I can't have a bird trying to have sex with my phone.

Alan Partridge (Steve Coogan), *I'm Alan Partridge*

If you say 'No' [to a selfie], they look at you like you just shot their child. Eventually you pull a face into the camera. He puts it on his page and before you know it, you google my name and that's the first picture to pop up. Looking shit!

Jennifer Saunders

The iPhone 2 led to the 3, but I didn't get the 4 or 5 because I'm holding out for the 7, which, I've heard on good authority, can also be used as a Taser. This will mean I'll have one less thing to carry around.

David Sedaris, *Let's Explore Diabetes with Owls*

My name is Fin, which means it's very hard for me to end emails without sounding pretentious.

Fin Taylor

I'm not interested in watching TV on my phone in the same way I don't want to take a shit in my oven.

Mark Watson

Teenagers

The biggest teenage taboo is being straitlaced. It's easy to tell a researcher you went to a house party that turned into an orgy. It's less easy to say you like eating toast and watching *QI*.

Charlie Brooker

The average teenager watches six hours of television every day. At least with drugs, you're out – you're singing, you're dancing. You're meeting people. You're breaking into homes. You're networking.

David Feldman

Hey, Lois, give Chris a break. I mean, no TV? So he failed a class, it's not like he felt up his cousin in the garage that one time when I was nineteen.

Peter Griffin (Seth MacFarlane), *Family Guy*

I don't want to be a traitor to my generation and all but I don't get how guys dress today. I mean, come on, it looks like they just fell out of bed and put on some baggy pants and took their greasy hair – ew – and covered it up with a backwards cap and, like, we're expected to swoon? I don't think so.

Cher Horowitz (Alicia Silverstone), *Clueless*

Teenagers are obviously God's punishment for having sex in the first place.

Kathy Lette

Having a teenage daughter is like living with the Taliban: a mum is not allowed to laugh, sing, dance or wear short skirts.

Kathy Lette

When I try to hug her, it's as if I'm a Russian spy full of plutonium. She keeps me very much at arm's length.

Kathy Lette

Teenagers complain there's nothing to do, then stay out all night doing it.

Bob Phillips

Raising a teenager makes the terrible twos seem like a holiday in Hawaii.

Ruby Wax, *A Mindfulness Guide for the Frazzled*

Teeth

I had to have a brace because I had big teeth. If I'd gone to Africa, I would have got poached.

Alan Carr

My girlfriend gets mad when I use her toothbrush but I ask you: how else am I meant to get dog shit out of the carpet?

Jimmy Carr

I finally have a dental plan. I chew on the other side.

Janine Ditullio

Have you ever looked at Kylie [Minogue]'s teeth? Those teeth are proportional to the teeth of a camel in the mouth of a toddler.

Jeremy Hardy

Margaret Meldrew (Annette Crosbie): What time's your appointment with the dentist this morning?

Victor Meldrew (Richard Wilson): Eleven-thirty.

Margaret Meldrew: Thank God for that. I've seen enough of those temporary crowns to last me a lifetime. It's like being kissed goodnight by Bugs Bunny.

One Foot in the Grave

Hank Kingsley (Jeffrey Tambor): What about the time I chipped my tooth on the bathroom urinal? What the fuck is so comical about that?

Larry Sanders (Garry Shandling): It was a back tooth, Hank . . . I don't know how you did it.

The Larry Sanders Show

'You have what we in France call "Good-time teeth",' she said. 'Why on earth would you want to change them?' 'Um, because I can floss with the sash to my bathrobe?'

David Sedaris, *Let's Explore Diabetes with Owls*

My extra-sensitive toothpaste doesn't like it when I use other toothpastes.

@senderblock23, Twitter

I've got very sensitive teeth. They'll probably be upset I've told you.

Gordon Southern

Television

Did you know it's possible on Netflix to run out of genocide documentaries?

Maria Bamford

Does anyone ever find it ironic how a programme aimed at old people is called *Countdown*?

Frankie Boyle

Working Lunch, a show for people who are so good at business they're sat at home watching TV in the middle of the day.

Frankie Boyle, *Mock the Week*

I think that people only get so offended by television because they rely on it as a babysitter and the sole educator of their kids.

Kyle Broflovski (Matt Stone), *South Park*

MasterChef is the best television show in broadcasting history, if you ignore all the other ones.

Charlie Brooker

In many ways *Big Brother* is the present day equivalent of a 1980s' Club 18–30 holiday: flirting, sunbathing, silly little organised games and lots of people you'd like to remove from the gene pool with a cricket bat.

Charlie Brooker

There are few things quite so effortlessly enjoyable as watching an eminent person getting in a huff and flouncing out of a television interview, often with microphone trailing.

Craig Brown

The best that can be said for Norwegian television is that it gives you the sensation of a coma without the worry and inconvenience.

Bill Bryson, *Neither Here Nor There: Travels in Europe*

The teenage masturbators of today are the television executives of tomorrow.

Melissa Cabriolet (Letitia Dean), *Drop the Dead Donkey*

I don't like to think of there being winners and losers in the *Big Brother* house. To me, they're all losers.

Jimmy Carr, *8 Out of 10 Cats*

In the olden days, it was easy to make a television work. You plugged an aerial cable into the back, then bashed the top with your fist until, eventually, Hughie Green stopped jumping up and down.

Jeremy Clarkson, *Is It Really Too Much to Ask?*

Fox News gives you both sides of every story: the president's side and the vice president's side.

Stephen Colbert, on the network during the George W. Bush presidency

Friday night on BBC One, we'll discover who has won *Fame Academy*, as the BBC plucks someone from obscurity and, with the help of designers, choreographers and a million-pound prize, throws them straight back into obscurity.

Continuity announcer, *Dead Ringers*

Unlikely things a TV continuity announcer would say . . . 'If you were affected by any of the issues raised in tonight's episode of *Balamory* . . .'

Hugh Dennis, *Mock the Week*

Gok Wan has a programme telling us what to wear, now what to eat. I feel like I'm in an abusive relationship with Channel 4.

Hayley Ellis

I would like to be able to watch the evening news with my family without having to explain what oral sex means to my wife.

David Feldman

I saw a documentary on how ships are kept together. Riveting!

Stewart Francis

Nothing ages a woman so rapidly as a diet of relentless Jeremy Kyle and *Emmerdale*. Evidenced by Grandmama, who carries the horrific strains and scars of years of loyal service to both of these demanding mistresses.

Dawn French, *A Tiny Bit Marvellous*

I wish there was a knob on the TV so you could turn up the intelligence. They've got one marked 'brightness', but it doesn't work, does it?

Gallagher

I watch hours on end of the History Channel and Discovery Channel. Just back and forth, History Channel and Discovery Channel. Ask me anything about sharks and Nazis.

Ricky Gervais

Nowadays, you can't let your kids watch TV. You don't know what's happening – a breast might pop out, somebody might lick somebody. It's, like, 'Hey, turn off that damn Disney Channel!'

Adele Givens

If John Logie Baird had been born in 1971, would he have been a genius? The only thing we know with any certainty is that he wouldn't have invented the television. Some people believe he would have still established his genius; that he would have simply found another arena in which to work. I disagree. I think he would have been distracted from such brainy pursuits by all that television.

Dave Gorman

Reality TV is the perfect antidote for people who don't have enough self-centred douchebags in their life.

Dana Gould

Things you wouldn't hear in a period drama . . . 'Mr Darcy, I do believe you've poked me on Facebook.'

Russell Howard, *Mock the Week*

Like anybody both adult and sane I had no intention of watching *Game of Thrones* . . . I place a total embargo on dragons.

Clive James, *Play All*

Sarah Lund [in *The Killing*] is a thin bundle of neuroses plunged into the gloom of a bad sweater.

Clive James, *Play All*

Rick Spleen (Jack Dee): Was that OK?
Jamie, TV commercial director (Ben Willbond): It was great, Rick. It's daytime TV, isn't it? It's for pond life, jobless morons stuffing their faces full of crisps, fat, single mums with eight kids from different dads . . .

Lead Balloon

TV networks are dying. The death throes of religion give us jihads. The death throes of television give us reality shows.

Penn Jillette

I don't see why people are so snooty about Channel 5. It has some respectable documentaries about the Second World War. It also devotes considerable airtime to investigations into lap dancing and other related and vital subjects.

Boris Johnson

The Bachelor is the show that answers the question: how much wine do you have to drink until the guy making out with twenty different women seems like he'd make a good husband?

Jimmy Kimmel

All [pub] landlords are like bad TV chat show hosts. So are all TV chat show hosts.

Miles Kington

I know what you're thinking. You're thinking, Oh, the script's not funny, it's lowest common denominator, and, you know, you're right. But don't worry about it. Because people will watch anything, all right? Particularly if it's after *EastEnders* and they haven't got to change the channel. Those sort of morons will help us win the ratings war. And, you know, ratings in the end are what count. And merchandise.

Theatrical agent Darren Lamb (Stephen Merchant), *Extras*

Sarah Palin made her debut as a Fox News analyst. They finally found a job that she's not under-qualified for.

David Letterman

You ever see *The Dating Game*? That's a weird game show. The prize on that show: another contestant. Talk about cheap.

Norm Macdonald

The only people who are desperate to go on the show are people we're desperate *not* to have on the show.

Chat show host Graham Norton

Let's face it, Fox [News], you'll miss me when I'm gone. It will be harder to convince the American people that Hillary was born in Kenya.

Barack Obama

A Trump administration official said that whenever the media criticises the president, they will call it 'fake news'. And whenever the media praises the president, they will call it 'Fox News'.

Conan O'Brien

Rex Harrison told me that he wouldn't talk about his ex-wives, and I said, 'Rex, you've been married six times. That's going to leave a pretty big gap.' He said, 'Yes, I suppose you're right, dear boy.'

Michael Parkinson

In my television paradise there would be no more property programmes, no more police-chasing-yobbos-in-cars programmes and, most of all – and please God – no more so-called documentary shows with titles like *My Twenty-Ton Tumour*, *My Big Fat Head*, *Wolf Girl*, *Embarrassing Illnesses* and *The Fastest Man on No Legs*.

Michael Parkinson

I've watched all of Bear Grylls' shows, and there doesn't seem to be a problem that can't be solved by drinking your own piss.

Chris Ramsey

I went on *Bake Off* and made vegan brownies, because I am one.

Romesh Ranganathan

I'm definitely going to watch the Emmys this year. My make-up team is nominated for Best Special Effects.

Joan Rivers

I knew I'd conquered America when Mike Tyson told me I was one mean lady.

Anne Robinson

Mandy, you're going to be a reality TV star! It's what every pretty girl with no specific talent dreams of.

Marc St James (Michael Urie), *Ugly Betty*

I don't like reality television. I think real people should not be on television; it's for special people like us, people who have trained and studied to appear to be real.

Garry Shandling

ITV is celebrating its fiftieth birthday this week. Coincidentally, 1955 was also the year James Dean was killed in a fatal car crash. Yes, fifty years ago, they both hit the screen.

Frank Skinner

Every time you watch *Jersey Shore*, a book commits suicide.

Professor Snape, Twitter

I have high-definition television because I felt the lack of resolution was affecting my ability to solve cases on *CSI*.

Daniel Tosh

I saw that show, *50 Things To Do Before You Die*. I would have thought the obvious one was shout for help.

Mark Watson

My favourite news story was at the time of the Californian forest fires. I was watching the news and this guy said that, in the blaze, three hundred mobile homes had been destroyed. Now, I don't know whether there are that many advantages to a mobile home, if any, but one of the main ones, the big selling-point of the mobile home, is that you're not really tied down to an area. Especially if the said area is on fucking fire!

Jack Whitehall

Netflix shows shouldn't remind us what happened on the last episode. They should remind us what happened since the last time we went outside.

Michelle Wolf, Twitter

You know daytime television? You know what it's supposed to be for? It's to keep unemployed people happy. It's supposed to stop them running to the social security demanding mad luxuries like cookers and windows.

Victoria Wood

I thought *Benefits Street* was a budget box of chocolates that you could buy at Lidl.

Imran Yusuf

Tennis

During the warming-up training before play I prayed. Not for victory, but that my hairpiece wouldn't fall off.

Andre Agassi, *Open*, about the French Open 1990

Like many men who play tennis, when I hit a ball into the net, I tend to look daggers at my racket, reproaching it for playing so badly when I myself have been trying so hard.

Craig Brown

Roger Federer's only weakness is heavy metal music.

Andrew Castle

Female tennis players must be able to control their grunting. Can't they just try and pretend that their parents are in the next room?

Jeremy Hardy

I've seen better tennis playing in a tampon commercial.

Helen's stepson (Matt Bennett), *Bridesmaids*

Tim Henman is going to be a father again. So that means at least one British seed got through.

Lenny Henry, 2004

(of Maria Sharapova's grunts): She sounds like a live pig being slaughtered.

Frew McMillan

In the women's game, why does the pretty one always lose to the moose?

David Mitchell

You can't improve at tennis after you're fifty. You get to be in your forties, and suddenly you're a doubles player.

Jack Nicholson

Serena Williams' breasts alone must weigh more than Justine Henin-Hardenne.

Matthew Norman

She was beside herself, which, come to think of it, would make a great doubles team.

> Scott Ostler, on a Martina Navratilova outburst

It's weird when you watch women's tennis now, with all the grunting and shouting. It's a bit like phone sex. So you have to be very careful not to get too excited.

> Robin Williams

Terrorism

I suppose you could be a member of a terrorist organisation in a non-violent way, in the laundry or the catering department.

> Bill Bailey

Did you see that guy they jailed the other month – Osama bin London? Is that the stage it has got to? Fucking tribute acts?!

> Frankie Boyle

I hate all this terrorist business. I used to love the days when you could look at an unattended bag on the train or bus and think, 'I'm having that!'

> Frankie Boyle

Who are we blowing up in Iraq? IS [Islamic State]. Remember last year when they said: 'We need to bomb Syria! Help the rebels – they're the good guys.' Who are the rebels? IS. They're the same people! They've gone from being loved to hated and despised in a year, and they haven't had to win *The X Factor* to make that happen.

> Frankie Boyle

On the airlines they're confiscating tweezers and shaving equipment. What do they think you'll do – give someone a makeover?

> Ed Byrne

Remember the good old days when the only bomb you had to worry about on a plane was the Rob Schneider movie?

> Jay Leno

Susan Boyle is an important weapon in the war on terror. Young extremists are thinking twice about blowing themselves up because they now know what a virgin looks like.

Sean Lock

Men who blow themselves up are promised seventy-two virgins in paradise. That's a high price to pay for a shag.

Shazia Mirza

They say being a hostage is difficult, but I could do that with my hands tied behind my back.

Phil Nichol

You know who I feel bad for? Arab-Americans who truly want to get into crop dusting. It could be their lifelong dream, but every time they ask for a pamphlet, all hell breaks loose.

Brian Regan

Nobody starts something hoping it will fail – except maybe a suicide bombing.

Katherine Ryan

Theatre

Miss, these seats are dreadful. They're facing the stage.

Roland T. Flakfizer (John Turturro), *Brain Donors*

I had a real allergy to Shakespeare. I thought it was very much the reserve of middle-class white people with tights and a cabbage down the front.

Lenny Henry

Linda La Hughes (Kathy Burke): I've been on stage. I was the Virgin Mary in the young offenders' nativity play.
Tom Farrell (James Dreyfus): You played our virgin mother, you blasphemous bint?
Linda: I was a virgin . . . till the dress rehearsal, anyway.

Gimme Gimme Gimme

Star quality is if you're on stage and a cat walks on, and they [the audience] still watch you.

Jack Nicholson

When I do a play, it's like agreeing to be ill for a couple of months.

Bill Nighy

[Jukebox musicals] get heterosexuals and the working classes going to the theatre, which is a good thing I suppose, but the amount of Pringles these peasants consume during performances is astonishing. Theatres these days reek of sour cream and chive.

Sir Tim Rice (himself), *Brian Pern: A Life in Rock*

Daffyd Thomas (Matt Lucas): The audition was a complete waste of time, the director said he couldn't see me as Hamlet. I'm sorry, Myfanwy, but the Llanddewi Brefi Amateur Dramatics Society is completely homophobist.
Myfanwy (Ruth Jones): What audition speech did you do?
Daffyd Thomas: 'It's Raining Men' by the Weather Girls.

Little Britain

Rose Nylund (Betty White): Well, I thought she was good in *The Diary of Anne Frank*.
Dorothy Zbornak (Bea Arthur): Rose, please! During the entire second act the audience kept screaming: 'She is in the attic! She is in the attic!'

The Golden Girls

Therapy

I am not going out there as a woman pretending to be a man pretending to be Tina Turner. I can't afford therapy on my salary.

Sam Fuller (Regina King), *Miss Congeniality 2: Armed and Fabulous*

Support groups? In my day when something bad happened you'd stay at home, get drunk and bite on a shoe!

Blanche Hunt (Maggie Jones), *Coronation Street*

Anyone living in Los Angeles who says they don't need a psychiatrist, needs a psychiatrist.

Kathy Lette

I'm in therapy at the moment. I don't need it, obviously, but I got all these psychiatrist gift vouchers for Christmas which my family clubbed together for. What I wanted was a crossbow.

Sean Lock

Being in therapy is great. I spend an hour just talking about myself. It's like being the guy on a date.

Caroline Rhea

Gabrielle Solis (Eva Longoria): I love therapy!
Carlos Solis (Ricardo Antonio Chavira): Really?
Gabrielle Solis: Yeah! It's like a talk show, where I'm the guest and the only topic is me.

Desperate Housewives

Time

To a man standing on the shore, time passes quicker than to a man on a boat – especially if the man on the boat is with his wife.

Woody Allen, *Mere Anarchy*

I don't understand people who say they need more 'me time'. What other time is there? Do these people spend part of their day in someone else's body?

Jarod Kintz, *This Book is Not for Sale*

Now, where did I leave my time machine? Oh, I know, next Wednesday.

Hugh Laurie, *The Gun Seller*

I bought a clock, but the big hand broke off it. So I just added 'ish' to every number.

Demetri Martin

Del Trotter (David Jason): It's closed! You said it was open twenty-four hours a day.

Trigger (Roger Lloyd Pack): Yeah, but not at night.

Only Fools and Horses

There's never enough time to do all the nothing you want.

Bill Watterson, *Calvin and Hobbes*

Toys

Lego is always opened and then left lying around so adults have something to tread on when they are prowling around the house at two in the morning, in bare feet, looking for the source of a noise.

Jeremy Clarkson, *And Another Thing . . .*

I tried to throw a yo-yo away. It was impossible.

Mitch Hedberg

The Etch A Sketch is the toy for drawing that makes drawing almost impossible. It simulates what drawing would be like if you had crippling arthritis.

Jared Logan

It's very easy to turn a toy into an adult toy; location, location, location.

Demetri Martin

Tradespeople

Margaret Meldrew (Annette Crosbie): Well? Any joy?

Victor Meldrew (Richard Wilson): I think it's safe to say I've had a very good day, all told. In the morning, I turned some water into wine, and then I healed a few lepers and, after lunch, I popped over and parted the waters of the Red Sea.

Margaret: Did the man come about the roof?

Victor: No, but you can't expect miracles.

One Foot in the Grave

Jesus was a carpenter, A tradesman. You can tell he was a tradesman because he disappeared off the face of the earth for three days with no rational explanation.

Al Murray, The Pub Landlord

Last Tuesday I was hosting the National Plumbers' Awards. It was meant to be on Monday, but I thought, 'Bollocks, they do it to me!'

Rick Spleen (Jack Dee), *Lead Balloon*

Transport and Travel

Ali G (Sacha Baron Cohen): When is man going to walk on da sun?
Buzz Aldrin: It's much too hot on the sun.
Ali G: We could go in da winter, when it's colder.

Da Ali G Show

If it's sent by ship then it's a cargo, if it's sent by road then it's a shipment.

Dave Allen

What was wrong with train toilet doors that just locked – instead of this multiple-choice system? If anything goes wrong, you'll be sitting there while the whole toilet wall slowly slides away, like a prize on a quiz show. For five hundred points, a shitting woman!

Frankie Boyle

It is an extraordinary fact but a true one that there are thousands of men in Britain who will never need Viagra as long as steam trains are in operation.

Bill Bryson, *The Road to Little Dribbling: More Notes from a Small Island*

Caravans are a fun way of telling your kids that you're poor.

Jimmy Carr

I don't understand bus lanes. Why do poor people have to get to places quicker than I do?

Jeremy Clarkson

I want to hang a map of the world in my house, then I'm gonna put pins into all the locations that I've travelled to. But first I'm gonna have to travel to the top two corners of the map so it won't fall down.

Mitch Hedberg

They're called Virgin Trains because they don't go all the way.

Simon Hoggart

I forgot that to rely on a train, in Blair's Britain, is to engage in a crap-shoot with the devil.

Boris Johnson

Trains in Britain can be late for all sorts of reasons: speed restrictions, livestock on the track, or a totally substandard rail infrastructure that's publicly funded, privately run and answerable to no one. All sorts of reasons.

Miles Jupp

Don't go to Casablanca expecting it to be like the film. In fact, if you're not too busy and your schedule allows it, don't go to Casablanca at all.

Hugh Laurie, *The Gun Seller*

Whenever I travel I like to keep the seat next to me empty. I found a great way to do it. When someone walks down the aisle and says to you, 'Is someone sitting there?' just say, 'No one except the Lord.'

Carol Leifer

My best friend got a truck. She didn't want to be trendy, so she got a UPS truck. You might laugh, but she can park it anywhere.

Wendy Liebman

England's transport system is great – we've got the best rail replacement bus service in the world.

Lee Nelson (Simon Brodkin)

Let me tell you something about the *Titanic*. People forget that on the *Titanic*'s maiden voyage there were over one thousand miles of uneventful, very pleasurable cruising before it hit the iceberg

Alan Partridge (Steve Coogan), *Knowing Me,*
Knowing You with Alan Partridge

The train system is so chronic now that any journey you undertake by train in Britain is identical to the one taken by Omar Sharif in *Doctor Zhivago* . . . Ancient, knackered rolling-stock limping painfully across the land, shuddering to a halt for no apparent reason . . . Desperate women in headscarves running alongside the carriages, throwing their babies into the train, shouting: 'I'll never see Purley Oaks, but my child might!'

Linda Smith

Getting stuck on a train for three days because a swan in the next county has decided to sit quite near the track.

Rob Temple, *Very British Problems*

When you've got an empty seat by you in a train and you don't want anybody to sit there, the trick is, as they approach, you smile at them and pat the seat.

Johnny Vaughan, *QI*

Tim Bisley (Simon Pegg): Where are you?
Mike Watt (Nick Frost): Er, Sheffield.
Tim: What are you doing in Sheffield?
Mike: Fell asleep on the tube.
Tim: The tube doesn't go to Sheffield, Mike.
Mike: Yeah, I know. I must have changed at King's Cross.

Spaced

Transvestites and Transgender

Rita Marshall (Doris Belack): I'd like to make her [Dorothy Michaels] look a little more attractive. How far can you pull back?
Cameraman: How do you feel about Cleveland?

Tootsie

Eddie Izzard is a straight man who identifies as a man, who likes to dress as a female estate agent from the eighties.

Bridget Christie

I am a professional transvestite, so I can run about in heels and not fall over. If a woman falls over wearing heels, that's embarrassing, but if a bloke falls over wearing heels, you have to kill yourself. It's the end of your life.

Eddie Izzard

I saw a transvestite wearing a T-shirt that said 'Guess'.

Demetri Martin

Roz Doyle (Peri Gilpin): This uncle of yours – does he dress like a woman all the time?
Daphne Moon (Jane Leeves): No, certainly not for work. His congregation would never stand for it.

Frasier

We are no longer allowed to incite hatred against lesbians, gays, and transgenders, but it's OK, we can still make jokes about them, which is lucky, isn't it, especially when it comes to transgenders. If you take a lady home and find out she's got a cock, you want to be able to have a bloody good laugh about it!

Andy Parsons

Donald Trump

Orange is the new black.

Anon, after Trump succeeded Barack Obama in November 2016

What does Melania see in Donald Trump? Ten billion dollars and high cholesterol.

Anon

All Americans must be accompanied by an adult.

Sign outside a London pub after Trump's election victory

We shall overcomb.

Sign at a 2017 anti-Trump protest march in London

Americans know Trump is a sexist bigot. They just don't care. A lot of voters have decided that racism and sexism aren't great but they're not a deal-breaker, kind of like a sandwich with too much mayo – they think they can just scrape off the extra white nonsense.

Samantha Bee

(on Trump's election win): Our democracy just hawked up a marmalade hairball with the whole world watching.

Samantha Bee

Say what you want about Trump, he is not stupid. He is a smart man with a deep understanding of what stupid people want.

Andy Borowitz

It's not just that he's the worst person for the job, he might even be the worst mammal.

Frankie Boyle

His face looks like a novelty jug made in a secure unit pottery class . . . his hair looks like a slovenly post-coital cat.

Frankie Boyle

He doesn't really have policies – they're more the sort of things a drunk would say on a bus when he gets shaken awake by a pothole.

Frankie Boyle

Apparently the Trump Foundation bought a six-foot portrait of Donald. It's very realistic; the hands seem to follow you around the room.

Jo Brand

It's bad news for minorities and women and everyone else he's insulted, but it's a progressive move inasmuch as they've elected the most openly crazy man to the most powerful office in the world.

Charlie Brooker, *Have I Got News for You*

Donald Trump looks like a guinea pig staring at you through the porthole on a washing machine.

Charlie Brooker

His strange hair, like an airplane on a launch pad.

Craig Brown

He's a child impersonating an adult, isn't he?

Morrissey

This man ejected a crying baby from a rally. And for that reason, Donald Trump should not have the authority to deploy US troops. Not if he's threatened by a crying baby. I don't even think the baby was armed.

Bridget Christie

People look at the Statue of Liberty and they see a proud symbol of our history as a nation of immigrants, a beacon of hope for people around the world. Donald looks at the Statue of Liberty and sees a four. Maybe a five, if she loses the torch and tablet and changes her hair.

Hillary Clinton

John McCain thinks Trump could be a 'capable leader'. I'm sorry, but that's not very reassuring. If you are about to have an operation and they tell you that your doctor could be a capable surgeon, you would be like, 'You know what? It was a minor heart attack. I'm good. Don't worry.'

James Corden, *The Late Late Show*

Republicans hope he'll keep his promise to build the wall and Democrats hope he'll keep his promise not to accept the election results.

Jimmy Fallon, the day after Trump's victory

According to his campaign staff, Donald Trump won't take any vacations as president. I think that's because he has offended so many other countries he can't leave this one.

Jimmy Fallon

Donald Trump showed his birth certificate to reporters. Who cares about his birth certificate? I want to know if that thing on his head has had its vaccinations.

Craig Ferguson

The trouble now with political jokes is that they have started to get elected.

William Hague

Hillary allegedly deletes her email history; now we've got a guy who will delete all history.

> Rich Hall

The inside of Trump Tower is fantastic – it's sort of late-Gaddafi, perhaps early-Saddam; it's a riot of vulgar dictator chic.

> Ian Hislop, *Have I Got News for You*

Donald Trump is giving narcissism a bad name.

> Madeleine Begun Kane

At first, Donald Trump came out with guns blazing, saying he's going to kick all the Mexicans out and build a wall to keep them from coming back in. But he could be softening. He's now agreed to give immigrants a thirty-minute head start before he tries to catch them with a net.

> Jimmy Kimmel

The one guy Donald Trump has nothing bad to say about is Vladimir Putin. Maybe he is afraid Putin will cut off his supply of wives.

> Jimmy Kimmel

Haven't voters noticed that Trump has the sort of look usually reserved for a ranting person bursting into McDonald's holding a chainsaw?

> Kathy Lette

When Trump bangs a supermodel, he closes his eyes and imagines he's jerking off.

> Seth MacFarlane

There are schizophrenics with Tourette's who have more control over what comes out of their mouths than Donald Trump.

> Bill Maher

Donald Trump is nuts, his party is chock full of nuts, too, and that is bad news for Americans with a nut allergy.

> Steve Merrick

Mike Pence is finding out that being Trump's vice president is like being a fireman who has an arsonist for a roommate.

> Seth Meyers

Donald Trump likes to say he's a friend to 'the blacks'. Unless the Blacks are a family of white people, I'm guessing he's mistaken.

Seth Meyers

President-elect Donald Trump visited President Obama in the White House today, which got Trump really excited to do his favourite thing: evict a black family from their home.

Seth Meyers

Barack Obama surprised his White House staffers with a private concert by Bruce Springsteen to thank them for their work over the last eight years. Meanwhile, Trump thanked his supporters with a performance by a Bruce Springsteen cover band's drummer's DJ friend.

Seth Meyers, on the eve of Trump's inauguration

Donald Trump comes closer than anyone else to being the archetype of the species; crossing genres, he exemplifies all the ways an asshole can capture our attention.

Geoffrey Nunberg, *Ascent of the A-Word: Assholism, the First Sixty Years*

Donald Trump insisted he's always had a great relationship with women. He said, 'I believe a woman can be anything she wants to be, whether that's Miss USA or Miss Universe. Either one.'

Conan O'Brien

Donald Trump's daughter Ivanka gave birth to a baby girl. The baby's name is Trump Granddaughter and Casino.

Conan O'Brien

A former speechwriter for John McCain said Donald Trump has an unstable personality. This is coming from the guy who wrote the words, 'Please welcome my running mate, Sarah Palin.'

Conan O'Brien

Sarah Palin said that God helped Donald Trump win the presidential election. When he heard this, a furious Satan said, 'Don't I get credit for anything?'

Conan O'Brien

Donald Trump is America's back mole. It may have seemed harmless a year ago but now that it's got frighteningly bigger, it's no longer wise to ignore it.

John Oliver, 2016

Donald Trump has had two foreign wives. It turns out that there really are jobs Americans won't do.

Mitt Romney

Donald Trump is the kind of person who goes to the Super Bowl and thinks the people in the huddle are talking about him.

Eric Schneiderman

If God gave comedians the power to invent people, the person we would invent is Donald Trump, God's gift to comedy.

Jerry Seinfeld

Now Melania is Trump's first lady, although I would think she's a way off that.

Frank Skinner

This feels like *House of Cards* on steroids.

Jon Sopel, after Trump sacked FBI chief James Comey

Hillary Clinton belongs in the White House; Donald Trump belongs on my show.

Jerry Springer

Trust

I don't trust that Homer Simpson. He's that rare combination of up to something and good for nothing.

Selma Bouvier (Julie Kavner), *The Simpsons*

Jeremy Usborne (Robert Webb): I only told you for a laugh. You promised not to tell.

Mark Corrigan (David Mitchell): Hitler promised not to invade Czechoslovakia, Jeremy. Welcome to the real world!

Peep Show

What we are about to have is a secret conversation, and I hope this time you can keep a fucking secret, because normally you're about as secure as a hymen in a south London comprehensive.

Jamie MacDonald (Paul Higgins), *The Thick of It*

Women have trust issues because you can buy two identical pants of the same size and only one of them will fit.

Jasmine Pierce, Twitter

Underwear

After two hours in a dancer's thong, my arse looks like a hot-cross bun.

Alan Carr

Women, stop buying the lingerie. It's a big rip off; eighteen bucks for panties this big? Come on, one trip through the dryer and it's a frilly bookmark.

Carol Leifer

Fit and comfort are a priority and I like colourful knickers but, most importantly, a great pair of knickers should be taken off with more joy than they were put on.

Elle Macpherson

I saw a pair of knickers today. On the front it said, 'I would do anything for love,' and on the back it said, 'but I won't do that.'

Sarah Millican

You know why I feel older? I went to buy sexy underwear and they automatically gift-wrapped it.

Joan Rivers

I saw this today in Victoria's Secret: a camouflage thong. On what battle-field are you finding it necessary to disguise yourself as shrubbery with a great ass?

Bill Santiago

Men want the same thing from their underwear that they want from women: a little bit of support and a little bit of freedom.

Jerry Seinfeld

What the hell is Victoria's Secret? My guess is that she likes to dress like a slut.

Carol Siskind

I can remember when pants were pants. You wore them for twenty years, then you cut them down for pan scrubs. Or quilts.

Victoria Wood

Vacation

My wife told me, 'Sex is better on holiday.' That wasn't a very nice post-card to receive.

Joe Bor

I don't like the beach. I think we have no business at the beach at all, as a species. We don't belong in the sea. The sea is full of things that bite us, sting us, hurt the soles of our feet and it's extremely cold. When are we going to take the hint that the things that live in the sea don't like us?

Billy Connolly

I promised some people that I would water their plants and take care of their animals while they went on vacation. Bad idea: the people are farmers.

Janine Ditullio

Dear Lillian: Soon I hope to take you on a Caribbean cruise, where we can hold hands on a soft summer's evening and watch that old Jamaican moon. Why that old Jamaican will be mooning us, I have no idea.

Roland T. Flakfizer (John Turturro), *Brain Donors*

My parents used to send me to spend summers with my grandparents. I hate cemeteries.

Chris Fonseca

Every year, my family would pile into the car for our vacation and drive eighty trillion miles just to prove we couldn't get along in any setting.

Janeane Garofalo

I'm packing you an extra pair of shoes and your 'angry' eyes just in case.

Mrs Potato Head (Estelle Harris) to Mr Potato Head, *Toy Story 2*

Asthmatics: avoid going on holiday to places where the scenery is described as breath-taking.

Top Tips, *Viz*

I went to a tourist information booth and said: 'Tell me about some people who were here last year.'

Steven Wright

Vanity

The ego is like a kid in the basement; it's best to keep him busy.

Tim Allen

Every time I'm wrong, the world makes a little less sense.

Frasier Crane (Kelsey Grammer), *Frasier*

(of Melvyn Bragg): I said he had love bites on his mirror and he was going through the tunnel of love holding his own hand.

Kathy Lette

But enough about me, let's talk about you. What do you think of me?

Bette Midler

It's really difficult to name a place after yourself. The thing to do as an explorer is to get there and then ask your assistant explorers if *they* can think of a name while reminding them how they got the job.

David Mitchell, *QI*

It is the vanity of women to spend hours in front of the mirror. It is the vanity of men not to bother.

Simon Munnery

Vegetarians

I'm a vegetarian. I'm not strict; I eat fish and duck. Well, they're nearly fish, aren't they? They're semi-submerged a lot of the time, they spend a lot of time in the water, they're virtually fish really. And pigs, cows, sheep, anything that lives near water. I'm not strict. I'm like a post-modern vegetarian; I eat meat ironically.

Bill Bailey

Hitler was a vegetarian. Just goes to show, vegetarianism, not always a good thing. Can in some extreme cases lead to genocide.

Bill Bailey

A vegetarian is a person who won't eat anything that can have children.

David Brenner

Tofu really is proof that nature abhors a vegan.

Marcus Brigstocke, *The Now Show*

My girlfriend bought a cookbook the other day called *Cheap and Easy Vegetarian Cooking*. Which is perfect for her, because not only is she vegetarian . . .

Jimmy Carr

Don't mess with vegans. Do not look vegans in the eye. If you get into an argument with a vegan say, 'I'm wrong', and run away as fast as you can. Do not fuck with vegans because they will fuck you up . . . because they're hungry!

Margaret Cho

Let's call a spade a spade. A lot of times when you are a vegetarian it is just a not very effective eating disorder.

Lena Dunham

I was vegan for a while. I lost six pounds, but most of that was personality.

Pippa Evans

I've gone vegetarian now. I mean, I know I had a sausage-roll yesterday, but it's not really meat, is it, y'know? I mean, there's no animal called a sausage.

Our Janine (Caroline Aherne), *The Fast Show*

What's the most evil snack imaginable for a vegetarian? Philosophically speaking, it's a Scotch egg because it's got death on the outside and potential for life within.

Russell Kane

Keziah (Emma Bernard): I'm a fruitarian . . . We believe that fruits and vegetables have feelings, so we think cooking is cruel. We only eat things that have actually fallen off a tree or bush – that are, in fact, dead already.
Will Thacker (Hugh Grant): Right. Right. Interesting stuff. So these carrots . . .
Keziah: Have been murdered, yes.

Notting Hill

I recently became vegan because I felt that, as a Jewish lesbian, I wasn't part of a small enough minority. So now I'm a Jewish lesbian vegan.

Carol Leifer

I make a lot of jokes about vegetarians in my act but most of them don't have the strength to protest.

Ardal O'Hanlon

You can either choose to be a vegan or you can choose to enjoy life.

Romesh Ranganathan

A vegetarian? Oh, it's a shame . . . Could she have wafer-thin ham, Barbara?

Norma Speakman (Liz Smith), *The Royle Family*

Virginity

Becky Conner (Lecy Goranson): Look what I found!
Darlene Conner (Sara Gilbert): Your virginity? No, wait, you left that behind the dumpster at K-Mart.

Roseanne

I lost my virginity under a bridge. I was having sex with this poor girl and I was trying my best, but I was like Scotland at a World Cup – just pleased to be there.

Russell Howard

(to daughter Saffy): Not one bloody boyfriend in the whole time that I've known you! I mean, you're not that bloody ugly! What's the matter with you? Huh? Have you read that *Karma Sutra* I gave you? No! That Dutch cap has only ever seen the light of day. I mean, God! Here I am, your mother, poised for your first sexual experience and, night after night, dry bloody sheets! I'm sorry, darling, but I don't want a little moustached virgin for a daughter, so do something about it!

Edina Monsoon (Jennifer Saunders), *Absolutely Fabulous*

I didn't lose my virginity until I was twenty-six – nineteen vaginally, but twenty-six what my boyfriend calls 'the real way'.

Sarah Silverman

Those who abstain from pre-marital sex will argue that the greatest gift a woman can offer a man is her virginity. Not necessarily – everything has a shelf life. I like cheesecake, but not if it's been sitting in the freezer for thirty years.

Jeff Stilson

She is a virgin in a world where men will even turn to soft fruit for pleasure.

Patsy Stone (Joanna Lumley), Absolutely Fabulous

I lost my virginity so late, that when it finally happened, I wasn't so much deflowered as deadheaded.

Holly Walsh

I lost my virginity to my cousin Jeanie. It was my uncle Murray's funeral, we were all back at my aunt Barbara's house. Our eyes locked over the pickled herring. We never meant for it to happen. To this day, I can't look at pickled herring without being aroused and ashamed.

Howard Wolowitz (Simon Helberg), The Big Bang Theory

Wales

In Wales, if a man sees a woman he likes in a nightclub, he says, 'Hello, love, I've got a Transit van in the car park. Let's go.'

Keith Barret (Rob Brydon), The Keith Barret Show

A Welsh satnav basically goes, 'Turning coming up now in about forty yards, get ready for it. Getting a bit closer now, get ready, here it comes . . . Ohh, you plank! You've missed it. Now do a u-ey, do a u-ey. Do it! No, don't. Pull over, attach a hose pipe to the exhaust and just end it all.'

Rob Brydon, QI

The hardest part of running competitively in Wales must be keeping up with the Joneses.

Gary Delaney

In the Bible, God made it rain for forty days and forty nights. That's a pretty good summer for us in Wales. That's a hosepipe ban waiting to happen. I was eight before I realised you could take a kagoule off.

Rhod Gilbert

We have al fresco dining in Cardiff now. Whose idea was that? My soup's filling up quicker than I can eat it!

Rhod Gilbert

Welsh is the only language you learn to be able to talk to fewer people.

A. A. Gill

The first time I went to Wales, I thought I'd landed in a land of hobbits. Everybody was really small.

David Hasselhoff

The Welsh are not meant to go out in the sun. They start to photosynthesise.

Rhys Ifans

Wales is one of those places where it feels like every day is Sunday.

Karl Pilkington

Bryn West (Rob Brydon): I cannot speak the Welsh language. It's a constant source of embarrassment to me, but Welsh is not my mother tongue.
Mick Shipman (Larry Lamb): Now why is that, Bryn? 'Cause every time I've been down there it seems none of you can speak it. I mean, you spend all that money on them signs and none of you can read 'em.

Gavin & Stacey

War

Field Marshal Haig is about to make yet another gargantuan effort to move his drinks cabinet six inches closer to Berlin.

Capt. Edmund Blackadder (Rowan Atkinson), *Blackadder Goes Forth*

War is never a picnic. Although obviously soldiers do end up eating outdoors a lot.

Mark Corrigan (David Mitchell), *Peep Show*

Just because I can give multiple orgasms to the furniture just by sitting on it doesn't mean that I'm not sick of this damn war: the blood, the noise, the endless poetry.

Lord Flashheart (Rik Mayall), *Blackadder Goes Forth*

The Afghan War has clearly reached a stage similar to that moment at your child's party where you realise you've forgotten to give the other parents a pick-up time.

Jeremy Hardy, 2009

No mode of warfare ever becomes truly obsolete. It always turns up again as an event in the Olympics.

Miles Kington

Vice President Dick Cheney was in Baghdad. While he was in Iraq, he said that it's a successful endeavour. At least I think that's what he said. It was hard to hear over the explosions.

David Letterman, 2008

War is the only game in which it doesn't pay to have home-court advantage.

Former basketball coach Dick Motta

Wherever there's injustice, oppression, and suffering, America will show up six months late and bomb the country next to where it's happening.

P. J. O'Rourke

I saw Vera Lynn once and she said, 'I don't think anyone else could have a career like mine because wars these days, they don't last long enough.' I remember thinking it's not a complaint you hear often.

Frank Skinner, *Have I Got News for You*

Wealth

Being wealthy when no one else is, is like being the only one at the party with a drink.

Tim Allen

There is no point in wasting any more moral or mental energy in being jealous of the very rich. They are no happier than anyone else; they just have more money. How does it hurt me, with my twenty-year-old Toyota, if somebody else has a swish Mercedes? We both get stuck in the same traffic.

Boris Johnson

I've got my own private jet – the rest of the jacuzzi belongs to my mum.

Milton Jones

Weapons

If the internet is any guide, a lot of people who are pro-gun are also anti-spelling.

Andy Borowitz

A lot of these people who keep a gun at home for safety are the same ones who refuse to wear a seat belt.

George Carlin

Guns don't kill people. People who say 'Guns don't kill people' kill people. With guns.

Rob Delaney

Instead of building newer and larger weapons of mass destruction, I think mankind should try to get more use out of the ones we have.

Jack Handey

You see, this is why birds and CID don't mix. You give a bloke a gun, it's a dream come true; you give a girl one, she moans it doesn't go with her dress.

DCI Gene Hunt (Philip Glenister), *Life on Mars*

What is that? I come here for a proper shootout! What are you gonna do with that rollin' pin? You gonna bake me a cake?

Ronnie Kray (Tom Hardy), *Legend*

There's no way I'm getting my wife a gun, because that would be like me saying, 'You know, I kinda want to kill myself, but I want it to be a surprise.'

Marc Maron

Firearms groups across the United States have declared today the first annual Gun Appreciation Day. So don't forget to set your clock back one hundred years.

Seth Meyers

Of course he had a gun. This is Texas! Everybody has a gun. My florist has a gun!

Kathy Morningside (Candice Bergen), *Miss Congeniality*

I keep hearing this thing that guns don't kill people, but people kill people. If that's the case, why do we give people guns when we go to war? Why not just send the people?

Ozzy Osbourne

A woman would never make a nuclear bomb. They would never make a weapon that kills. They'd make a weapon that makes you feel bad for a while.

Robin Williams

Weather

In Britain it had been a year without summer. Wet spring had merged imperceptibly into bleak autumn. For months the sky had remained a depthless grey. Sometimes it rained, but mostly it was just dull, a land without shadows. It was like living inside Tupperware.

> Bill Bryson, *The Lost Continent: Travels in Small-Town America*

I survived, Bear Grylls style, on nuts and berries – but I bought them at Marks & Spencer.

> Steve Coogan, stuck in his car for the night
> during the UK's Storm Desmond, 2015

In case you haven't noticed, Dad, it goes get a little damp around here [in Seattle]. For God's sake, the state flower is mildew!

> Frasier Crane (Kelsey Grammer), *Frasier*

Weathermen are the ponchoed buffoons who spend hurricanes outside, buffeted by winds, lashed by rains, struggling to stand erect; a mime's 'walking against the wind' routine come horribly to life. Whereas meteor-ologists – we're the people who sent them out there.

> John Hodgman, *The Daily Show*

I've discovered a delightful thing about winter in New York. When a bum throws up on you, you can chip it off.

> Richard Karinsky (Malcolm Gets), *Caroline in the City*

Ugh, I hate January. It's dark and freezing and everyone's wearing bulky coats; you can do some serious subway flirting before you realise the guy is homeless.

> Liz Lemon (Tina Fey), *30 Rock*

I used to get bummed out when it rained; then I realised it's God's way of washing hippies.

> Demetri Martin

It's raining so hard now, we're actually having mudslides here in LA. This morning I was driving to work and I was passed by a house.

Conan O'Brien

Snowflakes fell from the sky like tiny pieces of a snowman who had stood on a landmine.

Alan Partridge, *I, Partridge: We Need to Talk About Alan*

Starting in the south-east, where it should be dull and drizzly in the morning, a bit like waking up next to a corpse.

Weatherman Sylvester Stewart (David Schneider), *The Day Today*

Weddings

You know, there's nothing more off-putting in a wedding than a priest with an enormous erection.

Charles (Hugh Grant), *Four Weddings and a Funeral*

The wedding invite said 'Simon Feilder plus one'. So I turned up an hour late.

Simon Feilder

Think of your wedding as a driving test. You take it, you pass, and then you really start to learn how to drive. Or you crash.

Kate Jones (Emma Thompson), *The Love Punch*

I feel the same way about being a bridesmaid as you do about Botox. Painful and unnecessary.

Samantha Jones (Kim Cattrall), *Sex and the City: The Movie*

From time to time, my mother puts on her wedding dress. Not because she's sentimental, she just gets really far behind on her laundry.

Brian Kiley

I was promised sex. Everybody said it. 'You'll be a bridesmaid, you'll get sex, you'll be fighting 'em off.' But not so much as a tongue in sight.

Lydia (Sophie Thompson), *Four Weddings and a Funeral*

You're going to get back in there, you're going to say you're sorry and you're going to marry my son. I did not buy a five-hundred-pound suit and spend six weeks looking for a church with disabled access for you to just go.

Margaret (Di Botcher), *Pulling*

My wedding was like a fairytale. It wasn't magical; it's just that I've got an ugly sister.

Ellie Taylor

At American weddings, the quality of the food is in inverse proportion to the social position of the bride and groom.

Calvin Trillin

Weight

Statistically, skinny women die younger than fat women. Why? Because fat women are killing them.

Joy Behar

Only last month, I set up a brand new course to help the overweight come to terms with their self-image. First week, we have a light-hearted session with a measuring tape and second week . . . no one bothers to turn up.

Gordon Brittas (Chris Barrie), *The Brittas Empire*

The first few weeks of joining Weight Watchers, you're just finding your feet.

Jimmy Carr

He picked me up in his arms, as if I was as light as a feather, which I am not, unless it was a very heavy feather, maybe from a giant, prehistoric, dinosaur-type bird.

Helen Fielding: *Bridget Jones, Mad About the Boy*

My fitness goals are different from most people's. Most people want to lose enough weight so they look good in a bathing suit or they want to lower their cholesterol. I just want to lose enough so my stomach doesn't jiggle when I brush my teeth.

Kevin James

I went to the thirtieth reunion of my pre-school. I didn't want to go, because I've put on like a hundred pounds.

Wendy Liebman

I've put on some weight recently. My wife says it's just puppy fat, but I've been eating other things as well.

Gareth Richards

(of skinny models): The girls themselves resemble nothing so much as garden rakes, and bad-tempered, pouting garden rakes at that!

Sir Terry Wogan

Wisdom

Wisdom comes from experience. Experience is often a result of lack of wisdom.

Sir Terry Pratchett

Wives

My wife tries not to bring out the beast in me; she's afraid of mice.

Ronnie Corbett

I call my wife 'doll-face' because she's so pretty and missing an eye.

Stewart Francis

My wife is Cherokee Indian, which is great 'cause whenever we have sex, it rains.

Jay Mohr

I've had bad luck with both my wives. The first one left me and the second one didn't.

Patrick Murray

My wife gets all the money I make. I just get an apple and clean clothes every morning.

Ray Romano

I honestly thought my marriage would work, because me and my wife did share a sense of humour. We had to really, because she didn't have one.

Frank Skinner

My wife said to me recently that she hates couples who finish each other's sentences for them. I agreed that it was annoying, but it made me think that perhaps we were missing out on something, so now every time she says anything, I say 'full stop' at the end. I have been doing it for a full week now, and it has really kept the romance alive.

Danny Wallace, More Awkward Situations for Men

I met my wife in the Caribbean. I said, 'What are you doing here?'

Bradley Walsh

A friend of mine has a trophy wife, but apparently it wasn't first place.

Steven Wright

Women

Women are cursed, and men are the proof.

Roseanne Barr

Scientists are trying to invent Viagra for women. It's been around for years: they call it 'cash'.

Alonzo Bodden

Men may have discovered fire, but women discovered how to play with it.

Candace Bushnell, *Sex and the City*

That's the difference between girls and women: girls find men fascinating, women know better.

Candace Bushnell, *One Fifth Avenue*

A woman's mind is as complex as the contents of her handbag; even when you get to the bottom of it, there is always something at the bottom to surprise you.

Billy Connolly

If women are so perfect at multitasking, how come they can't have a headache and sex at the same time?

Billy Connolly

Have you ever seen a woman try to end a phone call? It takes my wife about an hour. She says: 'Bye . . . bye . . . bye . . . bye-bye . . . bye . . . bye . . . bye . . . bye . . . bye-bye . . . bye . . . bye . . . you're joking, really? . . .'

Micky Flanagan

There is a latent fairy in all women, but look how carefully we have to secrete her in order to be taken seriously. And fairies come in all shapes, colours, sizes and types, they don't have to be fluffy. They can be demanding and furious if they like. They do, however, have to wear a tiara. That much is compulsory.

Dawn French, *A Tiny Bit Marvellous*

A woman with clothes on has negotiating power.

Sally Harper (Kate Isitt), *Coupling*

Like a lot of women, I'm bisexual. Once I have sex with you . . . bye!

Carol Leifer

If God hadn't meant us to hunt men, he wouldn't have given us Wonderbras.

Kathy Lette

Show me a woman with both feet planted firmly on the ground, and I'll show you a girl who can't get her knickers off.

Kathy Lette, *To Love, Honour and Betray*

Women want to be treated as equals, not sequels.

Kathy Lette

They say a woman's work is never done. Maybe that's why they get paid less.

Sean Lock

I quite like women in a sad, baffled sort of way. But can we get a grip? Out of a workforce of five, at any given moment one will have pre-menstrual tension, one's panicking because she's not, someone's having a hot flush and someone else is having a nervous breakdown because her HRT patch has fallen in the minestrone!

Tony Martin (Andrew Dunn), *dinnerladies*

There are only two occasions where you're allowed to wake up a woman on a lie-in: it's snowing or the death of a celebrity.

Michael McIntyre

Women have no feelings. It's actually men who are the more romantic. Men are the people you will hear say, 'I've found somebody. She's amazing. If I don't get to be with this person, I can't carry on. I have a job, I have a flat, but they mean nothing. I have to be with her. Because if I can't, I'm going to end up in some bedsit, I'll be an alcoholic and I won't be able to walk the streets anymore.' That is how women feel about shoes.

Dylan Moran

Women are hens, puffed-up clucking creatures; little more than egg-laying machines, woken up each morning by a persistent cock.

Al Murray, The Pub Landlord

Toula Portokalos (Nia Vardalos): Ma, Dad is so stubborn. What he says goes. 'Ah, the man is the head of the house.'

Maria Portokalos (Lainie Kazan): Let me tell you something, Toula. The man is the head, but the woman is the neck. And she can turn the head any way she wants.

My Big Fat Greek Wedding

There are only three things women need in life: food, water and compliments.

Chris Rock

In US and A, they treat horses like we in Kazakhstan treat our women. They feed them two times a day. They have them sleep on straw in a small box. And for entertainment, they make them jump over fences while being whipped.

Borat Sagdiyev (Sacha Baron Cohen), *Borat: Cultural Learnings of America for Make Benefit Glorious Nation of Kazakhstan*

They had a Top Ten list of the most painful things in life that women have to endure and number one was having their nipples clamped. Surely having them towed away is worse.

Dave Spikey

It's all right, darling. I'll finish the financial report on my own. I can think clearly before sex and stay awake afterwards. That's one of the nice things about being a woman.

Barbara Taylor Bradford, *Power of a Woman*

There were people asking, 'Can women be funny?' People still ask that. It's like asking, 'Can women breathe in and out?'

Julie Walters

Words

No, Prime Minister, a clarification is not to make oneself clear. It is to put oneself *in* the clear.

> Sir Humphrey Appleby (Nigel Hawthorne), *Yes, Prime Minister*

In New York City, 'Fuck' isn't even a word; it's a comma.

> Lewis Black

Men in power always seem to get involved in sex scandals, but women don't even have a word for a male bimbo. Except maybe 'senator'.

> Elayne Boosler

Words have a life of their own. There is no telling what they will do. Within a matter of days, they can even turn turtle and mean the opposite.

> Craig Brown, on urban slang

I'm going to stop using hurtful words like 'fag' and 'retarded'. At least on my résumé.

> Tony Camin, Twitter

In 2016 there was a campaign to remove the term 'Essex girl' from the dictionary. I don't see the harm – it's not as if they're going to read it.

> Jimmy Carr

Maddy Magellan (Caroline Quentin): Enough with the pedanticism and let us eat.
Jonathan Creek (Alan Davies): The word is pedantry.

> *Jonathan Creek*

A sewage farm. In what way is it a farm? Is there a farm shop?

> Jack Dee

Merriam-Webster dictionary added over a thousand new words, including the word 'photobomb'. They didn't want to add 'photobomb', but it jumped in at the last second and kinda ruined the dictionary.

> Jimmy Fallon

So what if I can't spell 'Armageddon'? It's not the end of the world.

Stewart Francis

It is a cliché that most clichés are true, but then like most clichés, that cliché is untrue.

Stephen Fry

Whoever coined the phrase 'Killing two birds with one stone' not only hated birds but also thought we needed to conserve stones.

Dana Gould

I don't like the word 'alcoholic'. I like to think of myself as an advanced drinker.

Chelsea Handler

'Spiritual' is the word people use when they mean they want to be covered when they die but they're not getting up early on a Sunday.

Richard Jeni

I used to think sticks and stones could break my bones but words could never hurt me, until I fell into a printing press.

Milton Jones

'Sort of' is such a harmless thing to say. It's just a filler, it doesn't really mean anything. But after certain things, 'sort of' means everything. Like after, 'I love you' or, 'You're going to live' or, 'It's a boy'.

Demetri Martin

Scousers say 'boss' when something's really good. Everyone else uses 'boss' to mean person in charge at work, but of course they don't need a word for that in Liverpool.

Lee Nelson (Simon Brodkin)

As far as I'm concerned, 'whom' is a word that was invented to make everyone sound like a butler.

Calvin Trillin

Work

Hard work is rewarding. Taking credit for other people's hard work is rewarding and faster.

> Scott Adams, *Dilbert's Guide to the Rest of Your Life: Dispatches from Cubicleland*

I feel like every office has three people who do all the work and fifteen people who just walk around with salads.

> Alex Baze, Twitter

All right, kids, I gotta get to work. If I don't input those numbers . . . it doesn't make much of a difference.

> Chandler Bing (Matthew Perry), *Friends*

You ever hate your job with the passion that your boss claims you lack?

> Stuart Black

I can take a joke as well as anyone but, if it happens again, I'm taking it to an industrial tribunal.

> Mark Corrigan (David Mitchell), *Peep Show*

I had to get back to work. NBC has me under contract. The baby and I only have a verbal agreement.

> Tina Fey

I recently gave a talk to a group of backpackers. They were on the edge of their seats.

> Stewart Francis

Bob Porter (Paul Willson): Looks like you've been missing a lot of work lately.
Peter Gibbons (Ron Livingston): I wouldn't say I've been *missing* it, Bob.

> *Office Space*

I like to call in sick to work at places where I've never held a job. Then when the manager tells me I don't work there, I tell them I'd like to. But not today, as I'm sick.

> Jarod Kintz, *This Book is Not for Sale*

We had to get a live-in nanny 'cause that dead one wasn't working out.

Lee Mack

Employee of the month is a good example of how somebody can be both a winner and a loser at the same time.

Demetri Martin

(having just been fired by his boss) Ted Mosby (Josh Radnor): After he proposed a vocational paradigm shift, I made an impromptu presentation using a four-prong approach which really brought him to his knees.
Barney Stinson (Neil Patrick Harris): You hit him with a chair?
Ted: Yep.

How I Met Your Mother

I do have a rule that very few meetings are worth more than ten minutes.

Anne Robinson

You may look around and see two groups here. White collar, blue collar. But I don't see it that way. You know why not? Because I am collar-blind.

Michael Scott (Steve Carell), *The Office* (US)

Toby is in HR, which technically means he works for corporate, so he's really not a part of our family. Also, he's divorced, so he's really not a part of *his* family.

Michael Scott (Steve Carell), *The Office* (US)

The paintballing is meant to be a bonding exercise to boost morale. I'm not having it abused by people just out to enjoy themselves!

Sharon (Siobhan Redmond), *The Smoking Room*

Homer Simpson (Dan Castellaneta): You don't have to follow in my foot-steps, son.
Bart Simpson (Nancy Cartwright): Don't worry, I don't even like using the bathroom after you.

The Simpsons

Dr Caroline Todd (Tamsin Greig): How was the interview?

Dr 'Mac' Macartney (Julian Rhind-Tutt): Not sure . . . Think I might have used the words 'job', 'stick', 'up' and 'arse' all in one sentence. Is that a bad thing?

Dr Todd: Well, I think tone of voice is very important.

Green Wing

Jack McFarland (Sean Hayes): So I've decided to take my career in a whole new direction.

Will Truman (Eric McCormack): Forward?

Will & Grace

My mate asked me, 'What do you think of voluntary work?' I said, 'I wouldn't do it if you paid me.'

Tim Vine

Retirement is coming to all of us and, as my accountant said to me lately, 'You'd better think of taking your pension soon, otherwise it won't be worth your while.'

Sir Terry Wogan

Youth

For boys, puberty is like turning into the Incredible Hulk – but very, very slowly.

John Bishop

When I was a teenager I worked in Boots. I told boys I fancied that I worked on the make-up counter. But all I actually did was stack the feminine hygiene section, so they'd come into the shop and I'd be on my knees surrounded by huge piles of sanitary towels.

Jenny Eclair

My fondest childhood memory is I made out with my babysitter. She stops in the middle of everything, 'We have to stop this, I feel like such a whore.' I said, 'Why? I'm not paying you – my parents are! Come here!'

Adam Ferrara

There's one thing I have over any twenty-one-year-old: a proud history of accumulated neuroses.

Ray Romano

I have been in a youth hostel . . . You are put in a kitchen with seventeen venture scouts with behavioural difficulties and made to wash swedes.

Victoria Wood

All my friends started getting boyfriends, but I didn't want a boyfriend. I wanted a thirteen-colour biro.

Victoria Wood

Zombies

I love zombies. If any monster could Riverdance, it would be zombies.

Craig Ferguson

You wanna see some real zombies, check out the red carpet at the Tony Awards.

Martha Rodgers (Susan Sullivan), *Castle*

Index